William Congreve

Dramatic Works

Vol. 2

William Congreve

Dramatic Works
Vol. 2

ISBN/EAN: 9783337303204

Printed in Europe, USA, Canada, Australia, Japan

Cover: Foto ©Thomas Meinert / pixelio.de

More available books at **www.hansebooks.com**

THE

ATIC

LONDON

Printed for S. CROWDER, C. WARE, and T. PAYNE.

M.DCC.LXXIII.

THE

CONTENTS.

A 2

MOURNING BRIDE.

A

T R A G E D Y.

" ——Neque enim lex æquior ulla,
" Quam necis artifices arte perire fua."

Ovid. de Arte Am.

HER ROYAL HIGHNESS,

T H E

P R I N C E S S.

MADAM,

THAT high ftation, which by your birth you hold above the people, exacts from every one, as a duty, whatever honours they are capable of paying to your Royal Highnefs: but that more exalted place, to which your virtues have raifed you above the reft of princes, makes the attribute of our admiration and praife rather a choice more immediately preventing that duty.

The public gratitude is ever founded on a public benefit; and what is univerfally bleffed, is always an univerfal bleffing. Thus from yourfelf we derive the offerings which we bring; and that incenfe which arifes to your name, only returns to its original, and but naturally requites the parent of its being.

From hence it is that this poem, conftituted on a moral, whofe end is to recommend and to encourage virtue, of confequence has recourfe to your Royal Highnefs's patronage; afpiring to caft itfelf beneath your feet, and declining approbation, 'till you fhall condefcend to own it, and vouchfafe to fhine upon it as on a creature of your influence.

It is from the example of princes that virtue becomes a fashion in the people; for even they, who
are averse to instruction, will yet be fond of imitation.

But there are multitudes, who never can have
means nor opportunities of so near an access, as to
partake of the benefit of such examples. And to
these, Tragedy, which distinguishes itself from the
vulgar poetry by the dignity of its characters, may
be of use and information. For they who are at
that distance from original greatness, as to be de-
prived of the happiness of contemplating the perfec-
tions and real excellencies of your Royal Highness's
person in your court, may yet behold some small
sketches and imagings of the virtues of your mind,
abstracted, and represented on the theatre.

Thus poets are instructed, and instruct; not alone
by precepts, which persuade, but also by examples
which illustrate. Thus is delight interwoven with
instruction; when not only virtue is prescribed, but
also represented.

But if we are delighted with the liveliness of a
feigned representation of great and good persons
and their actions, how must we be charmed with
beholding the persons themselves! If one or two
excelling qualities, barely touched in the single action and small compass of a play, can warm an
audience, with a concern and regard even for the
seeming success and prosperity of the actor; with
what zeal must the hearts of all be filled for the
continued and increasing happiness of those, who
are the true and living instances of elevated and

perfifting virtue ! Even the vicious themfelves muft have a fecret veneration for thofe peculiar graces and endowments, which are daily fo eminently confpicuous in your Royal Highnefs; and though repining, feel a pleafure which, in fpite of envy, they perforce approve.

If in this piece, humbly offered to your Royal Highnefs, there fhall appear the refemblance of any of thofe many excellencies which you fo promifcuoufly poffefs, to be drawn fo as to merit your leaft approbation, it has the end and accomplifhment of its defign. And however imperfect it may be in the whole, through the inexperience or incapacity of the author, yet, if there is fo much as to convince your Royal Highnefs, that a play may be with induftry fo difpofed (in fpite of the licentious practice of the modern theatre) as to become fometimes an innocent, and not unprofitable entertainment; it will abundantly gratify the ambition, and recompenfe the endeavours of,

Your Royal Highnefs's moft obedient,

and moft humbly devoted fervant,

WILLIAM CONGREVE,

PROLOGUE,

Spoken by Mr BETTERTON.

THE time has been when plays were not so plenty,
And a less number now would well content ye.
New plays did then like almanacs appear;
And one was thought sufficient for a year:
Tho' they are more like almanacs of late;
For in one year, I think, they're out of date.
Nor were they without reason join'd together;
For just as one prognosticates the weather,
How plentiful the crop, or scarce the grain,
What peals of thunder, and what show'rs of rain;
So t'other can foretel, by certain rules,
What crops of coxcombs, or what floods of fools.
In such like prophesies were poets skill'd,
Which now they find in their own tribe fulfill'd:
The dearth of wit they did so long presage,
Is fall'n on us, and almost starves the stage.
Were you not griev'd, as often as you saw
Poor actors thrash such empty sheafs of straw;
Toiling and lab'ring at their lungs expence,
To start a jest, or force a little sense.
Hard fate for us! still harder in th' event;
Our authors sin, but we alone repent.
Still they proceed, and, at our charge, write worse;
'Twere some amends if they could reimburse:
But there's the devil, tho' their cause is lost,
There's no recovering damages or cost.
  Good wits, forgive this liberty we take,
Since custom gives the losers leave to speak.
But if provok'd, your dreadful wrath remains,
Take your revenge upon the coming scenes:

For that damn'd poet's fpar'd who damns a brother,
As one thief 'fcapes that executes another.
Thus far alone does to the wits relate;
But from the reft we hope another fate.
To pleafe and move has been our poet's theme,
Art may direct, but nature is his aim ;
And nature mifs'd, in vain he boafts his art,
For only nature can affect the heart.
Then freely judge the fcenes that fhall enfue;
But as with freedom, judge with candour too.
He wou'd not lofe thro' prejudice his caufe ;
Nor wou'd obtain precarioufly applaufe,
Impartial cenfure he requefts from all,
Prepar'd by juft decrees to ftand or fall.

Dramatis Personæ.

M E N.

MANUEL, the King of Granada, Mr VERBRUGGEN.
GONSALEZ, his favourite, Mr SANDFORD.
GARCIA, son to Gonsalez, Mr SCUDAMOUR.
PEREZ, captain of the guards, Mr FREEMAN.
ALONZO, an officer, creature to } Mr ARNOLD.
 Gonsalez,. }
OSMYN, a noble prisoner, Mr BETTERTON.
HELI, a prisoner, his friend, Mr BOWMAN.
SELIM, an eunuch, Mr BAILY.

W O M E N.

ALMERIA, the princess of Gra- } Mrs BRACEGIRDLE.
 nada, }
ZARA, a captive queen, Mrs BARRY.
LEONORA, a chief attendant on } Mrs BOWMAN.
 the Princess, }

Women, Eunuchs, and Mutes attending Zara; Guards, &c.

The SCENE, GRANADA.

MOURNING BRIDE.

ACT I. SCENE I.

A Room of State.

The Curtain, rifing flowly to foft Mufic, difcovers ALMERIA *in Mourning,* LEONORA *waiting in Mourning.*

After the Mufic, Almeria *rifes from her Chair, and comes forward.*

ALMERIA.

MUSIC has charms to foothe a favage breaft,
To foften rocks, or bend a knotted oak.
I've read, that things inanimate have mov'd,
And, as with living fouls, have been inform'd,
By magic numbers and perfuafive found.
What then am I? Am I more fenfelefs grown
Than trees or flint? O force of conftant woe!
'Tis not in harmony to calm my griefs.
Anfelmo fleeps, and is at peace; laft night
The filent tomb receiv'd the good old king;
He and his forrows now are fafely lodg'd
Within its cold but hofpitable bofom.
Why am not I at peace?

Leon. Dear Madam, ceafe,
Or moderate your griefs; there is no caufe——

Alm. No caufe! peace, peace; there is eternal caufe,
And mifery eternal will fucceed.
Thou canft not tell—thou haft indeed no caufe.

Leon. Believe me, Madam, I lament Anfelmo,
And always did compaffionate his fortune:
Have often wept to fee how cruelly
Your father kept in chains his fellow-king:
And oft at night when all have been retir'd,

Have stol'n from bed, and to his prison crept;
Where, while his jailor slept, I thro' the grate
Have softly whisper'd, and enquir'd his health;
Sent in my sighs and pray'rs for his deliv'rance;
For sighs and prayers were all that I could offer.

Alm. Indeed thou hast a soft and gentle nature,
That thus couldst melt to see a stranger's wrongs.
O Leonora, hadst thou known Anselmo,
How wou'd thy heart have bled to see his suff'rings!
Thou hadst no cause, but general compassion.

Leon. Love of my royal mistress gave me cause,
My love of you begot my grief for him;
For I had heard that when the chance of war
Had bless'd Anselmo's arms with victory,
And the rich spoil of all the field, and you,
The glory of the whole, were made the prey
Of his success; that then, in spite of hate,
Revenge, and that hereditary feud
Between Valentia's and Granada's kings,
He did endear himself to your affection,
By all the worthy and indulgent ways
His most industrious goodness cou'd invent;
Proposing by a match between Alphonso
His son, the brave Valentia prince, and you,
To end the long dissention, and unite
The jarring crowns.

Alm. Alphonso! O Alphonso!
Thou too art quiet—long hast been at peace—
Both, both—father and son are now no more.
Then why am I? O when shall I have rest?
Why do I live to say you are no more?
Why are all these things thus—Is it of force?
Is there necessity I must be miserable?
Is it of moment to the peace of Heav'n
That I shou'd be afflicted thus?—If not,
Why is it thus contriv'd? Why are things laid
By some unseen hand so, as of sure consequence,
They must to me bring curses, grief of heart,
The last distress of life, and sure despair?

Leon. Alas, you search too far, and think too deeply.

Alm. Why was I carried to Anselmo's court?
Or there, why was I us'd so tenderly?
Why not ill-treated like an enemy?
For so my father would have us'd his child.
O Alphonso! Alphonso!
Devouring seas have wash'd thee from my sight,
No time shall rase thee from my memory;
No, I will live to be thy monument;
The cruel ocean is no more thy tomb:
But in my heart thou art interr'd; there, there,
Thy dear resemblance is for ever fix'd;
My love, my lord, my husband still, though lost.

Leon. Husband! O heavens!

Alm. Alas, what have I said?
My grief has hurried me beyond all thought:
I wou'd have kept the secret; though I know
Thy love and faith to me deserve all confidence.
But 'tis the wretch's comfort still to have
Some small reserve of near and inward woe,
Some unsuspected hoard of darling grief,
Which they unseen may wail, and weep and mourn,
And, glutton-like, alone devour.

Leon. Indeed
I knew not this.

Alm. O no, thou know'st not half,
Know'st nothing of my sorrows.—If thou didst—
If I shou'd tell thee, wouldst thou pity me?
Tell me; I know thou would'st, thou art compassionate.

Leon. Witness these tears——

Alm. I thank thee—Leonora,
Indeed I do, for pitying thy sad mistress:
For 'tis, alas, the poor prerogative
Of greatness, to be wretched and unpitied——
But I did promise I would tell thee—What?
My miseries? thou dost already know 'em;
And when I told thee thou didst nothing know,
It was because thou didst not know Alphonso:

For to have known my lofs, thou muft have known
His worth, his truth, and tendernefs of love.

    Leon. The memory of that brave prince ftands fair
In all report——
And I have heard imperfectly his lofs ;
But fearful to renew your troubles paft,
I never did prefume to afk the ftory.

    Alm. If for my fwelling heart I can, I'll tell thee.
I was a welcome captive in Valentia,
Ev'n on the day when Manuel, my father,
Led on his conqu'ring troops, high at the gates
Of King Anfelmo's palace; which in rage,
And heat of war, and dire revenge, he fir'd.
The good king flying to avoid the flames,
Started amidft his foes, and made captivity
His fatal refuge——Wou'd that I had fallen
Amid thofe flames—but 'twas not fo decreed.
Alphonfo, who forefaw my father's cruelty,
Had borne the queen and me on board a fhip
Ready to fail; and when this news was brought,
We put to fea ; but being betray'd by fome
Who knew our flight, we clofely were purfu'd,
And almoft taken ; when a fudden ftorm
Drove us, and thofe that follow'd, on the coaft
Of Afric ; there our veffel ftruck the fhore,
And bulging 'gainft a rock was dafh'd in pieces !
But Heav'n fpar'd me for yet much more affliction !
Conducting them who follow'd us to fhun
The fhoal, and fave me floating on the waves,
While the good king and my Alphonfo perifh'd.

    Leon. Alas ! were you then wedded to Alphonfo ?

    Alm. That day, that fatal day, our hands were join'd.
For when my Lord beheld the fhip purfuing,
And faw her rate fo far exceeding ours ;
He came to me, and begg'd me by my love,
I wou'd confent the prieft fhou'd make us one ;
That whether death or victory enfu'd,
I might be his beyond the power of fate :

The Queen too did affift his fuit——I granted ;
And in one day, was wedded, and a widow.
 Leon. Indeed 'twas mournful——
 Alm. 'Twas—as I have told thee——
For which I mourn, and will for ever mourn ;
Nor will I change thefe black and difmal robes,
Or ever dry thefe fwoln and watry eyes ;
Or ever tafte content, or peace of heart,
While I have life, and thought of my Alphonfo.
 Leon. Look down, good Heav'n, with pity on her forrows,
And grant that time may bring her fome relief.
 Alm. O no, time gives increafe to my afflictions.
The circling hours, that gather all the woes,
Which are diffus'd through the revolving year,
Come, heavy-laden with th' oppreffing weight,
To me ; with me, fucceffively they leave
The fighs, the tears, the groans, the reftlefs cares,
And all the damps of grief, that did retard their flight ;
They fhake their downy wings, and fcatter all
The dire collected dews on my poor head ;
Then fly with joy and fwiftnefs from me.
 Leon. Hark !
The diftant fhouts proclaim your father's triumph ;
       [*Shouts at a diftance.*
O ceafe, for Heaven's fake, affuage a little
This torrent of your grief ; for much I fear,
'Twill urge his wrath to fee you drown'd in tears,
When joy appears in every other face.
 Alm. And joy he brings to ev'ry other heart,
But double, double weight of woe to mine ;
For with him Garcia comes—Garcia, to whom
I muft be facrific'd, and all the vows
I gave my dear Alphonfo bafely broken.
No, it fhall never be ; for I will die ;
Firft, die ten thoufand deaths——Look down, look down,
         [*Kneels.*
Alphonfo, hear the facred vow I make ;
One moment ceafe to gaze on perfect blifs,
     B 3

And bend thy glorious eyes on earth and me ;
And thou, Anſelmo, if yet thou art arriv'd,
Thro' all impediments of purging ſire,
To that bright heav'n, where my Alphonſo reigns,
Behold thou alſo, and attend my vow.
If ever I do yield, or give conſent,
By any action, word, or thought, to wed
Another lord; may then juſt Heav'n ſhow'r down
Unheard-of curſes on me, greater far
(If ſuch there be in angry Heaven's vengeance)
Than any I have yet endur'd——And now   [Riſing.
My heart has ſome relief; having ſo well
Diſcharg'd this debt, incumbent on my love.
Yet one thing more I wou'd engage from thee.

  Leon. My heart, my life and will, are only yours.
  Alm. I thank thee   'Tis but this ; anon when all
Are wrapp'd and buſied in the general joy,
Thou wilt withdraw, and privately with me
Steal forth, to viſit good Anſelmo's tomb.
  Leon. Alas, I fear ſome fatal reſolution.
  Alm. No, on my life, my faith, I mean no ill,
Nor violence.   I feel myſelf more light,
And more at large, ſince I have made this vow.
Perhaps I would repeat it there more ſolemnly.
'Tis that, or ſome ſuch melancholy thought,
Upon my word no more.
  Leon. I will attend you.

S C E N E II.

ALMERIA, LEONORA, ALONZO.

  Alon. The Lord Gonſalez comes to tell your Highneſs
The King is juſt arrived.
  Alm. Conduct him in.   [*Exit* Alon.
That's his pretence; his errand is, I know,
To fill my ears with Garcia's valiant deeds;
And gild and magnify his ſon's exploits.

But I am arm'd with ice around my heart,
Not to be warm'd with words, or idle eloquence.

S C E N E III.

GONSALEZ, ALMERIA, LEONORA.

Gon. Be ev'ry day of your long life like this.
The fun, bright conqueft, and your brighter eyes,
Have all confpir'd to blaze promifcuous light,
And blefs this day with moft unequal'd luftre.
Your Royal Father, my victorious Lord,
Loaden with fpoils, and ever-living laurel,
Is entering now in martial pomp the palace.
Five hundred mules precede his folemn march,
Which groan beneath the weight of Moorifh wealth.
Chariots of war adorn'd with glittering gems,
Succeed ; and next, a hundred neighing fteeds,
White as the fleecy rain on Alpine hills ;
That bound and foam, and champ the golden bit,
As they difdain'd the victory they grace.
Prifoners of war in fhining fetters follow :
And captains of the nobleft blood of Afric
Sweat by his chariot wheel, and lick and grind,
With gnafhing teeth, the duft his triumphs raife.
The fwarming populace fpread every wall,
And cling, as if with claws they did enforce
Their hold thro' clifted ftones, ftretching and ftaring,
As if they were all eyes, and every limb
Would feed its faculty of admiration.
While you alone retire and fhun this fight ;
This fight, which is indeed not feen (tho' twice
The multitude fhould gaze) in abfence of your eyes.

Alm. My Lord, my eyes ungratefully behold
The gilded trophies of exterior honours.
Nor will my ears be charm'd with founding words,
Or pompous phrafe ; the pageantry of fouls.
But that my father is return'd in fafety,
I bend to Heav'n with thanks.

Gon. Excellent princefs !

But 'tis a talk unfit for my weak age,
With dying words, to offer at your praife.
Garcia, my fon, your beauty's loweft flave,
Has better done; in proving with his fword
The force and influence of your matchlefs charms.

Alm. I doubt not of the worth of Garcia's deeds,
Which had been brave, tho' I had ne'er been born.

Leon. Madam, the King.   [*Flourifh.*

Alm. My women. I would meet him.

                    [*Attendants to* Almeria *enter in mourning.*

S C E N E IV.

Symphony of warlike mufic. Enter the K I N G, *attended by*
G A R C I A *and feveral officers. Files of Prifoners in chains,
and Guards, who are ranged in order round the ftage.* A L M E-
R I A *meets the King, and kneels; afterwards* G O N S A-
L E Z *kneels and kiffes the King's hand, while Garcia does the
fame to the Princefs.*

King. Almeria, rife————My beft Gonfalez, rife.
What, tears! my good old friend!

Gon. But tears of joy.
Believe me, Sir, to fee you thus has fill'd
My eyes with more delight than they can hold.

King. By Heav'n thou lov'ft me, and I'm pleas'd thou do'ft.
Take it for thanks, old man, that I rejoice
To fee thee weep on this occafion—fome.
Here are, who feem to mourn at our fuccefs!
Why is't, Almeria, that you meet our eyes,
Upon this folemn day, in thefe fad weeds?
In oppofition to my brightnefs, you
And yours are all like daughters of affliction.

Alm. Forgive me, Sir, if I offend.
The year, which I have vow'd to pay to Heav'n
In mourning and ftrict life, for my deliverance
From wreck and death, wants yet to be expir'd.

King. Your zeal to Heav'n is great, fo is your debt:
Yet fomething too is due to me, who gave
That life, which Heav'n preferv'd. A day beftow'd
In filial duty, had aton'd and given

A difpenfation to your vow—No more.
'Twas weak and wilful—and a woman's error.
Yet—upon thought, it doubly wounds my fight,
To fee that fable worn upon the day
Succeeding that, in which our deadlieft foe,
Hated Anfelmo, was inter'd——By Heav'n,
It looks as thou didft mourn for him: juft fo,
Thy fenfelefs vow appear'd to bear its date,
Not from that hour wherein thou wert preferv'd.
Ha ? What ? thou doft not weep to-think of that.

Gon. Have patience, Royal Sir; the Princefs weeps
To have offended you. If fate decreed,
One pointed hour fhould be Alphonfo's lofs,
And her deliverance; is fhe to blame?

King. I tell thee fhe's to blame, not to have feafted
When my firft foe was laid in earth, fuch enmity,
Such deteftation, bears my blood to his;
My daughter fhould have revell'd at his death,
She fhould have made thefe palace-walls to fhake,
And all this high and ample roof to ring
With her rejoicings. What, to mourn, and weep;
Then, then to weep, and pray, and grieve? By Heav'n,
There's not a flave, a fhackled flave of mine,
But fhould have fmil'd that hour, through all his care,
And fhook his chains in tranfport and rude harmony.

Gon. What fhe has done, was in excefs of goodnefs;
Betray'd by too much piety, to feem
As if fhe had offended.——Sure, no more.

King. To feem is to commit, at this conjuncture.
I wo' not have a feeming forrow feen
To-day——Retire, diveft yourfelf with fpeed
Of that offenfive black; on me be all
The violation of your vow: for you,
It fhall be your excufe, that I command it.

Gar. kneeling.] Your pardon, Sir, if I prefume fo far,
As to remind you of your gracious promife.

King. Rife, Garcia——I forgot. Yet ftay, Almeria.

Alm. My boding heart!——What is your pleafure, Sir?

King. Draw near, and give your hand; and, Garcia, yours:
Receive this Lord, as one whom I have found
Worthy to be your hufband, and my fon.

Gar. Thus let me kneel to take——O not to take——
But to devote, and yield myfelf for ever
The flave and creature of my royal miftrefs.

Gon. O let me proftrate pay my worthlefs thanks——

King. No more; my promife long fince pafs'd, thy fervices,
And Garcia's well-try'd valour, all oblige me.
This day we triumph: but to morrow's fun,
Garcia, fhall fhine to grace thy nuptials———

Alm. Oh!   [*Faints.*

Gar. She faints! help to fupport her.

Gon. She recovers.

King. A fit of bridal fear; how is't, Almeria?

Alm. A fudden chilnefs feizes on my fpirits.
Your leave, Sir, to retire.

King. Garcia, conduct her.

            [Garcia *leads* Almeria *to the door and returns.*
This idle vow hangs on her woman's, fears.
I'll have a prieft fhall preach her from her faith,
And make it fin, not to renounce that vow
Which I'd have broken. Now, what would Alonzo?

SCENE V.

KING, GONSALEZ, GARCIA, ALONZO, *Attendants.*

Alon. Your beauteous captive, Zara, is arriv'd,
And with a train as if fhe ftill were wife
To Abucacim, and the Moor had conquer'd.

King. It was our will fhe fhould be fo attended.
Bear hence thefe prifoners. Garcia, which is he,
Of whofe mute valour you relate fuch wonders?

                              [*Prifoners 'ed off.*

Gar. Ofmyn, who led the Moorifh horfe; but he,
Great Sir, at her requeft, attends on Zara.

King. He is your prifoner; as you pleafe difpofe him.

Gar. I would oblige him, but he fhuns my kindnefs;

And with a haughty mein, and ftern civility,
Dumbly declines all offers : if he fpeak,
'Tis fcarce above a word ; as he were born
Alone to do, and did difdain to talk;
At leaft, to talk where he muft not command.

King. Such fullennefs, and in a man fo brave,
Muft have fome other caufe than his captivity.
Did Zara, then, requeft he might attend her ?

Gar. My Lord, fhe did.

King. That, join'd with his behaviour,
Begets a doubt. I'd have 'em watch'd ; perhaps
Her chains hang heavier on him than his own.

S C E N E VI.

KING, GONSALEZ, GARCIA, ALONZO, ZA-
RA and OSMYN *bound. conducted by* PEREZ *and a
Guard, and attended by* SELIM *and feveral Mutes and Eu-
nuchs in a train.*

King. What welcome, and what honours, beauteous Zara,
A king and conqueror can give, are yours.
A conqueror indeed, where you are won ;
Who with fuch luftre ftrike admiring eyes,
That had our pomp been with fuch prefence grac'd,
Th' expecting croud had been deceiv'd; and feen
Their monarch enter not triumphant, but
In pleafing triumph led; your beauty's flave.

Zara. If I on any terms could condefcend
To like captivity, or think thofe honours
Which conquerors in courtefy beftow,
Of equal value with unborrow'd rule,
And native right to arbitrary fway;
I might be pleas'd, when I behold the train
With ufual homage wait But when I feel
Thefe bonds, I look with lothing on myfelf;
And fcorn vile flavery, tho' doubly hid
Beneath mock-praifes, and diffembling ftate.

King. Thofe bonds 'Twas my command you fhou'd be
How durft you, Perez, difobey ?   [free.

Per. Great Sir,
Your order was, she shou'd not wait your triumph;
But at some distance follow, thus attended.

King. 'Tis false; 'twas more; I bid she should be free:
If not in words, I bid it by my eyes.
Her eyes did more than bid——Free her and hers
With speed——yet stay——my hands alone can make
Fit reftitution here——Thus I release you,
And by releafing you, enflave myself.

Zara. Such favours so conferr'd, tho' when unfought,
Deferve acknowledgement from noble minds.
Such thanks, as one hating to be oblig'd——
Yet hating more ingratitude, can pay,
I offer.

King. born to excel, and to command!
As by tranfcendent beauty to attract
All eyes, so by pre-eminence of foul
To rule all hearts.
Garcia, what's he, who with contracted brow

           [*Beholding* Ofmyn *as they unbind him.*
And fullen port, glooms downward with his eyes;
At once regardlefs of his chains, or liberty?

Gar. That, Sir, is he of whom I fpoke; that's Ofmyn.

King. He anfwers well the character you gave him.
Whence comes it, valiant Ofmyn, that a man
So great in arms, as thou art faid to be,
So hardly can endure captivity,
The common chance of war?

Ofm. Becaufe captivity
Has robb'd me of a dear and juft revenge.

King. I underftand not that.

Ofm I would not have you.

Zara. That gallant Moor in battle loft a friend,
Whom more than life he lov d; and the regret,
Of not revenging on his foes that lofs,
Has caus'd this melancholy and defpair.

King. She does excufe him: 'tis as I expected. [*To* Gon.

Gon. That friend may be herfelf; feem not to heed
His arrogant reply: fhe looks concern'd.

King. I'll have inquiry made; perhaps his friend
Yet lives, and is a prisoner. His name?

Zara. Heli.

King. Garcia, that search shall be your care:
It shall be mine to pay devotion here;
At this fair shrine to lay my laurels down,
And raise love's altar on the spoils of war.

    Conquest and triumph, now, are mine no more:
Nor will I victory in camps adore:
For, ling'ring there, in long suspence she stands,
Shifting the prize in unresolving hands:
Unus'd to wait, I broke through her delay,
Fix'd her by force, and snatch'd the doubtful day.
Now late I find that war is but her sport;
In love the goddess keeps her awful court:
Fickle in fields, unsteadily she flies,
But rules with settled sway in Zara's eyes.

ACT II.   SCENE I.

Representing the Isle of a Temple.

GARCIA, HELI, PEREZ.

GARCIA.

THIS way, we're told, Osmyn was seen to walk;
   Choosing this lonely mansion of the dead,
To mourn, brave Heli, thy mistaken fate.

    Heli. Let Heav'n with thunder to the centre strike me,
If to arise in very deed from death,
And to revisit with my long-clos'd eyes
This living light, could to my soul, or sense,
Afford a thought, or show a glimpse of joy,
In least proportion to the vast delight
I feel, to hear of Osmyn's name; to hear
That Osmyn lives, and I again shall see him.

    Gar. I've heard, with admiration, of your friendship.

    Per. Yonder, my Lord, behold the noble Moor.

    Heli. Where? where?

    Gar. I saw him not, nor any like him——

Per. I faw him, when I fpoke, thwarting my view,
And ftriding with diftemper'd hafte; his eyes
Seem'd flame, and flafh'd upon me with a glance;
Then forward fhot their fires, which he purfu'd,
As to fome object frightful, yet not fear'd.

Gar. Let's hafte to follow him, and know the caufe.

Heli. My Lord, let me intreat you to forbear:
Leave me alone to find, and cure the caufe.
I know his melancholy, and fuch ftarts
Are ufual to his temper. It might raife him
To act fome violence upon himfelf,
So to be caught in an unguarded hour,
And when his foul gives all her paffion way
Secure and loofe in friendly folitude.
I know his noble heart would burft with fhame,
To be furpris'd by ftrangers in its frailty.

Gar. Go, gen'rous Heli, and relieve your friend.
Far be it from me, officioufly to pry
Or prefs upon the privacies of others.

SCENE II.

GARCIA, PEREZ.

Gar. Perez, the King expects from our return
To have his jealoufy confirm'd or clear'd,
Of that appearing love which Zara bears
To Ofmyn; but fome other opportunity
Muft make that plain.

Per. To me 'twas long fince plain,
And ev'ry look from him and her confirms it.

Gar. If fo, unhappinefs attends their love,
And I cou'd pity 'em. I hear fome coming.
The friends perhaps are met; let us avoid 'em.

SCENE III.

ALMERIA, LEONORA.

Alm. It was a fancy'd noife, for all is hufh'd.

Leon. It bore the accent of a human voice.

Alm. It was thy fear, or elfe fome tranfient wind
Whiftling thro' hollows of this vaulted ifle.
We'll liften ———

 Leon. Hark!

 Alm. No, all is hufh'd, and ftill as death—'Tis dreadful!
How reverend is the face of this tall pile,
Whofe ancient pillars rear their marble heads,
To bear aloft its arch'd and pond'rous roof,
By its own weight made ftedfaft and immoveable,
Looking tranquillity. It ftrikes an awe
And terror on my aching fight ; the tombs
And monumental caves of death look cold,
And fhoot a chilnefs to my trembling heart.
Give me thy hand, and let me hear thy voice ;
Nay, quickly fpeak to me, and let me hear
Thy voice ———my own affrights me with its echoes.

 Leon. Let us return ; the horror of this place,
And filence, will increafe your melancholy.

 Alm. It may my fears, but cannot add to that.
No, I will on ; fhew me Anfelmo's tomb,
Lead me o'er bones and fkulls and mould'ring earth
Of human bodies ; for I'll mix with them.
Or wind me in the fhroud of fome pale coarfe
Yet green in earth, rather than be the bride
Of Garcia's more detefted bed : that thought
Exerts my fpirits ; and my prefent fears
Are loft in dread of greater ill. Then fhew me,
Lead me, for I am bolder grown : lead on
Where I may kneel, and pay my vows again
To him, to Heav'n, and my Alphonfo's foul.

 Leon. I go : but Heaven can tell with what regret.

S C E N E   IV.

The SCENE *opening difcovers a place of tombs. One monument
    fronting the view greater than the reft.*

 Heli. I wander through this maze of monuments,
Yet cannot find him——Hark ! fure 'tis the voice
Of one complaining.—There it founds——I'll follow it.

SCENE V.

ALMERIA, LEONORA.

Leon. Behold the sacred vault, within whose womb,
The poor remains of good Anselmo reft;
Yet fresh and unconsum'd by time or worms:
What do I see? O Heaven; either my eyes
Are false, or still the marble door remains
Unclos'd: the iron grates that lead to death
Beneath, are still wide-stretch'd upon their hinge,
And staring on us with unfolded leaves.

Alm. Sure 'tis the friendly yawn of death for me;
And that dumb mouth, significant in show,
Invites me to the bed where I alone
Shall reft; shew me the grave, where nature, weary,
And long opprefs'd with woes and bending cares,
May lay the burden down, and sink in slumbers
Of peace eternal.   Death, grim death, will fold
Me in his leaden arms, and press me close
To his cold clayie breast: my father then
Will ceafe his tyranny; and Garcia too
Will fly my pale deformity with loathing.
My foul, enlarg'd from its vile bonds, will mount,
And range the starry orbs, and milky ways,
Of that refulgent world, where I shall swim
In liquid light, and float on seas of bliss
To my Alphonso's foul.   O joy too great!
O ecstasy of thought! Help me, Anselmo;
Help me, Alphonfo: take me, reach thy hand;
To thee, to thee I call, to thee, Alphonfo:
O Alphonfo!

SCENE VI.

ALMERIA, LEONORA, OSMYN *ascending from the tomb.*

Ofm. Who calls that wretched thing that was Alphonfo?
Alm. Angels, and all the hoft of heav'n, fupport me!
Ofm. Whence is that voice, whose fhrilness, from the grave,

And growing to his father's fhrowd, roots up
Alphonfo?

Alm. Mercy! providence! O fpeak,
Speak to it quickly, quickly; fpeak to me;
Comfort me, help me, hold me, hide me, hide me,
Leonora, in thy bofom, from the light,
And from all eyes.

Ofm. Amazement and illufion!
Rivet and nail me where I ftand, ye powers; [*Coming forward*
That motionlefs I may be ftill deceiv'd.
Let me not ftir, nor breathe, left I diffolve
That tender, lovely form of painted air,
So like Almeria.   Ha! it finks, it falls;
I'll catch it ere it goes, and grafp her fhade.
'Tis life! 'tis warm! 'tis fhe! 'tis fhe herfelf!
Nor dead, nor fhade, but breathing and alive!
It is Almeria, yes, it is my wife!

S C E N E   VII.

ALMERIA, LEONORA, OSMYN, HELI.

Leon. Alas, fhe ftirs not yet, nor lifts her eyes;
He too is fainting——Help me, help me, ftranger,
Who-e'er thou art, and lend thy hand to raife
Thefe bodies.

Heli. Ha! 'tis he! and with Almeria!
O miracle of happinefs! O joy
Unhop'd for! does Almeria live!

Ofm. Where is fhe?
Let me behold and touch her; and be fure
'Tis fhe; fhew me her face, and let me feel
Her lips with mine———'Tis fhe, I'm not deceiv'd;
I tafte her breath, I warm'd her and am warm'd,
Look up, Almeria, blefs me with thy eyes;
Look on thy love, thy lover, and thy hufband.

Alm. I've fworn I'll not wed Garcia; why d'ye force me?
Is this a father?

Ofm. Look on thy Alphonfo,
Thy father is not here, my love, nor Garcia:

Nor am I what I feem, but thy Alphonfo.
Am I fo alter'd, or art thou fo chang'd,
That feeing my difguife, thou feeft not me?

Alm. It is, it is Alphonfo; 'tis his face,
His voice, I know him now, I know him all.
O take me to thy arms, and bear me hence,
Back to the bottom of the boundlefs deep,
To feas beneath, where thou fo long haft dwelt.
O how haft thou return'd? How haft thou charm'd?
The wildnefs of the waves and rocks to this?
That thus relenting, they have giv'n thee back
To earth, to light and life, to love and me.

Ofm. O I'll not afk, nor anfwer how, or why.
We both have backward trod the path of fate,.
To meet again in life; to know I have thee,
Is knowing more than any circumftance
Or means by which I have thee————
To fold thee thus, to prefs thy balmy lips,
And gaze upon thy eyes, is fo much joy,
I have not leifure to reflect, or know,
Or trifle time in thinking.

Alm. Stay a while————
Let me look on thee, yet a little more.

Ofm. What would'ft thou? thou doft put me from thee
Alm. Yes.

Ofm. And why? What doft thou mean? Why dol
thou gaze fo?

Alm. I know not; 'tis to fee thy face, I think——.
It is too much! too much to bear and live!
To fee him thus again is fuch profufion
Of joy, of blifs——I cannot bear——I muft
Be mad——I cannot be tranfported thus.

Ofm. Thou excellence, thou joy, thou heav'n of love!

Alm. Where haft thou been? and how art thou alive?
How is all this? All-powerful Heav'n, what are we!
O my ftrain'd heart!——let me again behold thee,
For I weep to fee thee——Art thou not paler?
Much, much; how art thou chang'd?

Ofm. Not in my love.

Alm. No, no, thy griefs, I know, have done this to thee.
Thou haſt wept much, Alphonſo ; and, I fear,
Too much, too tenderly lamented me.

Ofm. Wrong not my love, to ſay too tenderly.
No more, my life; talk not of tears or grief;
Affliction is no more, now thou art found.
Why doſt thou weep, and hold thee from my arms;
My arms which ake to fold thee faſt, and grow
To thee with twining? Come, come to my heart.

Alm. I will, for I ſhould never look enough.
They would have marry'd me; but I had ſworn
To Heav'n and thee, and ſooner wou'd have dy'd.

Ofm. Perfection of all faithfulneſs and love!

Alm. Indeed I wou'd——Nay, I wou'd tell thee all,
If I cou'd ſpeak; how I have mourn'd and pray'd;
For I have pray'd to thee, as to a ſaint:
And thou haſt heard my prayer; for thou art come
To my diſtreſs, to my deſpair, which Heav'n
Could only by reſtoring thee have cur'd.

Ofm. Grant me but life, good Heav'n, but length of days,
To pay ſome part, ſome little of this debt,
This countleſs ſum of tenderneſs and love,
For which I ſtand engag'd to this all-excellence:
Then bear me in a whirlwind to my fate,
Snatch me from life, and cut me ſhort unwarn'd;
Then, then 'twill be enough——I ſhall be old,
I ſhall have liv'd beyond all æra's then
Of yet unmeaſur'd time; when I have made
This exquiſite, this moſt amazing goodneſs,
Some recompence of love and matchleſs truth.

Alm. 'Tis more than recompence, to ſee thy face;
If heav'n is greater joy, it is no happineſs,
For 'tis not to be borne——What ſhall I ſay?
I have a thouſand things to know, and aſk,
And ſpeak——That thou art here, beyond all hope,
All thought; that all at once thou art before me,
And with ſuch ſuddenneſs haſt hit my ſight,

Is such surprize, such mystery, such ecstasy!
It hurries all my soul, and stuns my sense.
Sure from thy father's tomb thou didst arise.

Osm. I did; and thou, my love, didst call me; thou.

Alm. True; but how cam'st thou there? Wert thou

Osm. I was, and lying on my father's lead,   [alone?
When broken echoes of a distant voice
Disturb'd the sacred silence of the vault,
In murmurs round my head. I rose and listned,
And thought I heard thy spirit call Alphonso;
I thought I saw thee too; but O, I thought not
That I indeed should be so blest to see thee——

Alm. But still, how cam'st thou hither? How thus?—Ha?
What's he, who like thyself is started here
Ere seen?

Osm. Where? ha! What do I see? Antonio?
I'm fortunate indeed——my friend too, safe!

Heli. Most happily, in finding you thus bless'd.

Alm. More miracles! Antonio too escap'd!

Osm. And twice escap'd, both from the rage of seas:
And war: for in the fight I saw him fall.

Heli. But fell unhurt, a prisoner as yourself,
And as yourself made free; hither I came
Impatiently to seek you, where I knew
Your grief would lead you, to lament Anselmo.

Osm. There are no wonders, or else all is wonder.

Heli. I saw you on the ground, and rais'd you up.
When with astonishment, I saw Almeria.

Osm. I saw her too, and therefore saw not thee.

Alm. Nor I; nor could I, for my eyes were yours.

Osm. What means the bounty of all-gracious Heav'n,
That persevering still, with open hand,
It scatters good, as in a waste of mercy!
Where will this end! but Heav'n is infinite
In all, and can continue to bestow,
When scanty number shall be spent in telling.

Leon. Or i'm deceiv'd, or I beheld the glimpse
Of two in shining habits cross the isle;
Who by their pointing seem to mark this place.

Alm. Sure I have dream'd, if we muſt part ſo ſoon.

Oſm. I wiſh, at leaſt, our parting were a dream,
Or we could ſleep 'till we again were met.

Heli. Zara with Selim, Sir; I ſaw and know 'em :
You muſt be quick, for love will lend her wings.

Alm. What love ? Who is ſhe ? Why are you alarm'd ?

Oſm. She's the reverſe of thee; ſhe's my unhappineſs.
Harbour no thought that may diſturb thy peace;
But gently take thyſelf away, leſt ſhe
Should come, and ſee the ſtraining of my eyes
To follow thee. I'll think how we may meet
To part no more. My friend will tell thee all;
How I eſcap'd, how I am here, and thus;
How I'm not call'd Alphonſo, now, but Oſmyn;
And he Heli. All, all he will unfold,
Ere next we meet————

Alm. Sure we ſhall meet again————

Oſm. We ſhall; we part not but to meet again.
Gladneſs and warmth of ever-kindling love
Dwell with thee, and revive thy heart in abſence.

SCENE VIII.

OSMYN *alone.*

Yet I behold her————yet————And now no more.
Turn your lights inward, eyes, and view my thought,
So ſhall you ſtill behold her————'twill not be.
O impotence of ſight ! Mechanic ſenſe,
Which to exterior objects ow'ſt thy faculty,
Not ſeeing of election, but neceſſity.
Thus do our eyes, as do all common mirrours,
Succeſſively reflect ſucceeding images :
Not what they would, but muſt; a ſtar, or toad:
Not ſo the mind, whoſe undetermin'd view
Revolves, and to the preſent adds the paſt:
Eſſaying further to futurity ;
But that in vain. I have Almeria here————
At once, as I before have ſeen her often————

SCENE IX.

ZARA, SELIM, OSMYN.

Zara. See where he ftands, folded and fix'd to earth,
Stiff'ning in thought, a ftatue among ftatues.
Why, cruel Ofmyn, doft thou fly me thus?
Is it well done? Is this then the return
For fame, for honour, and for empire loft?
But what is lofs of honour, fame and empire!
Is this the recompence referv'd for love;
Why doft thou leave my eyes, and fly my arms,
To find this place of horror and obfcurity?
Am I more loathfome to thee than the grave,
That thou doft feek to fhield thee there, and fhun
My love? But to the grave I'll follow thee————
He looks not, minds not, hears not; barbarous man,
Am I neglected thus? Am I defpifed?
Not heard! ungrateful Ofmyn.

Ofm. Ha, 'tis Zara!

Zara. Yes, traitor; Zara, loft, abandon'd Zara,
Is a regardlefs fuppliant, now, to Ofmyn,
The flave, the wretch that fhe redeem'd from death,
Difdains to liften now, or look on Zara.

Ofm. Far be the guilt of fuch reproaches from me;
Loft in myfelf, and blinded by my thoughts,
I faw you not, 'till now.

Zara. Now then you fee————
But with fuch dumb and thanklefs eyes you look,
Better I was unfeen, than feen thus coldly.

Ofm. What would you from a wretch that came to mourn,
And only for his forrows chofe this folitude?
Look round; joy is not here, nor chearfulnefs.
You have purfu'd misfortune to its dwelling,
Yet look for gaiety and gladnefs there.

Zara. Inhuman! why, why doft thou rack me thus?
And with perverfenefs, from the purpofe anfwer?
What is't to me, this houfe of mifery?
What joy do I require? if thou doft mourn,

I come to mourn with thee; to fhare thy griefs,
And give thee, for 'em, in exchange my love.

 Ofm. O that's the greateft grief————I am fo poor,
I have not wherewithal to give again.

 Zara. Thou haft a heart, tho' 'tis a favage one;
Give it me as it is; I afk no more
For all I've done, and all I have endur'd:
For faving thee, when I beheld thee firft,
Driven by the tide upon my country's coaft,
Pale and expiring, drench'd in briny waves,
Thou and thy friend, 'till my compaffion found thee;
Compaffion! fcarce will't own that name, fo foon,
So quickly was it love; for thou wert god-like
Ev'n then. Kneeling on earth, I loos'd my hair,
And with it dry'd thy wat'ry cheeks; then chaf'd
Thy temples, 'till reviving blood arofe,
And like the morn vermilion'd o'er thy face.
O Heav'n! how did my heart rejoice and ake,
When I beheld the day-break of thy eyes,
And felt the balm of thy refpiring lips!

 Ofm. O call not to my mind what you have done;
It fets a debt of that account before me,
Which fhews me poor, and bankrupt even in hopes.

 Zara. The faithful Selim, and my women know
The dangers which I tempted to conceal you.
You know how I abus'd the credulous king;
What arts I us'd to make you pafs on him,
When he receiv'd you as the Prince of Fez;
And as my kinfman, honour'd and advanc'd you.
O, why do I relate what I have done?
What did I not? Was't not for you this war
Commenc'd? not knowing who you were, nor why
You hated Manuel, I urg'd my hufband
To this invafion; where he late was loft,
Where all is loft, and I am made a flave.
Look on me now, from empire fall'n to flavery;
Think on my fuff'rings firft, then look on me;
Think on the caufe of all, then view thyfelf:

I

Reflect on Ofmyn, and then look on Zara,
The fall'n, the loft, and now the captive Zara,
And now abandon'd——fay, what then is Ofmyn?

  Ofm. A fatal wretch——a huge ftupendous ruin,
That tumbling on its prop, crufh'd all beneath,
And bore contiguous palaces to earth.

  Zara. Yet thus, thus fall'n, thus levell'd with the vileft,
If I have gain'd thy love, 'tis glorious ruin ;
Ruin ! 'tis ftill to reign, and to be more
A queen; for what are riches, empire, power,
But larger means to gratify the will ?
The fteps on which we tread, to rife, and reach
Our wifh ; and that obtain'd, down with the fcaffolding
Of fceptres, crowns, and thrones ; they've ferv'd their end,
And are, like lumber to be left and fcorn'd.

  Ofm. Why was I made the inftrument to throw
In bonds the frame of this exalted mind ?

  Zara. We may be free ; the conqueror is mine ;
In chains unfeen I hold him by the heart,
And can unwind or ftrain him as I pleafe.
Give me thy love, I'll give thee liberty.

  Ofm. In vain you offer, and in vain require
What neither can beftow: fet free yourfelf,
And leave a flave the wretch that would be fo.

  Zara. Thou an'ft not mean fo poorly as thou talk'ft.

  Ofm. Alas, you know me not.

  Zara Not who thou art :
But what this laft ingratitude declares,
This groveling bafenefs——Thou fay'ft true, I know
Thee not, for what thou art yet wants a name :
But fomething fo unworthy, and fo vile,
That to have lov'd thee makes me yet more loft,
Than all the malice of my other fate.
Traitor, monfter, cold and perfidious flave ;
A flave, not daring to be free! nor dares
To love above him, for 'tis dangerous :
'Tis that I know ; for thou doft look, with eyes
Sparkling defire, and trembling to poffefs.

I know my charms have reach'd thy very soul,
And thrill'd thee through with darted fires; but thou
Doſt fear ſo much, thou dar'ſt not wiſh.   The King!
There, there's the dreadful ſound, the King's thy rival!

Sel. Madam, the King is here, and entering now.

Zara. As I could wiſh; by Heav'n I'll be reveng'd.

S C E N E X.

ZARA, OSMYN, SELIM, the KING, PEREZ,
and Attendants.

King. Why does the faireſt of her kind withdraw
Her ſhining from the day, to gild this ſcene
Of death and night? Ha! what diſorder's this?
Somewhat I heard of king and rival mention'd.
What's he that dares be rival to the King?
Or lift his eyes to like, where I adore?

Zara. There, he; your priſoner, and that was my ſlave.

King. How? Better than my hopes! does ſhe accuſe him?
                                                    [*Aſide.*

Zara. Am I become ſo low by my captivity,
And do your arms ſo leſſen what they conquer,
That Zara muſt be made the ſport of ſlaves?
And ſhall the wretch, whom yeſter ſun beheld
Waiting my nod, the creature of my pow'r,
Preſume to-day to plead audacious love,
And build bold hopes on my dejected fate?

King. Better for him to tempt the rage of Heav'n,
And wrench the bolt red-hiſſing from the hand
Of him that thunders, than but think that inſolence.
'Tis daring for a God.   Hence, to the wheel
With that Ixion, who aſpires to hold
Divinity embrac'd, to whips and priſons
Drag him with ſpeed, and rid me of his face.
                                        [*Guards ſeize* Oſmyn.

Zara. Compaſſion led me to bemoan his ſtate,
Whoſe former faith had merited much more;
And through my hopes in you, I undertook

VOL. II.   D

He fhould be fet at large ; thence fprung his infolence,
And what was charity he conftru'd love.

   King. Enough ; his punifhment be what you pleafe.
But let me lead you from this place of forrow,
To one, where young delights attend ; and joys
Yet new, unborn, and blooming in the bud,
Which wait to be full-blown at your approach,
And fpread like rofes to the morning fun :
Where ev'ry hour fhall roll in circling joys,
And love fhall wing the tedious-wafting day :
Life without love is load ; and time ftands ftill ;
   What we refufe to him, to death we give ;
   And then, then only, when we love, we live.

ACT III. SCENE I.

A PRISON.

OSMYN *alone, with a paper.*

BUT now, and I was clos'd within the tomb
    That holds my father's afhes ; and but now,
Where he was pris'ner, I am too imprifon'd.
Sure 'tis the hand of Heav'n that leads me thus,
And for fome purpofe points out thefe remembrances.
In a dark corner of my cell I found
This paper, what it is this light will fhow.
   " If my Alphonfo"——Ha !   [*Reading.*
   " If my Alphonfo live, reftore him, Heav'n ;
   " Give me more weight, crufh my declining years
   " With bolts, with chains, imprifonment and want ;
   " But blefs my fon, vifit not him for me."

It is his hand ; this was his prayer—yet more :

   " Let ev'ry hair, which forrow by the roots   [*Reading.*
   " Tears from my hoary and devoted head,
   " Be doubled in thy mercies to my fon :
   " Not for myfelf, but him, hear me, all-gracious"——

'Tis wanting what fhould follow—Heav'n fhould follow,
But 'tis torn off—Why fhould that word alone

Be torn from his petition ? 'Twas to Heav'n,
But Heav'n was deaf, Heav'n heard him not ; but thus,
Thus as the name of Heav'n from this is torn,
So did it tear the ears of mercy from
His voice, shutting the gates of pray'r against him.
If piety be thus debarr'd accefs
On high, and of good men the very beft
Is fingled out to bleed, and bear the fcourge,
What is reward ? or what is punifhment ?
But who fhall dare to tax eternal juftice !
Yet I may think——I may, I muft ; for thought
Precedes the will to think, and error lives
Ere reafon can be born. Reafon, the power
To guefs at right and wrong, the twinkling lamp
Of wand'ring life, that winks by turns,
Fooling the follower, betwixt fhade and fhining.
What noife ! Who's there ! My friend ! How com'ft thou
    hither ?

S C E N E II.

OSMYN, HELI.

Heli. The time's too precious to be fpent in telling ;
The captain, influenc'd by Almeria's power,
Gave order to the guards for my admittance.

   Ofm. How does Almeria ? But I know fhe is
As I am. Tell me, may I hope to fee her ?

   Heli. You may : anon, at midnight when the King
Is gone to reft, and Garcia is retir'd,
(Who takes the privilege to vifit late,
Prefuming on a bridegroom's right) fhe'll come.

   Ofm. She'll come ! 'tis what I wifh, yet what I fear.
She'll come ! but whither, and to whom ? O Heav'n !
To a vile prifon, and a captiv'd wretch ;
To one, whom had fhe never known, fhe had
Been happy : Why, why was that heav'nly creature
Abandon'd o'er to love what Heav'n forfakes ?
Why does fhe follow, with unwearied fteps,

One who has tir'd misfortune with purfuing?
One, driven about the world like blaſted leaves
And chaff, the fport of adverfe winds; 'till late
At length, imprifon'd in fome cleft of rock,
Or earth, it refts, and rots to filent duſt.

   Heli. Have hopes, and hear the voice of better fate.
I've learn'd there are diforders ripe for mutiny
Among the troops, who thought to ſhare the plunder,
Which Manuel to his own ufe and avarice
Converts. This news has reach'd Valentia's frontiers;
Where many of your fubjects, long opprefs'd
With tyranny and grievous impofitions,
Are rifen in arms, and call for chiefs to head
And lead them to regain their rights and liberty.

   Ofm. By Heav'n thou'ſt rous'd me from my lethargy.
The fpirit which was deaf to my own wrongs,
And the loud cries of my dead father's blood;
Deaf to revenge——nay, which refus'd to hear
The piercing fighs and murmurs of my love
Yet unenjoy'd; what not Almeria could
Revive, or raife, my people's voice has waken'd.
O my Antonio, I am all on fire,
My foul is up in arms, ready to charge
And bear amidſt the foe, with conqu'ring troops.
I hear 'em call to lead 'em on to liberty,
To victory; their fhouts and clamours rend
My ears, and reach the heav'n: where is the King?
Where is Alphonfo? ha! Where, where indeed?
O I could tear and burſt the ſtrings of life,
To break thefe chains. Off, off, ye ſtains of royalty,
Off, flavery. O curfe! that I alone
Can beat and flutter in my cage, when I
Would foar and ſtoop at victory beneath.

   Heli. Our poſture of affairs, and fcanty time,
My Lord, require you ſhould compofe yourfelf,
And think on what we may reduce to practice.
Zara, the caufe of your reſtraint, may be
The means of liberty reſtor'd. That gain'd,
Occafion will not fail to point out ways

For your efcape. Mean time, I've thought already
With fpeed and fafety to convey myfelf
Where not far off fome malecontents hold council
Nightly; who hate this tyrant; fome, who love
Anfelmo's memory, and will, for certain,
When they fhall know you live, affift your caufe.

Ofm. My friend and counfellor, as thou think'ft fit,
So do. I will with patience wait my fortune.

Heli. When Zara comes, abate of your averfion.

Ofm. I hate her not, nor can diffemble love:
But as I may, I'll do. I have a paper
Which I would fhew thee, friend, but that the fight
Would hold thee here, and clog thy expedition.
Within I found it, by my father's hand
'Twas writ; a pray'r for me, wherein appears
Paternal love prevailing o'er his forrows;
Such fanctity, fuch tendernefs fo mix'd
With grief as would draw tears from inhumanity.

Heli. The care of Providence fure left it there,
To arm your mind with hope. Such piety
Was never heard in vain: Heav'n has in ftore
For you thofe bleffings it with-held from him.
In that affurance live : which time, I hope,
And our next meeting will confirm.

Ofm. Farewel,
My friend; the good thou doft deferve attend thee.

S C E N E III.

O S M Y N *alone.*

I've been to blame, and queftion'd with impiety
The care of Heav'n. Not fo my father bore
More anxious grief. This fhould have better taught me:
This leffon, in fome hour of infpiration,
By him fet down; when his pure thoughts were born,
Like fumes of facred incenfe, o'er the clouds,
And wafted thence, on angels wings, thro' ways
Of light, to the bright fource of all. For there
He in the book of prefcience faw this day.

And waking, to the world, and mortal fenfe,
Left this example of his refignation,
This his laft legacy to me, which, here,
I'll treafure as more worth than diadèms,
Or all extended rule of regal pow'r.

SCENE IV.

OSMYN, ZARA *veiled*.

Ofm. What brightnefs breaks upon me thus thro' fhades,
And promifes a day to this dark dwelling?
Is it my love ?——

Zara. O that thy heart had taught   [*Lifting her veil.*
Thy tongue that faying.

Ofm. Zàra! I am betray'd
By my furprize.   [*Afide.*

Zara. What, does my face difpleafe thee ?
That having feen it, thou doft turn thy eyes
Away, as from deformity and horror.
If fo, this fable curtain fhall again
Be drawn, and I will ftand before thee feeing,
And unfeen. Is it my love? afk again
That queftion, fpeak again in that foft voice,
And look again with wifhes in thy eyes.
O no, thou canft not, for thou fee'ft me now,
As fhe whofe favage breaft has been the caufe
Of thefe thy wrongs; as fhe whofe barbarous rage
Has loaded thee with chains and galling irons :
Well doft thou fcorn me, and upbraid my falfenefs :
Could one who lov'd, thus torture whom fhe lov'd?
No, no, it muft be hatred, dire revenge,
And deteftation, that could ufe thee thus.
So thou doft think; then do but tell me fo;
Tell me, and thou fhalt fee how I'll revenge
Thee on this falfe one, how I'll ftab and tear
This heart of flint 'till it fhall bleed; and thou
Shalt weep for mine, forgetting thy own miferies.

Ofm. You wrong me, beauteous Zara, to believe
bear my fortunes with fo low a mind,

As ſtill to meditate revenge on all
Whom chance, or fate, working by ſecret cauſes,
Has made perforce ſubſervient to that end
The heav'nly pow'rs allot me; no, not you,
But deſtiny and inauſpicious ſtars
Have caſt me down to this low being : or,
Granting you had, from you I have deſerv'd it.

   Zara. Can'ſt thou forgive me then ? wilt thou believe
So kindly of my fault, to call it madueſs ?
O, give that madneſs yet a milder name,
And call it paſſion ; then, be ſtill more kind,
And call that paſſion love.

   Oſm. Give it a name,
Or being as you pleaſe, ſuch I will think it.   [neſs,

   Zira. O thou doſt wound me more with this thy good-
Than e'er thou could'ſt with bittereſt reproaches ;
Thy anger could not pierce thus to my heart.

   Oſm. Yet I could wiſh——
   Zara. Haſte me to know it ; what ?
   Oſm. That at this time I had not been this thing.
   Zara. What thing?
   Oſm. This ſlave.
   Zara. O Heav'n ! my fears interpret
This thy ſilence : ſomewhat of high concern,
Long faſhioning within thy labouring mind,
And now juſt ripe for birth, my rage has ruin'd:
Have I done this ? Tell me, am I ſo curs'd ?

   Oſm. Time may have ſtill one fated hour to come,
Which, wing'd with liberty, might overtake
Occaſion paſt.

   Zara. Swift as occaſion, I
Myſelf will fly ; and earlier than the morn
Wake thee to freedom. Now 'tis late; and yet
Some news few minutes paſt arriv'd which ſeem'd
To ſhake the temper of the king—Who knows
What racking cares diſeaſe a monarch's bed ?
Or love, that late at night ſtill lights his lamp,
And ſtrikes his rays thro' duſk, and folded lids,
Forbidding reſt, may ſtretch his eyes awake,

And force their balls abroad at this dead hour.
I'll try.

   Osm. I have not merited this grace;
Nor, shou'd my secret purpose take effect,
Can I repay, as you require, such benefit.

   Zara. Thou can'st not owe me more, nor have I more
To give, than I've already lost. But now,
So does the form of our engagements rest,
Thou hast the wrong, 'till I redeem thee hence;
That done, I leave thy justice to return.
My love. Adieu.

SCENE V.

OSMYN, *alone.*

   This woman has a soul
Of godlike mould, intrepid and commanding;
And challenges, in spite of me, my best
Esteem; to this she's fair, few more can boast
Of personal charms, or with less vanity
Might hope to captivate the heart of kings.
But she has passions which out-strip the wind,
And tear her virtues up, as tempests root
The sea. I fear when she shall know the truth,
Some swift and dire event of her blind rage
Will make all fatal. But behold she comes
For whom I fear, to shield me from my fears,
The cause and comfort of my boding heart.

SCENE VI.

ALMERIA. OSMYN.

   Osm. My life, my health, my liberty, my all!
How shall I welcome thee to this sad place?
How speak to thee the words of joy and transport?
How run into thy arms witheld by fetters;
Or take thee into mine, while I'm thus manacled,
And pinion'd like a thief or murderer?
Shall I not hurt or bruise thy tender body,
And stain thy body with the rust of these
Rude irons? must I meet thee thus, Almeria?

Alm. Thus, thus; we parted, thus to meet again,
Thou told'st me thou would'st think how we might meet
To part no more——Now we will part no more;
For these thy chains, or death, shall join us ever.

Osm. Hard means to ratify that word!—O cruelty,
That ever I should think beholding thee
A torture'—Yet, such is the bleeding anguish
Of my heart, to see thy sufferings——O heav'n!
That I could almost turn my eyes away,
Or wish thee from my sight.

Alm. O, say not so;
Tho' 'tis because thou lov'st me. Do not say,
On any terms, that thou dost wish me from thee.
No, no, 'tis better thus, that we together
Feed on each other's heart, devour our woes
With mutual appetite; and mingling in
One cup the common stream of both our eyes,
Drink bitter draughts, with never-slacking thirst,
Thus better, than for any cause to part.
What dost thou think? Look not so tenderly
Upon me——speak, and take me in thy arms——.
Thou canst not! thy poor arms are bound, and strive
In vain with the remorseless chains which gnaw
And eat into thy flesh, festring thy limbs
With rankling rust.

Osm. Oh! O——

Alm. Give me that sigh.
Why dost thou heave, and stifle in thy griefs?
Thy heart will burst, thy eyes look red and start;
Give thy soul way, and tell me thy dark thought.

Osm. For this world's rule, I wou'd not wound thy breast
With such a dagger as then stuck my heart.

Alm. Why? why? to know it cannot wound me more,
Than knowing thou hast felt it. Tell it me.
——Thou giv'st me pain with too much tenderness.

Osm. And thy excessive love distracts my sense!
O would'st thou be less killing, soft or kind,
Grief cou'd not double thus his darts against me.

Alm. Thou dost me wrong, and grief too robs my heart,

If there he fhoot not every other fhaft ;
Thy fecond felf fhou'd feel each other wound,
And woe fhou'd be in equal portions dealt.
I am thy wife——

 Ofm. O thou haft fearch'd too deep ;
There, there I bleed; there pull the cruel cords,
That ftrain my cracking nerves; engines and wheels,
That piece-meal grind, are beds of down and balm
To that foul-racking thought.

 Am. Then I am curs'd
Indeed, if that be fo ; if I'm thy torment,
Kill me, then kill me, dafh me with thy chains,
Tread on me ; what, am I thy bofom-fnake,
That fucks thy life-warm blood, and gnaws thy heart?
O that thy words had ftrength to break thefe bonds,
As they have ftrength to tear this heart afuuder ;
So fhould'ft thou be at large from all oppreffion.
Am I, am I of all thy woes the worft ?

 Ofm. My all of blifs, my everlafting life,.
Soul of my foul, and end of all my wifhes,
Why doft thou thus unman me with thy words,
And melt me down to mingle with thy weepings ?
Why doft thou afk ? Why doft thou talk thus piercingly ?
Thy forrows have difturb'd thy peace of mind,
And thou doft fpeak of miferies impoffible.

 Alm. Didft thou not fay, that racks and wheels were
And beds of eafe, to thinking me thy wife?   [balm,
 Ofm. No, no; nor fhou'd the fubtleft pains that hell,.
Or hell-born malice can invent, extort
A wifh or thought from me, to have thee other.
But thou wilt know what harrows up my heart:
Thou art my wife——nay, thou art yet my bride!
The facred union of connubial love
Yet unaccomplifh'd; his myfterious rites.
Delay'd ; nor has our Hymeneal torch
Yet lighted up his laft moft grateful facrifice ;
But dafh'd with rain from eyes, and fwell'd with fighs,
Burns dim, and glimmers with expiring light.
Is this dark cell a temple for that god ?

Or this vile earth an altar for such off'rings?
This den for slaves, this dungeon damp'd with woes;
Is this our marriage-bed? Are these our joys?
Is this to call thee mine? Oh, hold my heart!
To call thee mine? Yes; thus, even thus to call
Thee mine, were comfort, joy, extremest ecstasy.
But O, thou art not mine, not even in misery;
And 'tis deny'd to me to be so bless'd,
As to be wretched with thee.

  Alm. No; not that
The extremest malice of our fate can hinder:
That still is left us, and on that we'll feed,
As on the leavings of calamity.
There we will feast, and smile on past distress,
And hug, in scorn of it, our mutual ruin.

  Osm. O thou dost talk, my love, as one resolv'd
Because not knowing danger. But look forward;
Think on to-morrow, when thou shalt be torn
From these weak, struggling, unextended arms;
Think how my heart will heave, and eyes will strain,
To grasp and reach what is deny'd my hands;
Think how the blood will start, and tears will gush
To follow thee, my separating soul.
Think how I am, when thou shalt wed with Garcia!
Then will I smear these walls with blood, disfigure
And dash my face, and rive my clotted hair,
Break on the flinty floor my throbbing breast,
And grovel with gash'd hands to scratch a grave,
Stripping my nails, to tear this pavement up,
And bury me alive

  Alm. Heart-breaking horror!

  Osm. Then Garcia shall ly panting on thy bosom,
Luxurious revelling amidst thy charms;
And thou perforce must yield, and aid his transport.
Hell! hell! have I not cause to rage and rave?
What are all racks, and wheels, and whips to this?
Are they not soothing softness, sinking ease,
And wafting air to this! O my Almeria?
What do the damn'd endure, but to despair,

But knowing Heaven, to know it lost for ever?

Alm. O, I am struck; thy words are bolts of ice,
Which shot into my breast, now melt and chill me.
I chatter, shake, and faint, with thrilling fears.
No, hold me not——O let us not support,
But sink each other, deeper yet, down, down,
Where level'd low, no more we'll lift our eyes,
But prone, and dumb, rot the firm face of earth
With rivers of incessant scalding rain.

S C E N E VII.

ZARA, PEREZ, SELIM, OSMYN, ALMERIA.

Zara. Somewhat of weight to me requires his freedom,
Dare you dispute the king's command? Behold
The Royal signet.

Per. I obey; yet beg
Your Majesty one moment to defer
Your entering, 'till the princess is return'd
From visiting the noble prisoner.

Zara. Ha!
What say'st thou?

Osm. We are lost! undone! discover'd!
Retire, my life, with speed——Alas, we're seen:
Speak of compassion, let her hear you speak
Of interceding for me with the king?
Say somewhat quickly to conceal our loves,
If possible——

Alm. ——I cannot speak.

Osm. Let me
Conduct you forth, as not perceiving her,
But 'till she's gone; then bless me thus again.

Zara. Trembling and weeping as he leads her forth!
Confusion in his face, and grief in hers!
'Tis plain I've been abus'd——Death and destruction!
How shall I search into this mystery?
The bluest blast of pestilential air
Strike, damp, deaden her charms, and kill his eyes;
Perdition catch 'em both, and ruin part 'em.

Ofm. This charity to one unknown, and thus

[*Aloud to* Almeria *as she goes out.*

Diſtreſs'd, Heav'n will repay ; all thanks are poor.

S C E N E   VIII.

ZARA, SELIM, OSMYN.

Zara. Damn'd, damn'd diſſembler ! yet I will be calm,
Choke in my rage, and know the utmoſt depth
Of this deceiver——you ſeem much ſurprized.

Oſm. At your return ſo ſoon and unexpected !

Zara. And ſo unwiſh'd, unwanted too it ſeems.
Confuſion ! yet I will contain myſelf.
You're grown a favonrite ſince laſt we parted ;
Perhaps I'm ſaucy and intruding——

Oſm. ——Madam !

Zara. I did not know the Princeſs' favourite ;
Your pardon, Sir—miſtake me not ; you think
I'm angry ; you're deceiv'd.   I came to ſet
You free : but ſhall return much better pleas'd,
To find you have an intereſt ſuperior.

Oſm. You do not come to mock my miſeries ?

Zara. I do.

Oſm. I could at this time ſpare your mirth.

Zara. I know thou cou'dſt : but I'm not often pleas'd,
And will indulge it now.   What miſeries ?
Who wou'd not be thus happily confin'd,
To be the care of weeping Majeſty ?
To have contending queens, at dead of night,
Forſake their down, to wake with watry eyes,
And watch like tapers o'er your hours of reſt ?
O curſe ! I cannot hold——

Oſm. Come, 'tis too much.

Zara. Villain !

Oſm. How, Madam !

Zara. Thou ſhalt die.

Oſm. I thank you.

Zara. Thou lieſt ; for now I know for whom thou'd'ſt

Oſm. Then you may know for whom I'd die.   [live.

VOL. II.   E

Zara. Hell! Hell!
Yet I'll be calm—Dark and unknown betrayer!
But now the dawn begins, and the flow hand
Of fate is ftretch'd to draw the veil, and leave
Thee bare, the naked mark of public view.

Ofm. You may be ftill deceiv'd, 'tis in my power————

Zara. Who waits there? As you'll anfwer it, look this
    flave   [*To the Guard.*
Attempt no means to make himfelf away.
I've been deceiv'd. The public fafety now
Requires he fhould be more confin'd, and none,
No, not the princefs, fuffer'd or to fee,
Or fpeak with him: I'll quit you to the king.
Vile and ingrate! too late thou fhalt repent
The bafe injuftice thou haft done my love:
Yes, thou fhalt know, fpite of thy paft diftrefs,
  And all thofe ills which thou fo long haft mourn'd;
  Heav'n has no rage, like love to hatred turn'd,
  Nor hell a fury, like a woman fcorn'd.

ACT IV. SCENE I.

A Room of State.

ZARA, SELIM.

ZARA.

THOU haft already rack'd me with thy ftay;
  Therefore require me not to afk thee twice;
Reply at once to all. What is concluded?
 Sel. Your accufation highly has incens'd
The king, and were alone enough to urge
The fate of Ofmyn; but to that, frefh news
Is fince arriv'd, of more revolted troops.
'Tis certain Heli too is fled, and with him
(Which breeds amazement and diftraction) fome
Who bore high offices of weight and truft,
Both in the ftate and army. This confirms

The king, in full belief of all you told him,
Concerning Ofmyn and his correfpondence
With them who firft began the mutiny.
Wherefore a warrant for his death is fign'd,
And order given for public execution.

Zara. Ha! hafte thee! fly, prevent his fate and mine:
Find out the king, tell him I have of weight
More than his crown t'impart ere Ofmyn die.

Sel. It needs not, for the king will ftraight be here;
And as to your revenge, not his own intereft,
Pretend to facrifice the life of Ofmyn.

Zara. What fhall I fay? Invent, contrive, advife,
Somewhat to blind the king, and fave his life
In whom I live. Spite of my rage and pride,
I am a woman, and a lover ftill.
O, 'tis more grief but to fuppofe his death,
Than ftill to meet the rigour of his fcorn.
From my defpair my anger had its fource;
When he is dead I muft defpair for ever.
For ever! that's defpair—it was diftruft
Before: diftruft will ever be in love,
And anger in diftruft, both fhort-liv'd pains.
But in defpair, and ever-during death,
No term, no bound, but infinite of woe.
O torment, but to think! what then to bear?
Not to be borne——devife the means to fhun it,
Quick, or by Heav'n this dagger drinks thy blood.

Sel. My life is yours, nor wifh I to preferve it,
But to ferve you. I have already thought.

Zara. Forgive my rage; I know thy love and truth.
But fay, what's to be done? or when, or how,
Shall I prevent, or ftop th' approaching danger?

Sel. You muft ftill feem moft refolute and fix'd
On Ofmyn's death; too quick a change for mercy
Might breed fufpicion of the caufe. Advife
That execution may be done in private.

Zara. On what pretence?

Sel. Your own requeft's enough.
However, for a colour, tell him, you

Have cause to fear his guards may be corrupted,
And some of them bought off to Osmyn's interest,
Who, at the place of execution, will
Attempt to force his way for an escape.
The state of things will countenance all suspicions.
Then offer to the king to have him strangled
In secret by your mutes, and get an order,
That none but mutes may have admittance to him.
I can no more, the King is here.   Obtain
This grant——and I'll acquaint you with the rest.

S C E N E II.

KING, GONSALEZ, PEREZ, ZARA, SELIM.

King. Bear to the dungeon those rebellious slaves,
Th' ignoble curs, that help to fill the cry,
And spend their mouths in barking tyranny.
But for their leaders, Sancho and Ramirez,
Let 'em be led away to present death.
  Per. See it perform'd.
  Gon. Might I presume,
Their execution better were deferr'd
Till Osmyn die.   Meantime we may learn more
Of this conspiracy.
  King. Then be it so.
Stay, soldier; they shall suffer with the Moor.
Are none return'd of those who follow'd Heli?
  Gon. None, Sir. Some papers have been since discover'd
In Roderigo's house, who fled with him,
Which seem to intimate, as if Alphonso
Were still alive, and arming in Valentia:
Which wears indeed this colour of a truth,
They who are fled have that way bent their course.
Of the same nature divers notes have been
Dispers'd t' amuse the people; whereupon
Some ready of belief have rais'd this rumour;
That being sav'd upon the coast of Afric,
He there disclos'd himself to Albucacim,
And by a secret compact made with him,

Open'd and urg'd the way to this invaſion ;
While he himſelf returning to Valentia
In private, undertook to raiſe this tumult.

Zara. Ha ! hear'ſt thou that ? Is Oſmyn then Alphonſo !
O Heav'n ! a thouſand things occur at once
To my remembrance now, that makes it plain.
O certain death for him, as ſure deſpair
For me, if it be known——If not, what hope
Have I ? Yet 'twere the loweſt baſeneſs, now
To yield him up——No, I will ſtill conceal him,
And try the force of yet more obligations.

Gon. 'Tis not impoſſible. Yet, it may be
That ſome impoſtor has uſurp'd his name.
Your beauteous captive Zara can inform,
If ſuch a one, ſo 'ſcaping, was receiv'd,
At any time' in Albucacim's court.

King. Pardon, fair excellence, this long neglect :
An unforeſeen, unwelcome hour of buſineſs,
Has thruſt between us and our while of love;
But wearing now apace with ebbing ſand,
Will quickly waſte, and give again the day.

Zara. You're too ſecure ; the danger is more imminent
Than your high courage ſuffers you to ſee ;
While Oſmyn lives, you are not ſafe.

King. His doom
Is paſs'd ; if you revoke it not, he dies.

Zara. 'Tis well. By what I heard upon your entrance,
I find I can unfold what yet concerns
You more. One who did call himſelf Alphonſo
Was caſt upon my coaſt, as is reported,
And oft had private conference with the King;
To what effect I knew not then but he,
Alphonſo, ſecretly departed, juſt
About the time our arms embark'd for Spain.
What I know more is, that a triple league
Of ſtricteſt friendſhip, was profeſs'd between
Alphonſo, Heli, and the traitor Oſmyn.

King. Public report is ratified in this.

Zara. And Ofmyn's death requir'd of ftrong neceffity.

King. Give order ftraight that all the pris'ners die.

Zara. Forbear a moment; fomewhat more I have
Worthy your private car, and this your minifter.

King. Let all except Gonfalez leave the room.

S C E N E III.
'KING, GONSALEZ, ZARA, SELIM.

Zara. I am your captive, and you've us'd me nobly;
And in return of that, tho' otherwife
Your enemy, I have difcover'd Ofmyn
His private practice and confpiracy
Againft your ftate : and fully to difcharge
Myfelf of what I've undertaken, now
I think it fit to tell you, that your guards
Are tainted : fome among 'em have refolv'd
To refcue Ofmyn at the place of death.

King. Is treafon then fo near us as our guards!

Zara. Moft certain; tho' my knowledge is not yet
So ripe, to point at the particular men.

King. What's to be done?

Zara. That too I will advife.
I have remaining in my train fome mutes,
A prefent once from the Sultana queen,
In the Grand Seignior's court. Thefe, from their infancy
Are practis'd in the trade of death ; and fhall
(As there the cuftom is) in private ftrangle
Ofmyn.

Gon. My Lord, the Queen advifes well.

King. What off'ring, or what recompence remains
In me, that can be worthy fo great fervices?
To caft beneath your feet the crown you've fav'd,
Tho' on the head that wears it, were too little.

Zara. Of that hereafter; but, mean time, 'tis fit
You give ftrict charge, that none may be admitted
To fee the pris'ner, but fuch mutes as I
Shall fend.

King. Who waits there?

SCENE IV.

KING, GONSALEZ, ZARA, SELIM, PEREZ.

King. On your life take heed,
That only Zara's mutes, or such who bring
Her warrant, have admittance to the Moor.

Zara. They and no other, not the Princes' self.

Per. Your Majesty shall be obey'd.

King. Retire.

SCENE V.

KING, GONSALEZ, ZARA, SELIM.

Gon. That interdiction so particular,
Pronounc'd with vehemence against the Princess,
Shou'd have more meaning than appears barefac'd.
The King is blinded by his love, and heeds
It not.————Your Majesty sure might have spar'd
That last restraint; you hardly can suspect
The Princess is confederate with the Moor.

Zara. I've heard, her charity did once extend
So far, to visit him, at his request.

Gon. Ha!

King. How? She visit Osmyn! What, my daughter?

Sel. Madam, take heed; or you have ruin'd all.

Zara. And after did sollicit you on his
Behalf.

King. Never. You have been misinform'd.

Zara. Indeed? Then 'twas a whisper spread by some;
Who wish'd it so; a common art in courts.
I will retire, and instantly prepare
Instruction for my ministers of death.

SCENE VI.

KING, GONSALEZ.

Gon. There's somewhat yet of mystery in this;
Her words and actions are obscure and double,
Sometimes concur, and sometimes disagree;
I like it not.

King. What doſt thou think, Gonſalez?
Are we not much indebted to this fair one ?

Gon. I am a little ſlow of credit, Sir,
In the ſincerity of women's actions.
Methinks this Lady's hatred to the Moor
Diſquiets her too much ; which makes it ſeem
As if ſhe'd rather that ſhe did not hate him.
I wiſh her mutes are meant to be employ'd
As ſhe pretends——I doubt it now——Your guards
Corrupted! how ? by whom ? who told her ſo?
I'th' evening Oſmyn was to die; at midnight
She begg'd the royal ſignet to releaſe him ;
I'th' morning he muſt die again ; ere noon
Her mutes alone muſt ſtrangle him, or he'll
Eſcape. This put together ſuits not well.

King. Yet, that there's truth in what ſhe has diſcover'd,
Is manifeſt from every circumſtance.
This tumult, and the Lords who fled with Heli,
Are confirmation——that Alphonſo lives,
Agrees expreſly too with her report.

Gon. I grant it, Sir; and doubt not, but in rage
Of jealouſy, ſhe has diſcover'd what
She now repents. It may be I'm deceiv'd.
But why that needleſs caution of the Princeſs?
What if ſhe had ſeen Oſmyn ? tho' 'twere ſtrange.
But if ſhe had, what was't to her? unleſs
She fear'd her ſtronger charms might cauſe the Moor's
Affection to revolt.

King. I thank thee, friend.
There's reaſon in thy doubt, and I am warn'd.
But think'ſt thou that my daughter ſaw this Moor?

Gon. If Oſmyn be, as Zara has related,
Alphonſo's friend; 'tis not impoſſible,
But ſhe might wiſh on his account to ſee him.

King. Say'ſt thou ? By Heaven thou haſt rous'd a thought,
That like a ſudden earthquake ſhakes my frame;
Confuſion! then my daughter's an accomplice,
And plots in private with this helliſh Moor.

Gon. That were too hard a thought—but fee fhe comes :
'Twere not amifs to queftion her a little,
And try howe'er, if I have divin'd aright.
If what I fear be true, fhe'll be concern'd
For Ofmyn's death, as he's Alphonfo's friend.
Urge that, to try if fhe'll folicit for him.

SCENE VII.

KING, GONSALEZ, ALMERIA, LEONORA.

King. Your coming has prevented me, Almeria;
I had determin'd to have fent for you.
Let your attendant be difmifs'd ; I have   [*Leonora retires.*
To talk with you.   Come near; why doft thou fhake ?
What mean thofe fwollen and red-fleck'd eyes, that look
As they had wept in blood, and worn the night
In waking anguifh ? Why this, on the day
Which was defign'd to celebrate thy nuptials ;
But that the beams of light are to be ftain'd
With reeking gore, from traitors on the rack ?
Wherefore I have deferr'd the marriage rites ;
Nor fhall the guilty horrors of this day
Prophane that jubilee.

Alm. All days to me
Henceforth are equal ; this the day of death,
To-morrow, and the next, and each that follows,
Will undiftinguifh'd roll, and but prolong
One hated line of more extended woe.

King. Whence is thy grief ? give me to know the caufe,
And look thou anfwer me with truth ; for know,
I am not unacquainted with thy falfehood.
Why art thou mute ? bafe and degenerate maid !

Gon. Dear Madam, fpeak, or you'll incenfe the King.

Alm. What is't to fpeak ? or wherefore fhou'd I fpeak ?
What mean thefe tears, but grief unutterable !

King. They are the dumb confeffions of thy mind ;
They mean thy guilt ; and fay thou wert confed'rate
With damn'd confpirators to take my life.
O impious parricide ! now can'ft thou fpeak ?

Alm. O earth, behold, I kneel upon thy bofom,
And bend my flowing eyes, to ftream upon
Thy face, imploring thee that thou wilt yield;
Open thy bowels of compaffion, take
Into thy womb the laft and moft forlorn
Of all thy race.   Hear me, thou common parent;
——I have no parent elfe——be thou a mother,
And ftep between me and the curfe of him,
Who was——who was, but is no more a father,
But brands my innocence with horrid crimes;
And for the tender names of child and daughter,
Now calls me murderer and parricide.

King. Rife, I command thee rife——and if thou woud'ft
Acquit thyfelf of thofe detefted names,
Swear thou haft never feen that foreign dog,
Now doom'd to die, that moft accurfed Ofmyn.

Alm. Never, but as with innocence I might,
And free of all bad purpofes.   So Heaven's
My witnefs.

King. Vile equivocating wretch!
With innocence! O patience! hear——fhe owns it!
Confeffes it! by Heaven I'll have him rack'd,
Torn, mangled, flay'd, impal'd——all pains and tortures
That wit of man and dire revenge can think,
Shall he accumulated under-bear.

Alm. Oh, I'm loft——there fate begins to wound.

King. Hear me, then; if thou can'ft, reply; know,
I'm not to learn that curs'd Alphonfo lives;   [traitrefs,
Nor am I ignorant what Ofmyn is.

Aim. Then all is ended, and we both muft die.
Since thou'rt reveal'd, alone thou fhalt not die.
And yet alone wou'd I have died, Heaven knows,
Repeated deaths, rather than have reveal'd thee.
Yes, all my father's wounded wrath, tho' each
Reproach cuts deeper than the keeneft fword,
And cleaves my heart; I wou'd have born it all,
Nay, all the pains that are prepar'd for thee:
To the remorfelefs rack I wou'd have given

This weak and tender flesh, to have been bruis'd
And torn, rather than have reveal'd thy being.

King. Hell, hell! do I hear this, and yet endure!
What, dar'st thou to my face avow thy guilt?
Hence, ere I curse——fly my just rage with speed;
Lest I forget us both, and spurn thee from me.

Alm. And yet a father! think I am your child.
Turn not your eyes away——look on me kneeling;
Now curse me if you can, now spurn me off.
Did ever father curse his kneeling child!
Never ﹖ for always blessings crown that posture.
Nature inclines, and half-way meets that duty,
Stooping to raise from earth the filial reverence;
For bended knees returning folding arms,
With pray'rs, and blessings, and paternal love.
O hear me then, thus crawling on the earth——

King. Be thou advis'd, and let me go, while yet
The light impression thou hast made remains.

Alm. No, never will I rise, nor loose this hold,
'Till you are mov'd, and grant that he may live.

King. Ha! who may live? take heed, no more of that;
For on my soul he dies, tho' thou and I,
And all thou'd follow to partake his doom.
Away, off, let me go.——Call her attendants.

[Leonora *and women return.*

Alm. Drag me, harrow the earth with my bare bosom,
I'll not let go 'till you have spar'd my husband.

King. Ha! what say'st thou? Husband! husband!
What husband? which? who!   [damnation!

Alm. He is my husband.

King. Poison and daggers! who?

Alm. O——

Gonf. Help, support her.

Alm. Let me go, let me fall, sink deep——I'll dig,
I'll dig a grave, and tear up death; I will;
I'll scrape 'till I collect his rotten bones,
And clothe their nakedness with my own flesh:
Yes, I will strip off life, and we will change:

I will be death; then tho' you kill my husband,
He shall be mine, still and for ever mine.

King. What husband? who? whom dost thou mean?

Gonf. She raves!

Alm. O that I did. Osmyn, he is my husband.

King. Osmyn?

Alm. Not Osmyn, but Alphonso is my dear
And wedded husband——Heav'n, and air, and seas,
Ye winds and waves, I call ye all to witnes.

King. Wilder than winds or waves thyself dost rave.
Shou'd I hear more, I too shou'd catch thy madness.
Yet somewhat she must mean of dire import,
Which I'll not hear, 'till I am more at peace.
Watch her returning sense, and bring me word;
And look that she attempt not on her life.

SCENE VIII.

ALMERIA, GONSALEZ, LEONORA, *Attendants.*

Alm. O stay, yet stay; hear me, I am not mad.
I wou'd to Heaven I were—He's gone.

Gonf. Have comfort.

Alm. Curs'd be that tongue that bids me be of comfort;
Curs'd my own tongue, that cou'd not move his pity;
Curs'd these weak hands that cou'd not hold him here;
For he is gone to doom Alphonso's death.

Gonf. Your too excessive grief works on your fancy,
And deludes your sense. Alphonso, if living,
Is far from hence, beyond your father's power.

Alm. Hence, thou detested, ill-tim'd flatterer;
Source of my woes: thou and thy race be curs'd;
But doubly thou, who could alone have policy
And fraud, to find the fatal secret out,
And know that Osmyn was Alphonso.

Gonf. Ha!

Alm. Why dost thou start! what dost thou see or hear?
Was it the doleful bell, tolling for death?
Or dying groans from my Alphonso's breast?

See, fee, look yonder! where a grizzled, pale,
And ghaftly head glares by, all fmear'd with blood,
Gafping as it wou'd fpeak; and after, fee!
Behold a damp, dead hand has dropp'd a dagger:
I'll catch it——Hark! a voice cries murder! ah!
My father's voice! hollow it founds, and calls
Me from the tomb——I'll follow it; for there
I fhall again behold my dear Alphonfo.

S C E N E   IX.

GONSALEZ alone.

She's greatly griev'd; nor am I lefs furpriz'd.
Ofmyn Alphonfo! no; fhe over-rates
My policy: I ne'er fufpected it:
Nor now had known it, but from her miftake.
Her hufband too! ha! where is Garcia then?
And where the crown that fhou'd defcend on him,
To grace the line of my pofterity?
Hold, let me think——if I fhou'd tell the King——
Things come to this extremity; his daughter
Wedded already——what if he fhou'd yield?
Knowing no remedy for what is paft;
And urg'd by nature pleading for his child,
With which he feems to be already fhaken.
And tho' I know he hates beyond the grave
Anfelmo's race; yet if—that if concludes me.
To doubt, when I may be affur'd, is folly.
But how prevent the captive queen, who means
To fet him free? Ay, now 'tis plain; O well
Invented tale! He was Alphonfo's friend.
This fubtile woman will amufe the King,
If I delay——'twill do——or better fo.
One to my wifh. Alonzo, thou art welcome.

S C E N E   X.

GONSALEZ, ALONZO.

Alon. The King expects your Lordfhip,
VOL. II.   F

Gonf. 'Tis no matter.
I'm not i' the way at prefent, good Alonzo.

Alor. If't pleafe your Lordfhip, I'll return, and fay
I have not feen you.

Gon. Do, my beft Alonzo.
Yet ftay, I would—but go; anon will ferve——
Yet I have that requires thy fpeedy help.
I think thou woud'ft not ftop to do me fervice.

Alon. I am your creature.

Gon. Say thou art my friend.
I've feen thy fword do noble execution.

Alon. All that it can your Lordfhip fhall command.

Gon. Thanks; and I take thee at thy word; thou'ft feen
Amongft the followers of the captive queen,
Dumb men, who make their meaning known by figns?

Alon. I have, my Lord.

Gon. Couldft thou procure with fpeed
And privacy, the wearing garb of one
Of thofe, though purchas'd by his death, I'd give
Thee fuch reward as fhould exceed thy wifh.   [fhip?

Alon. Conclude it done. Where fhall I wait your Lord-

Gon. At my apartment. Ufe thy utmoft diligence;
And fay I've not been feen———hafte, good Alonzo.
So, this can hardly fail. Alphonfo flain,
The greateft obftacle is then remov'd.

Almeria widow'd, yet again may wed;
And I yet fix the crown on Garcia's head.

ACT V. SCENE I.

A Room of State.

KING, PEREZ, ALONZO.

KING.

NOT to be found? In an ill hour he's abfent.
None, fay you; what, not the fav'rite eunuch?
Nor fhe herfelf, nor any of her mutes,
Have yet requir'd admittance?

Per. None, my Lord.

King. Is Ofmyn fo difpos'd as I commanded ?

Per. Faft bound in double chains, and at full length
He lyes fupine on earth; with as much eafe
She might remove the centre of this earth,
As loofe the rivets of his bonds.

King. 'Tis well.

   [*A Mute appears, and feeing the King retires.*
Ha ! ftop, and feize that mute ; Alonzo follow him.
Ent'ring he met my eyes, and ftarted back,
Frighted, and fumbling one hand in his bofom,
As to conceal th' importance of his errand.

   [Alonzo *follows him, and returns with a paper.*
Alon. O bloody proof of obftinate fidelity !

King. What doft thou mean ?

Alon. Soon as I feized the man,
He fnatch'd from out his bofom this——and ftrove
With rath and greedy hafte, at once to cram
The morfel down his throat.   I catch'd his arm,
And hardly wrench'd his hand to wring it from him;
Which done, he drew his poniard from his fide,
And on the inftant plung'd it in his breaft.

King. Remove the body hence ere Zara fee it,

Alon. I'll be fo bold to borrow his attire;
'Twill quit me of my promife to Gonfalez.

S C E N E II.

KING, PEREZ.

Per. Whate'er it is, the King's complexion turns.

King. How's this ? my mortal foe beneath my roof !

   [*Having read the letter.*
O give me patience, all ye powers ! no, rather
Give me new rage, implacable revenge,
And trebled fury——Ha! who's there ?

Per. My Lord.

King. Hence, flave ! how dar'ft thou 'bide, to watch and
Into how poor a thing a king defcends ?   [pry

    F 2

How like thyfelf, when paffion treads him down!
Ha! ftir not, on thy life: for thou wert fix'd
And planted   e to fee me gorge the bait,
And lafh againft the hook———By Heav'n, you're all
Rank traitors; thou art with the reft combin'd;
Thou knew'ft that Ofmyn was Alphonfo, knew'ft
My daughter privately with him conferr'd ;
And wert the fpy and pandar to their meeting.

   Per. By all that's holy, I'm amaz'd——
   King. Thou ly'ft.
Thou art accomplice too with Zara : here
Where fhe fets down—" Still will I fet thee free"—[*Reading.*
That fomewhere is repeated—" I have power   [traitor.
" O'er them that are thy guards."———Mark that, thou
   Per. It was your Majefty's command, I fhould
Obey her order——
   King, reading.]——" And ftill will fet
" Thee free, Alphonfo"—Hell! curs'd, curs'd Alphonfo!
Falfe and perfidious Zara! Strumpet daughter!
Away, be gone, thou feeble boy, fond love,
All nature, foftnefs, pity and compaffion,
This hour I throw ye off, and entertain
Fell hate within my breaft, revenge and gall.
By Heav'n, I'll meet, and counterwork this treachery.
Hark thee, villain, traitor——anfwer me, flave.
   Per. My fervice has not merited thefe titles.
   King. Dar'ft thou reply? Take that——thy fervices?
    thine ?   [*Strikes him.*
What's thy whole life, thy foul, thy all, to my
One moment's eafe? Hear my command; and look
That thou obey, or horror on thy head.
Drench me thy dagger in Alphonfo's heart:
Why doft thou ftart? Refolve, or——
   Per.——Sir, I will.
   King. 'Tis well—that when fhe comes to fet him free,
His teeth may grin, and mock at her remorfe.

                    [*Perez going.*
——Stay thee——I've farther thought—I'll add to this.

And give her eyes yet greater difappointment :
When thou haft ended him, bring me his robe;
And let the cell where fhe'll expect to fee him
Be darken'd, fo as to amufe the fight.
I'll be conducted thither——mark me well——
There with his turbant, and his robe array'd,
And laid along as he now lyes fupine,
I fhall convict her to her face of falfehood.
When for Alphonfo's fhe fhall take my hand,
And breathe her fighs upon my lips for his,
Sudden I'll ftart, and dafh her with her guilt.
But fee fhe comes; I'll fhun th' encounter; thou,
Follow me, and give heed to my direction.

SCENE III.

ZARA, SELIM.

Zara. The mute not yet return'd! ha, 'twas the King!
The King that parted hence! frowning he went;
His eyes like meteors roll'd, then darted down
Their red and angry beams; as if his fight
Would, like the raging dog-ftar, fcorch the earth,
And kindle ruin in its courfe. Do'ft think
He faw me?
  Sel. Yes : but then, as if he thought
His eyes had err'd, he haftily recall'd
Th' imperfect look, and fternly turn'd away.
  Zara. Shun me when feen! I fear thou haft undone me,
Thy fhallow artifice begets fufpicion,
And, like a cob-web-veil, but thinly fhades
The face of thy defign; alone difguifing
What fhould have ne'er been feen; imperfect mifchief!
Thou, like the adder, venomous and deaf,
Haft ftung the traveller; and after hear'ft
Not his purfuing voice; ev'n where thou think'ft
To hide, the ruftling leaves and bended grafs
Confefs, and point the path which thou haft crept.
O fate of fools ! officious in contriving ;
In executing puzzled, lame and loft.

Sel. Avert it, Heav'n, that you should ever suffer
For my defect : or that the means which I
Devis'd to serve should ruin your design!
Prescience is Heav'n's alone, not given to man.
If I have fail'd in what, as being man,
I needs must fail; impute not as a crime
My nature's want, but punish nature in me :
I plead not for a pardon, and to live,
But to be punish'd, and forgiv'n. Here, strike;
I bare my breast to meet your just revenge.

 Zara. I have not leisure now to take so poor
A forfeit as thy life : somewhat of high
And more important fate requires my thought.
When I've concluded on myself, if I
Think fit, I'll leave thee my command to die.
Regard me well; and dare not to reply
To what I give in charge; for I'm resolv'd:
Give order, that the two remaining mutes
Attend me instantly, with each a bowl
Of such ingredients mix'd, as will with speed
Benumb the living faculties, and give
Most easy and inevitable death.
Yes, Osmyn, yes; be Osmyn or Alphonso,
I'll give thee freedom, if thou dar'st be free :
Such liberty as I embrace myself,
Thou shalt partake. Since fates no more afford,
I can but die with thee to keep my word.

SCENE IV.

SCENE *opening, shews the Prison.*

GONSALEZ *alone, disguised like a Mute, with a dagger.*

 Gon. Nor centinel, nor guard ! the doors unbarr'd !
And all as still as at the noon of night!
Sure death already has been busy here.
There lyes my way, that door too is unlock'd. [*Looks in.*
Ha! sure he sleeps——all's dark within, save what
A lamp, that feebly lifts a sickly flame,

By fits reveals——his face feems turn'd, to favour
Th' attempt. I'll fteal, and do it unperceiv'd.
What noife! Some body coming? 'ſt, Alonzo?
No body? Sure he'll wait without——I would
'Twere done——I'll crawl, and fting him to the heart:
Then caſt my ſkin, and leave it there to anfwer it. [Goes in.

SCENE V.

GARCIA, ALONZO.

Gar. Where? where, Alonzo? where's my Father? where
The King! confufion! all is on the rout!
All's loft, all ruin'd by furprife and treachery.
Where, where is he? why doft thou thus miflead me?
Alon. My Lord, he enter'd but a moment fince,
And cou'd not pafs me unperceiv'd—What, hoa!
My Lord, my Lord, what, hoa! my Lord Gonfalez!

SCENE VI.

GARCIA, ALONZO, GONSALEZ *bloody.*

Gon. Perdition choke your clamours—whence this rude-
nefs? Garcia!
Gar. Perdition, flavery, and death,
Are ent'ring now our doors. Where is the King?
What means this blood? and why this face of horror?
Gon. No matter——give me firft to know the caufe
Of thefe your rafh and ill-tim'd exclamations.
Gar. The eaftern gate is to the foe betray'd,
Who, but for heaps of flain that choke the paffage,
Had enter'd long ere now, and borne down all
Before 'em, to the palace walls. Unlefs
The King in perfon animate our men,
Granada's loft: and to confirm this fear,
The traitor Perez, and the captive Moor,
Are thro' a poftern fled, and join the foe.
Gon. Wou'd all were falfe as that; for whom you call
The Moor, is dead. That Ofmyn was Alphonfo;
In whofe heart's blood this poniard yet is warm.

Enter that chamber, and convince your eyes,
How much report has wrong'd your faith.

[*Garcia goes in.*

Alon. My Lord, for certain truth, Perez is fled;
And has declar'd the cause of his revolt,
Was to revenge a blow the King had giv'n him.

Gar. returning.] Ruin and horror! O heart-wounding
sight!

Gon. What says my son? what ruin? ha, what sorrow?

Gar. Blasted be my eyes, and speechless be my tongue,
Rather than or to see, or to relate
This deed——O dire mistake! O fatal blow!

Gon. Alon. The King——

Gar. Dead, welt'ring, drown'd in blood.
See, see, attir'd like Osmyn, where he lyes.   [*They look in.*
O whence, or how, or wherefore was this done?
But what imports the manner, or the cause!
Nothing remains to do, or to require,
But that we all should turn our swords against
Ourselves, and expiate with our own his blood.

Gon. O wretch, O curs'd, and rash, deluded fool!
On me, on me, turn your avenging sword.
I, who have spilt my Royal Master's blood,
Shou'd make atonement by a death as horrid;
And fall beneath the hand of my own son.

Gar. Ha! what? atone this murder with a greater!
The horror of that thought has damp'd my rage.
The earth already groans to bear this deed;
Oppress her not, nor think to stain her face
With more unnatural blood.   Murder my father?
Better with this to rip up my own bowels,
And bathe it to the hilt, in far less damnable
Self-murder.

Gon. O my son! from the blind dotage
Of a father's fondness these ills arose;
For thee I've been ambitious, base, and bloody:
For thee I've plung'd into this sea of sin;
Stemming the tide with only one weak hand,

While t'other bore the crown, (to wreath thy brow)
Whofe weight has funk me ere I reach'd the fhore.

Gon. Fatal ambition! Hark! the foe is enter'd : *[Shout.]*
The fhrilnefs of that fhout fpeaks 'em at hand,
We have no time to fearch into the caufe
Of this furprifing and moft fatal error.
What's to be done ? the King's death known, will ftrike
The few remaining foldiers with defpair,
And make 'em yield to mercy of the conqueror.

Alon. My Lord, I've thought how to conceal the body ;
Require me not to tell the means, 'till done,
Left you forbid what then you may approve.
               — *[Goes in. Shout.*

Gon. They fhout again ! whate'er he means to do,
'Twere fit the foldiers were amus'd with hopes ;
And in the mean time fed with expectation
To fee the King in perfon at their head.

Gar. Were it a truth, I fear 'tis now too late;
But I'll omit no care, nor hafte; and try
Or to repel their force, or bravely die.

S C E N E VII.

G O N S A L E Z, A L O N Z O.

Gon. What haft thou done, Alonzo ?

Alon. Such a deed
As but an hour ago I'd not have done,
Tho' for the crown of univerfal empire.
But what are kings reduc'd to common clay ?
Or who can wound the dead ? I've from the body
Sever'd the head, and in an obfcure corner
Difpos'd it, muffled in the mute's attire,
Leaving to view of them who enter next,
Alone the undiftinguifhable trunk :
Which may be ftill miftaken by the guards
For Ofmyn, if in feeking for the King
They chance to find it.

Gon. 'Twas an act of horror ;

And of a-piece with this day's dire misdeeds.
But 'tis no time to ponder or repent.
Haste thee, Alonzo, haste thee hence with speed,
To aid my son. I'll follow with the last
Reserve to re-inforce his arms: at least,
I shall make good, and shelter his retreat.

SCENE VIII.

ZARA, *followed by* SELIM, *and two* MUTES *bearing the bowls.*

Zara. Silence and solitude are ev'ry where!
Thro' all the gloomy ways and iron doors
That hither lead, nor human face nor voice
Is seen or heard. A dreadful din was wont
To grate the sense, when enter'd here; from groans
And howls of slaves condemn'd, from clink of chains,
And crash of rusty bars and creeking hinges:
And ever and anon the sight was dash'd
With frightful faces, and the meagre looks
Of grim and ghastly executioners.
Yet more this stilness terrifies my soul,
Than did that scene of complicated horrors.
It may be, that the cause of this my errand
And purpose, being chang'd from life to death,
Has also wrought this chilling change of temper.
Or does my heart bode more? what can it more
Than death?
Let 'em set down the bowls, and warn Alphonso
That I am here——so. You return and find
[*Mutes going in.*
The king; tell him, what he requir'd I've done,
And wait his coming to approve the deed.

SCENE IX.

ZARA *and* MUTES.

Zara. What have you seen? Ha! wherefore stare you
thus   [*The mutes return, and are affrighted.*
With haggard eyes? why are your arms a-cross?
Your heavy and desponding heads hung down?

Why is't you more than speak in these sad signs?
Give me more ample knowledge of this mourning.

[*They go to the Scene which opening she perceives the body.*

Ha! prostrate? bloody! headless! O——I'm lost.
O Osmyn! O Alpho! Cruel fate!
Cruel, cruel, O more than killing object!
I came prepar'd to die, and see thee die——
Nay, came prepared myself to give thee death—
But cannot bear to find thee thus, my Osmyn—
O this accursed, base, this treach'rous king!

S C E N E X.

ZARA, SELIM.

Sel. I've sought in vain, for no where can the king
Be found—

Zara. Get thee to hell, and seek him there. [*Stabs him.*
His hellish rage had wanted means to act,
But for thy fatal and pernicious counsel.

Sel. You thought it better then——but I'm rewarded:
The mute you sent by some mischance was seen,
And forc'd to yield your letter with his life:
I found the dead and bloody body stripp'd—
My tongue falters, and my voice fails—I sink——
Drink not the poison——for Alphonso is—— [*Dies.*

Zara. As thou art now——and I shall quickly be.
'Tis not that he is dead; for 'twas decreed
We both should die. Nor is't that I survive;
I have a certain remedy for that.
But oh, he dy'd unknowing in my heart.
He knew I lov'd, but knew not to what height:
Nor that I meant to fall before his eyes,
A martyr and a victim to my vows:
Insensible of this last proof he's gone.
Yet fate alone can rob his mortal part
Of sense; his soul still sees, and knows each purpose,
And fix'd event of my persisting faith.

Then, wherefore do I pause? give me the bowl
              [*A Mute kneels and gives one of the bowls.*
.Hover a moment, yet, thou gentle spirit,
Soul of my love, and I will wait thy flight:
This to our mutual bliss when join'd above.   [*Drinks.*
O friendly draught, already in my heart!
Cold, cold! my veins are icicles and frost.
I'll creep into his bosom, lay me there;
Cover us close—or I shall chill his breast,
And fright him from my arms——See, see, he slides
Still further from me; look he hides his face,
I cannot feel it— —quite beyond my reach
O now he's gone, and all is dark—   [*Dies.*
              [*The mutes kneel and mourn over her.*

SCENE XI.

ALMERIA, LEONORA, MUTES, *etc.*

Alm. O let me seek him in this horrid cell;
For in the tomb, or prison, I alone
Must hope to find him.
    Leon. Heav'ns! what dismal scene
Of death is this? The eunuch Selim slain!
    Alm. Shew me, for I am come in search of death;
But want a guide; for tears have dim'd my sight.
    Leon. Alas, a little farther, and behold
Zara all pale and dead! two frightful men,
Who seem the murderers, kneel weeping by,
Feeling remorse too late for what they've done.
But O forbear————lift up your eyes no more;
But haste away, fly from this fatal place,
Where miseries are multiply'd; return,
Return and look not on; for there's a dagger
Ready to stab the sight, and make your eyes
Rain blood————
    Alm. O I foreknow, foresee that object.
Is it at last then so! Is he then dead?
What, dead at last, quite, quite, for ever dead?

'There, there I see him; there he lyes, the blood
'Yet bubbling from his wounds——O more than savage!
Had they or hearts, or eyes, that did this deed!
Could eyes endure to guide such cruel hands?
Are not my eyes guilty alike with theirs,
That thus can gaze, and yet not turn to stone?
——I do not weep! The springs of tears are dry'd;
And on a sudden I am calm, as if
All things were well: and yet my husband's murder'd!
Yes, yes, I know to mourn! I'll sluce this heart,
The source of woe, and let the torrent loose.
——Those men have left to weep! they look on me!
I hope they murder all on whom they look.
Behold me well; your bloody hands have err'd,
And wrongfully have slain those innocents:
I am the sacrifice desig'd to bleed;
And come prepar'd to yield my throat——they shake
Their heads, in sign of grief and innocence!

                    [*They point at the bowl on the ground.*
And point! what mean they? Ha! a cup.   O well
I understand what medicine has been here.
O noble thirst! yet greedy to drink all——
——Oh for another draught of death—What mean they?

                    [*They point at the other cup.*
Ha! point again? 'tis there, and full, I hope.
Thanks to the liberal hand that fill'd thee thus;
I'll drink my glad acknowledgement——

  Leon. O hold
For mercy's sake; upon my knee I beg——
  Alm. With thee the kneeling world should beg in vain.
Seest thou not there? behold who prostrate lyes,
And pleads against thee? who shall then prevail?
Yet I will take a cold and parting leave,
From his pale lips; I'll kiss him, ere I drink,
Lest the rank juice shou'd blister on my mouth,
And stain the colour of my last adieu.

  VOL. II.   G

Horror! a headlcfs trunk! nor lips nor face,

      [Coming nearer the body, ftarts and lets fall the cup.

But fpouting veins, and mangled flefh! O, oh!

S C E N E, *The Laft.*

ALMERIA, LEONORA, ALPHONSO, HELI,
PEREZ, *with* GARCIA *prifoner, guards and attendants.*

Alph. Away, ftand off, where is fhe? let me fly,
Save her from death, and fnatch her to my heart.

Alm. Oh!

Alph. Forbear; my arms alone fhall hold her up,
Warm her to life, and wake her into gladnefs.
O let me talk to thy reviving fenfe,
The words of joy and peace; warm thy cold beauties,
With the new-flufhing ardour of my cheek;
Into thy lips pour the foft trickling balm
Of cordial fighs; and re-infpire thy bofom
With the breath of love. Shine, awake, Almeria,
Give a new birth to thy long-fhaded eyes,
Then double on the day reflected light.

Alm. Where am I? Heav'n! what does this dream
    intend?

Alph. O may'ft thou never dream of lefs delight,
Nor ever wake to lefs fubftantial joys.

Alm. Giv'n me again from death! O all ye pow'rs
Confirm this miracle! Can I believe
My fight, againft my fight? and fhall I truft
That fenfe, which in one inftant fhews him dead
And living? Yes I will; I've been abus'd
With apparitions and affrighting fantoms:
This is my Lord, my life, my only hufband:
I have him now, and we no more will part.
My father too fhall have compaffion——

Alph. O my heart's comfort; 'tis not giv'n to this
Frail life, to be entirely blefs'd. Even now,
In this extremeft joy my foul can tafte,
Yet am I dafh'd to think that thou muft weep;
Thy father fell, where he defign'd my death.

Gonfalez and Alonzo, both of wounds
Expiring, have with their laft breath confefs'd
The juft decrees of Heav'n, which on themfelves
Has turn'd their own moft bloody purpofes.
Nay, I muft grant, 'tis fit you fhou'd be thus——

[*She weeps.*

Let 'em remove the body from her fight.
Ill-fated Zara! Ha! a cup? Alas!
Thy error then is plain; but I were flint
Not to o'erflow in tribute to thy memory.
O Garcia!——.
Whofe virtue has renounc'd thy father's crimes;
Seeft thou, how juft the hand of Heav'n has been?
Let us, who thro' our innocence furvive,
    Still in the paths of honour, perfevere,
    And not from paft or prefent ills defpair:
    For bleffings ever wait on virtuous deeds;
    And tho' a late, a fure reward fucceeds.

[*Exeunt Omnes.*

G 2

EPILOGUE.

Spoken by Mrs BRACEGIRDLE.

THE tragedy thus done, I am, you know,
 No more a princefs, but in *ſtatu quo*:
And now as unconcern'd this mourning wear,
As if indeed a widow or an heir.
I've leifure now to mark your fev'ral faces,
And know each critic by his four grimaces.
To poifon plays, I fee fome where they fit;
Scatter'd, like rats-bane, up and down the pit;
While others watch, like parifh-fearchers hir'd
To tell of what difeafe the play expir'd.
O with what joy they run to fpread the news
Of a damn'd poet, and departed mufe!
But if he 'fcape, with what regret they're feiz'd!
And how they're difappointed when they're pleas'd!
Critics to plays for the fame end refort,
That furgeons wait on trials in a court;
For innocence condemn'd they've no refpect,
Provided they've a body to diffect.
As Suffex men, that dwell upon the fhore,
Look out when ftorms arife, and billows roar,
Devoutly praying, with uplifted hands,
That fome well-laden fhip may ftrike the fands;
To whofe rich cargo they may make pretence,
And fatten on the fpoils of providence:
So critics throng to fee a new play fplit,
And thrive and profper on the wrecks of wit.
Small hope our poet from thefe profpects draws;
And therefore to the fair commends his caufe.
Your tender hearts to mercy are inclin'd,
With whom, he hopes, this play will favour find,
Which was an off'ring to the fex defign'd.

THE

WAY OF THE WORLD.

A

C O M E D Y.

" Audire eſt operæ pretium, procedere recte
" Qui mœchos non vultis"———   Hor. Sàt. 2. Lib. 2.
" Metuat, doti deprenſa."——   Ibid.

To the Right Honourable

R A L P H,

Earl of MONTAGUE, &c.

My LORD,

WHETHER the world will arraign me of vanity or not, that I have prefumed to dedicate this comedy to your Lordfhip, I am yet in doubt; though, it may be, it is fome degree of vanity even to doubt of it. One who has at any time had the honour of your Lordfhip's converfation, cannot be fuppofed to think very meanly of that which he would prefer to your perufal; yet it were to incur the imputation of too much fufficiency, to pretend to fuch a merit as might abide the teft of your Lordfhip's cenfure.

Whatever value may be wanting to this play while yet it is mine, will be fufficiently made up to it, when it is once become your Lordfhip's; and it is my fecurity, that I cannot have over-rated it more by my dedication, than your Lordfhip will dignify it by your patronage.

That it fucceeded on the ftage, was almoft beyond my expectation; for but little of it was prepared for the general tafte which feems now to be predominant in the palates of our audience.

Those characters which are meant to be ridiculed in most of our comedies, are of fools so gross, that, in my humble opinion, they should rather disturb than divert the well-natured and reflecting part of an audience; they are rather objects of charity than contempt; and instead of moving our mirth, they ought very often to excite our compassion.

This reflection moved me to design some characters, which should appear ridiculous, not so much through a natural folly (which is incorrigible, and therefore not proper for the stage) as through an affected wit; a wit, which at the same time that it is affected, is also false. As there is some difficulty in the formation of a character of this nature, so there is some hazard which attends the progress of its success upon the stage; for many come to a play, so over-charged with criticism, that they very often let fly their censure, when through their rashness they have mistaken their aim. This I had occasion lately to observe; for this play had been acted two or three days, before some of these hasty judges could find the leisure to distinguish betwixt the character of a Witwoud and a Truewit.

I must beg your Lordship's pardon for this digression from the true course of this epistle; but that it may not seem altogether impertinent, I beg that I may plead the occasion of it, in part of that excuse of which I stand in need, for recommending this comedy to your protection. It is only by the countenance of your Lordship, and the *few* so qualified, that such who write with care and pains can hope to be diftinguifhed; for the proftituted name of *poet* promifcuoufly levels all that bear it.

Terence, the moft correct writer in the world, had a Scipio and a Lælius, if not to affift him, at leaft to fupport him in his reputation; and notwithftanding his extraordinary merit, it may be their countenance was not more than neceffary.

The purity of his ftyle, the delicacy of his turns, and the juftnefs of his characters, were all of them beauties, which the greater part of his audience were incapable of tafting; fome of the coarfeft ftrokes of Plautus, fo feverely cenfured by Horace, were more likely to affect the multitude; fuch, who come with expectation to laugh at the laft act of a play, and are better entertained with two or three unfeafonable jefts, than with the artful folution of the *fable*.

As Terence excelled in his performances, fo had he great advantages to encourage his undertakings; for he built moft on the foundations of Menander; his plots were generally modelled, and his characters ready drawn to his hand. He copied Menander, and Menander had not lefs light in the information of his characters, from the obfervations of Theophraftus, of whom he was a difciple; and Theophraftus, it is known, was not only the difciple, but the immediate fucceffor of Ariftotle, the firft and greateft judge of poetry. Thefe were great models to defign by; and the further advantage which Terence poffeffed, towards giving his play the due

ornaments of purity of ftyle, and juftnefs of manners, was not lefs confiderable, from the freedom
of converfation, which was permitted him with
Lælius and Scipio, two of the greateft and moft
polite men of his age. And indeed the privilege
of fuch a converfation is the only certain means of
attaining to the perfection of dialogue.

If it has happened in any part of this comedy,
that I have gained a turn of ftyle, or expreffion more
correct, or at leaft more corrigible than thofe which
I have formerly written, I muft, with equal pride
and gratitude, afcribe it to the honour of your
Lordfhip's admitting me into your converfation,
and that of a fociety where every body elfe was fo
well worthy of you, in your retirement laft fummer
from the town ; for it was immediately after, that
this comedy was written. If I have failed in my
performance, it is only to be regretted, where there
were fo many, not inferior either to a Scipio or a
Lælius, that there fhould be one wanting, equal in
capacity to a Terence.

If I am not miftaken, poetry is almoft the only
art which has not yet laid claim to your Lordfhip's patronage. Architecture and painting, to
the great honour of our country, have flourifhed
under your influence and protection. In the mean
time, poetry, the eldeft fifter of all arts, and parent
of moft, feems to have refigned her birth-right, by
having neglected to pay her duty to your Lordfhip,
and by permitting others of a later extraction, to
prepoffefs that place in your efteem, to which none

can pretend a better title. Poetry, in its nature, is sacred to the good and great; the relation between them is reciprocal, and they are ever propitious to it.' It is the privilege of poetry to addrefs them, and it is their prerogative alone to give it protection.

This received maxim is a general apology for all writers who confecrate their labours to great men; but I could wifh at this time, that this addrefs was exempted from the common pretence of all dedications; and that as I can diftinguifh your Lordfhip even among the moft deferving, fo this offering might become remarkable by fome particular inftance of refpect, which fhould affure your Lordfhip, that I am with all due fenfe of your extreme worthinefs and humanity,

.My LORD,

Your Lordfhip's moft obedient,

.and moft obliged humble fervant,

WILLIAM CONGREVE.

T O

Mr CONGREVE.

Occasioned by his COMEDY

C A L L E D

The WAY of the WORLD.

WHEN pleasure's falling to the low delight,
In the vain joys of the uncertain fight;
No sense of wit when rude spectators know,
But in distorted gesture, farce and show;
How could, great author, your aspiring mind
Dare to write only to the few refin'd!
Yet tho' that nice ambition you pursue,
'Tis not in Congreve's power to please but few.
Implicitly devoted to his fame,
Well-dress'd Barbarians know his awful name.
Though senseless they're of mirth, but when they laugh,
As they feel wine, but when, 'till drunk, they quaff.

On you, from fate a lavish portion fell
In ev'ry way of writing to excell.
Your muse applause to Arabella brings,
In notes as sweet as Arabella sings.
Whene'er you draw an undissembled woe,
With sweet distress your rural numbers flow.
Pastora's the complaint of ev'ry swain,
Pastora still the echo of the plain!
Or if your muse describe, with warming force,
The wounded Frenchman falling from his horse;
And her own William glorious in the strife,
Bestowing on the prostrate foe his life:
You the great act as generously rehearse,
And all the English fury's in your verse.

By your selected scenes, and handsome choice,
Ennobled comedy exalts her voice;.
You check unjust esteem and fond desire,
And teach to scorn, what else we should admire;
The just impression taught by you we bear,
The player acts the world, the world the player;
Whom still that world unjustly disesteems,
Though he, alone, professes what he seems:
But when your muse assumes her tragic part,
She conquers and she reigns in ev'ry heart.
To mourn with her men cheat their private woe,
And gen'rous pity's all the grief they know:
The widow, who, impatient of delay,
From the town joys must mask it to the play,
Joins with your Mourning Bride's resistless moan,
And weeps a loss she slighted, when her own;
You give us torment, and you give us ease,
And vary our afflictions as you please.
Is not a heart so kind as yours in pain,
To load your friends with cares you only feign;
Your friends in grief, compos'd yourself, to leave?
But 'tis the only way you'll e'er deceive.
Then still, great Sir, your moving pow'r employ,
To lull our sorrow, and correct our joy.

RICHARD STEELE.

PROLOGUE.

Spoken by Mr BETTERTON.

OF thofe few fools who with ill ftars are curft,
    Sure fcribbling fools, call'd poets, fare the worft:
For they're a fort of fools which Fortune makes,
And after fhe has made 'em fools, forfakes.
With Nature's oafs 'tis quite a diff'rent cafe,
For Fortune favours all her ideot-race.
In her own neft the cuckow-eggs we find,
O'er which fhe broods to hatch the changling-kind.
No portion for her own fhe has to fpare,
So much fhe doats on her adopted care.

    Poets are bubbles, by the town drawn in,
Suffer'd at firft fome trifling ftakes to win:
But what unequal hazards do they run!
Each time they write they venture all they've won:
The fquire that's butter'd ftill, is fure to be undone.
This author, heretofore, has found your favour;
But pleads no merit from his paft behaviour.
To build on that might prove a vain prefumption,
Shou'd grants, to poets made, admit refumption:
And in Parnaffus he might lofe his feat,
If that be found a forfeited eftate.

    He owns with toil he wrought the following fcenes;
But, if they're naught, ne'er fpare him for his pains:
Damn him the more; have no commiferation
For dulnefs on mature deliberation,
He fwears he'll not refent one hifs'd-off fcene,
Nor, like thofe peevifh wits, his play maintain,
Who, to affert their fenfe, your tafte arraign.

Some plot we think he has, and some new thought;
Some humour too, no farce; but that's a fault.
Satire, he thinks, you ought not to expect;
For so reform'd a town, who dares correct?
To please, this time, has been his sole pretence,
He'll not instruct, lest it should give offence.
Shou'd he by chance a knave or fool expose,
That hurts none here, sure here are none of those:
In short, our play shall (with your leave to shew it)
Give you one instance of a passive poet,
Who to your judgments yields all resignation;
So save or damn, after your own discretion.

H 2.

Dramatis Personæ.

M E N.

FAINALL, in love with Mrs Marwood,	Mr BETTERTON.
MIRABELL, in love with Mrs Millamant,	Mr VERBRUGGEN.
WITWOUD, } followers of Mrs	Mr BOWEN.
PETULANT, } Millamant,	Mr BOWMAN.
Sir WILFUL WITWOUD, half brother to Witwoud, and nephew to Lady Wishfort,	Mr UNDERHILL.
WAITWELL, servant to Mirabell,	Mr BRIGHT.

W O M E N.

Lady WISHFORT, enemy to Mirabell, for having falsly pretended love to her,	Mrs LEIGH.
Mrs MILLAMANT, a fine lady, niece to Lady Wishfort, and loves Mirabell,	Mrs BRACEGIRDLE.
Mrs MARWOOD, friend to Mr Fainall, and likes Mirabell,	Mrs BARRY.
Mrs FAINALL, daughter to lady Wishfort, and wife to Fainall, formerly friend to Mirabell,	Mrs BOWMAN.
FOIBLE, woman to Lady Wishfort,	Mrs WILLIS.
MINCING, woman to Mrs Millamant,	Mrs PRINCE.

Dancers, Footmen and Attendants.

SCENE, LONDON.

The time equal to that of the representation.

THE

WAY OF THE WORLD.

ACT I. SCENE I.

A Chocolate-houfe.

MIRABELL *and* FAINALL [*rifing from cards*]
BETTY *waiting.*

MIRABELL.

YOU are a fortunate man, Mr Fainall.

Fain. Have we done?

Mira. What you pleafe. I'll play on to entertain you.

Fain. No, I'll give you your revenge another time, when you are not fo indifferent; you are thinking of fome-thing elfe now, and play too negligently; the coldnefs of a lofing gamfter leffens the pleafure of the winner. I'd no more play with a man that flighted his ill fortune, than I'd make love to a woman who undervalued the lofs of her reputation.

Mira. You have a tafte extremely delicate, and are for refining on your pleafures.

Fain. Pr'ythee, why fo referv'd? Something has put you out of humour.

Mira. Not at all: I happen to be grave to-day, and you are gay; that's all.

Fain. Confefs, Millamant and you quarrell'd laft night after I left you; my fair coufin has fome humours that would tempt the patience of a Stoic. What, fome cox-

H. 3

comb came in, and was well receiv'd by her, while you
were by!

Mir. Witwoud and Petulant; and what was worse,
her aunt, your wife's mother, my evil genius; or to fum up
all in her own name, my old Lady Wishfort came in——

Fain. O there it is then——she has a lasting passion for
you, and with reason.———What, then my wife was
there?

Mir. Yes, and Mrs Marwood, and three or four
more, whom I never saw before; seeing me, they all put
on their grave faces, whisper'd one another; then complained aloud of the vapours, and after fell into a pro-
found silence.

Fain. They had a mind to be rid of you.

Mir. For which reason I resolved not to stir. At last
the good old lady broke thro' her painful taciturnity, with
an invective against long visits. I would not have under-
stood her, but Millamant joining in the argument, I rose,
and with a constrain'd smile, told her, I thought nothing
was so easy as to know when a visit began to be trouble-
some; she redden'd, and I withdrew, without expecting
her reply.

Fain. You were to blame to resent what she spoke only
in compliance with her aunt.

Mir. She is more mistress of herself, than to be under
the necessity of such a resignation.

Fain. What? tho' half her fortune depends upon her
marrying with my Lady's approbation?

Mir. I was then in such a humour, that I should have
been better pleas'd if she had been less discreet.

Fain. Now, I remember, I wonder not they were weary
of you; last night was one of their cabal nights; they
have 'em three times a-week, and meet by turns, at one
another's apartments, where they come together like the
coroner's inquest, to sit upon the murder'd reputations of
the week. You and I are excluded; and it was once pro-
pos'd, that all the male sex should be excepted; but some-
body mov'd that, to avoid scandal, there might be one

man of the community; upon which motion Witwoud and Petulant were inroll'd members.

Mir. And who may have been the foundress of this sect? My Lady Wishfort, I warrant, who publishes her detestation of mankind; and full of the vigour of fifty-five; declares for a friend and ratifia; and let posterity shift for itself, she'll breed no more.

Mir. The discovery of your sham addresses to her to conceal your love to her niece, has provoked this separation; had you dissembled better, things might have continu'd in the state of nature.

Mir. I did as much as man could, with any reasonable conscience; I proceeded to the very last act of flattery with her, and was guilty of a song in her commendation. Nay, I got a friend to put her into a lampoon, and compliment her with the imputation of an affair with a young fellow, which I carried so far, that I told her the malicious town took notice that she was grown fat of a sudden; and when she lay in of a dropsy, persuaded her she was reported to be in labour. The devil's in't, if an old woman is to be flatter'd further, unless a man shou'd endeavour downright personally to debauch her; and that my virtue forbad me. But for the discovery of this amour, I am indebted to your friend, or your wife's friend Mrs Marwood.

Fain. What should provoke her to be your enemy, unless she has made you advances which you have slighted? Women do not easily forgive omissions of that nature.

Mir. She was always civil to me 'till of late; I confess I am not one of those coxcombs who are apt to interpret a woman's good manners to her prejudice, and think that she who does not refuse 'em ev'ry thing, can refuse 'em nothing

Fain. You are a gallant man, Mirabell; and though you may have cruelty enough not to satisfy a lady's longing, you have too much generosity not to be tender of her honour. Yet you speak with an indifference which seems to be affected, and confesses you are conscious of a negligence

Mir. You pursue the argument with a distrust that seems to be unaffected, and confesses you are conscious of a concern for which the Lady is more indebted to you than is your wife.

Fain. Fy, fy, friend; if you grow censorious I must leave you;———I'll look upon the gamesters in the next room.

Mir. Who are they?

Fain. Petulant and Witwoud———Bring me some chocolate.

Mir. Betty, what says your clock?

Bet. Turn'd of the last canonical hour, Sir.

Mir. How pertinently the jade answers me! há! almost one o' clock! [*Looking on his watch.*] O, y'are come——

SCENE II.

MIRABEL *and* FOOTMAN.

Mir. Well, is the grand affair over? You have been something tedious.

Serv. Sir, there's such coupling at Pancras, that they stand behind one another, as 'twere a country dance. Ours was the last couple to lead up; and no hopes appearing of dispatch; besides, the parson growing hoarse, we were afraid his lungs would have fail'd before it came to our turn; so we drove round to Duke's-place; and there we were rivetted in a trice.

Mir. So, so, you are sure they are married.

Serv. Married and bedded, Sir: I am a witness.

Mir. Have you the certificate?

Serv. Here it is, Sir.

Mir. Has the tailor brought Waitwell's clothes home, and the new liveries?

Serv. Yes, Sir.

Mir. That's well. Do you go home again, d'ye hear, and adjourn the consummation 'till farther orders;

bid Waitwell shake his ears, and Dame Partlet rustle up
her feathers, and meet me at one o' clock by Rosamond's
pond; that I may see her before she returns to her lady;
and as you tender your ears be secret.

S C E N E III.

MIRABELL, FAINALL, BETTY.

Fain. Joy of your success, Mirabell; you look pleas'd.

Mir. Ay; I have been engag'd in a matter of some
sort of mirth, which is not ripe for discovery. I am glad
this is not a cabal-night. I wonder, Fainall, that you
who are married, and of consequence should be discreet,
will suffer your wife to be of such a party.

Fain. Faith, I am not jealous. Besides, most who are
engag'd are women and relations; and for the men, they
are of a kind too contemptible to give scandal.

Mir. I am of another opinion. The greater the coxcomb, always the more the scandal : for a woman, who
is not a fool, can have but one reason for associating with
a man who is one.

Fain. Are you jealous as often as you see Witwoud entertain'd by Millamant ?

Mir. Of her understanding I am, if not of her person.

Fain. You do her wrong; for, to give her her due, she
has wit.

Mir. She has beauty enough to make any man think
so; and complaisance enough not to contradict him who
shall tell her so.

Fain. For a passionate lover, methinks you are a man
somewhat too discerning in the failings of your mistress.

Mir. And for a discerning man, somewhat too passionate a lover; for I like her with all her faults; nay,
like her for her faults. Her follies are so natural, or so
artful, that they become her; and those affections
which in another woman would be odious, serve but to

make her more agrecable. I'll tell thee, Fainall, she, once us'd me with that infolence, that in revenge I took her to pieces ; fifted her, and feparated her failings ; I ftudied 'em, and got 'em by rote. The catalogue was fo large, that I was not without hopes one day or other to hate her heartily : to which end I fo us'd myfelf to think of 'em, that at length, contrary to my defign and expectation, they gave me every hour lefs and lefs difturbance; 'till in a few days it became habitual to me to remember 'em without being difpleas'd. They are now grown as familiar to me as my own frailties ; and in all probability in a little time longer I fhall like 'em as. well.

Fain. Marry her, marry her; be half as well acquainted with her charms, as you are with her defects, and my life on't, you are your own man again.

Mir. Say you fo?

Fain. Ay, ay, I have experience : I have a wife, and fo forth.

SCENE IV.

[*To them*] MESSENGER.

Mess. Is one Squire Witwoud here?

Bet. Yes, what's your bufinefs?

Mess. I have a letter for him, from his brother Sir Wilful, which I am charg'd to deliver into his own hands.

Bet. He's in the next room, friend——that way.

SCENE V.

MIRABELL, FAINALL, BETTY.

Mir. What, is the chief of that noble family in town, Sir Wilful Witwoud?

Fain. He is expected to-day. Do you know him ?

Mir. I have feen him, he promifes to be an extraor-

dinary perfon; I think you have the honour to be related
to him.

Fain. Yes; he is half brother to this Witwoud by a
former wife, who was fifter to my Lady Wifhfort, my
wife's mother. If you marry Millamant, you muft call
coufins too.

Mir. I had rather be his relation than his acquaintance.

Fain. He comes to town in order to equip himfelf for
travel.

Mir. For travel! why, the man that I mean is above
forty.

Fain. No matter for that; 'tis for the honour of England, that all Europe fhould know we have blockheads of
all ages.

Mir. I wonder there is not an act of parliament to fave
the credit of the nation, and prohibit the exportation of
fools.

Fain. By no means; 'tis better as 'tis; 'tis better to trade
with a little lofs, than to be quite eaten up with being
overftocked.

Mir. Pray, are the follies of this knight-errant, and
thofe of the Squire his brother, any thing related?

Fain. Not at all; Witwoud grows by the knight, like
a medlar grafted on a crab. One will melt in your mouth,
and t'other fet your teeth on edge; one is all pulp, and
the other all core.

Mir. So one will be rotten before he be ripe, and the
ether will be rotten without being ripe at all.

Fain. Sir Wilfull is an odd mixture of bafhfulnefs and
obftinacy——But when he's drunk he's as loving as the
monfter in the Tempeft, and much after the fame manner.
To give t'other his due, he has fomething of good nature,
and does not always want wit.

Mir. Not always; but as often as his memory fails
him, and his common-place of comparifons. He is a
fool with a good memory, and fome fcraps of other folks
wit. He is one whofe converfation can never be approv'd,
yet it is now and then to be endur'd. He has indeed one

good quality, he is not exceptious; for he so paſſionately affects the reputation of underſtanding raillery, that he will conſtrue an affront into a jeſt; and call downright rudeneſs and ill language, ſatire and fire.

Fain. If you have a mind to finiſh this picture, you have an opportunity to do it at full length. Behold the original.

S C E N E VI.

[To them] WITWOUD.

Wit. Afford me your compaſſion, my dears; pity me, Fainall; Mirabell, pity me.

Mir. I do from my ſoul.

Fain. Why, what's the matter?

Wit. No letters for me, Betty?

Bet. Did not a meſſenger bring you one but now, Sir?

Wit. Ay, but no other?

Bet. No, Sir.

Wit. That's hard, that's very hard;——A meſſenger, a mule, a beaſt of burden! he has brought me a letter from the fool my brother, as heavy as a panegyric in a funeral ſermon, or a copy of commendatory verſes from one poet to another: and what's worſe, 'tis as ſure a forerunner of the author, as an epiſtle dedicatory.

Mir. A fool, and your brother, Witwoud!

Wit. Ay, ay, my half brother. My half brother he is, no nearer upon honour.

Mir. Then 'tis poſſible he may be half a fool.

Wit. Good, good, Mirabell, le Drole! good, good; hang him, don't let's talk of him:——Fainall, how does your Lady? Gad, I ſay any thing in the world to get this fellow out of my head. I beg pardon that I ſhou'd aſk a man of pleaſure, and the town, a queſtion at once ſo foreign and domeſtic. But I talk like an old maid at a marriage; I don't know what I ſay: but ſhe's the beſt woman in the world.

I

Fain. 'Tis well you don't know what you fay, or elfe your commendation wou'd go near to make me either vain or jealous.

Wit. No man in town lives well with a wife but Fainall. Your judgment, Mirabell.

Mir. You had better ftep and afk his wife, if you wou'd be credibly inform'd.

Wit. Mirabell?

Mir. Ay.

Wit. My dear, I afk ten thoufand pardons;————gad I have forgot what I was going to fay to you.

Mir. I thank you heartily, heartily.

Wit. No, but pr'ythee excufe me,————my memory is fuch a memory.

Mir. Have a care of fuch apologies, Witwoud;———— for I never knew a fool but he affected to complain, either of the fpleen or his memory.

Fain. What have you done with Petulant?

Wit. He's reckoning his money————my money it was ————I have no luck to-day.

Fain. You may allow him to win of you at play;———— for you are fure to be too hard for him at repartee; fince you monopolize the wit that is between you, the fortune muft be his of courfe.

Mia. I don't find that Petulant confefies the fuperiority of wit to be your talent, Witwoud.

Wit. Come, come, you are malicious now, and wou'd breed debates————Petulant's my friend, and a very honeft fellow, and a very pretty fellow, and has a fmattering———— faith and troth a pretty deal of an odd fort of a fmall wit: nay, I'll do him juftice. I'm his friend, I won't wrong him. ————And if he had any judgment in the world,———— he wou'd not be altogether contemptible. Come, come, don't detract from the merit of my friend.

Fain. You don't take your friend to be over-nicely bred?

Wit. No, no, hang him, the rogue has no manners at all, that I muft own————no more breeding than a bum

baily, that I can grant you—'tis pity; the fellow has fire
and life.

Mir. What courage?

Wit. Hum, faith I don't know as to that, I can't say as
to that.——Yes, faith, in a controverfy, he'll contradict
any body.

Mir. Tho' 'twere a man whom he fear'd, or a woman
whom he lov'd.

Wit. Well, well, he does not always think before he
fpeaks;—we have all our failings : you are too hard upon
him, you are, faith. Let me excufe him——I can defend
moft of his faults, except one or two : one he has, that's
the truth on't; if he were my brother. I cou'd not acquit
him—that indeed I cou'd wifh were otherwife.

Mir. Ay marry, what's that, Witwoud?

Wit. O pardon me——expofe the infirmities of my
friend?——No, my dear, excufe me there.

Fain. What, I warrant he's unfincere, or 'tis fome fuch
trifle.

Wit. No, no, what if he be? 'tis no matter for that, his
wit will excufe that : a wit fhou'd no more be fincere,
than a woman conftant; one argues a decay of parts, as
t'other of beauty.

Mir. May be you think him too pofitive?

Wit. No, no, his being pofitive is an incentive to argument, and keeps up converfation.

Fain. Too illiterate?

Wit. That! that's his happinefs——his want of learning gives him the more opportunities to fhew his natural
parts.

Mir. He wants words?

Wit. Ay: but I like him for that now; for his want
of words gives me the pleafure very often to explain his
meaning.

Fain. He's impudent?

Wit. No, that's not it.

Mir. Vain?

Wit. No.

Mir. What! he fpeaks unfeafonable truths fometimes, becaufe he has not wit enough to invent an evafion?

Wit. Truths! ha, ha, ha! no, no; fince you will have it,———I mean, he never fpeaks truth at all,———that's all. He will lie like a chambermaid, or a woman of quality's porter. Now that is a fault.

SCENE VII.

[*To them*] COACHMAN.

Coach. Is Mafter Petulant here, Miftrefs?

Bet. Yes.

Coach. Three gentlewomen in a coach wou'd fpeak with him.

Fain. O brave Petulant! three!

Bet. I'll tell him.

Coach. You muft bring two difhes of chocolate and a glafs of cinnamon-water.

SCENE VIII.

MIRABELL, FAINALL, WITWOUD.

Wit. That fhou'd be for two fafting ftrumpets, and a bawd troubled with wind. Now you may know what the three are.

Mira. You are very free with your friend's acquaintance.

Wit. Ay, ay, friendfhip without freedom is as dull as love without enjoyment, or wine without toafting; but to tell you a fecret, thefe are trulls whom he allows coach hire, and fomething more, by the week, to call on him once a-day at public places.

Mir. How!

Wit. You fhall fee he won't go to 'em, becaufe there's no more company here to take notice of him———why

this is nothing to what he us'd to do:—before he found
out this way, I have known him call for himself——

Fain. Call for himself! what doft thou mean?

Wit. Mean, why he wou'd flip you out of this chocolate-
houfe, juft when you had been talking to him————as
foon as your back was turn'd——whip he was gone;——
then trip to his lodging, clap on a hood and fcarf, and a
mafk, flap into a hackney-coach, and drive hither to the
door again in a trice; where he wou'd fend in for himfelf,
that is I mean, call for himfelf, wait for himfelf, nay, and
what's more, not finding himfelf, fometimes leave a letter
for himfelf.

Mir. I confefs this is fomething extraordinary——
I believe he waits for himfelf now, he is fo long a coming:
O I afk his pardon.

S C E N E   IX.

PETULANT, MIRABELL, FAINALL, WIT-
WOUD, BETTY.

Bet. Sir, the coach ftays.

Pet. Well, well; I come;——'Sbud, a man had as good
be a profefs'd midwife, as a profefs'd whoremafter, at this
rate; to be knock'd up and rais'd at all hours, and in all
places. Pox on 'em, I won't come————d'ye hear, tell
'em I won't come——let 'em fnivel and cry their hearts
out.

Fain. You were very cruel, Petulant.

Pet. All's one, let it pafs——I have a humour to be
cruel.

Mir. I hope they are not perfons of condition that you
ufe at this rate.

Pet. Condition, condition's a dry'd fig, if I am not in
humour——by this hand, if they were your——a——a—
your what d'ye-call-'ems themfelves, they muft wait or rub
off, if I want appetite.

Mir. What d'ye-call-'ems! what are they, Witwoud?

Wit. Empreffes, my dear—by your what-d'ye-call-'cms he means Sultana Queens.

Pet. Ay, Roxolana's.

Mir. Cry you mercy.

Fain. Witwoud fays they are——

Pet. What does he fay th'are?

Wit. I? fine ladies, I fay.

Pet. Pafs on, Witwoud—hark'ee, by this light his relations—two co-heireffes his coufins, and an old aunt, who loves caterwauling better than a conventicle.

Wit. Ha, ha, ha, I had a mind to fee how the rogue wou'd come off—ha, ha, ha, gad I can't be angry with him, if he had faid they were my mother and my fifters!

Mir. No?

Wit. No; the rogue's wit and readinefs of invention charm me, dear Petulant.

Bet. They are gone, Sir, in great anger.

Pet. Enough, let 'em trundle. Anger helps complection, faves paint.

Fain. This continence is all diffembled; this is in order to have fomething to brag of the next time he makes court to Millamant, and fwear he has abandoned the whole fex for her fake.

Mir. Have you not left off your impudent pretenfion there yet? I fhall cut your throat fome time or other, Petulant, about that bufinefs.

Pet. Ay, ay, let that pafs—there are other throats to be cut——

Mir. Meaning mine, Sir?

Pet. Not I—I mean no body—I know nothing—but there are uncles and nephews in the world—and they may be rivals—what then! All's one for that——

Mir. How! hark'ee, Petulant, come hither——explain, or I fhall call your interpreter.

Pet. Explain! I know nothing—why; you have an uncle, have you not, lately come to town, and lodges by my Lady Wifhfort's?

Mir. True.

Pet. Why, that's enough—you and he are not friends ; and if he fhou'd marry and have a child, you may be difinherited, ha ?

Mir. Where haft thou ftumbled upon all this truth ?

Pet. All's one for that; why then fay I know fomething.

Mir. Come, thou art an honeft fellow, Petulant, and fhalt make love to my miftrefs, thou fha't faith. What haft thou heard of my uncle ?

Pet. I? nothing, I. If throats are to be cut, let fwords clafh; fnug's the word, I fhrug and am filent.

Mir. O raillery, raillery. Come, I know thou art in the womens fecrets——what, you're a cabalift; I know you ftaid at Millamant's laft night, after I went. Was there any mention made of my uncle or me ? tell me. If thou hadft but good nature equal to thy wit, Petulant, Tony Witwoud, who is now thy competitor in fame, wou'd fhew as dim by thee as a dead whiting's eye by a pearl of orient ; he wou'd no more be feen by thee, than Mercury is by the fun. Come, I'm fure thou wo't tell me.

Pet. If I do, will you grant me common fenfe then, for the future ?

Mir. Faith, I'll do what I can for thee, and I'll pray that Heav'n may grant it thee in the mean time.

Pet. Well, hark'ee.

Fain. Petulant and you both will find Mirabell as warm a rival as a lover.

Wit. Pfhaw, pfhaw, that fhe laughs at Petulant is plain. And for my part——but that it is almoft a fafhion to admire her, I fhou'd—hark'ee—to tell you a fecret, but let it go no further——between friends, I fhall never break my heart for her.

Fain. How !

Wit. She's handfome; but fhe's a fort of an uncertain woman.

Fain. I thought you had died for her.

Wit. Umh—no—

Fain. She has wit.

Wit. 'Tis what she will hardly allow any body else——
now, demme, I shou'd hate that, if she were as handsome
as Cleopatra. Mirabell is not so sure of her as he thinks
for.

Fain. Why do you think so?

Wit. We staid pretty late there last night : and heard
something of an uncle to Mirabell, who is lately come to
town—and is between him and the best part of his estate ;
Mirabell and he are at some distance, as my Lady Wishfort has been told ; and you know she hates Mirabell worse
than a quaker hates a parrot, or than a fishmonger hates
a hard frost. Whether this uncle has seen Mrs Millamant
or not I cannot say, but there were items of such a treaty
being in embryo ; and if it shou'd come to life, poor Mirabell wou'd be in some sort unfortunately fobb'd, i'faith.

Fain. 'Tis impossible Millamant shou'd hearken to it.

Wit. Faith, my dear, I can't tell ; she's a woman, and
a kind of humourist.

Mir. And this is the sum of what you could collect last
night?

Pet. The quintessence. May be Witwoud knows more,
he staid longer——besides, they never mind him ; they say
any thing before him.

Mir. I thought you had been the greatest favourite.

Pet. Ay, *tete a tete*, but not in public, because I make
remarks.

Mir. You do?

Pet. Ay, ay ; pox, I'm malicious, man. Now he's soft
you know ; they are not in awe of him—the fellow's well-
bred ; he's what you call a——what-d'ye-call-ems, a fine
gentleman ; but he's silly withal.

Mir. I thank you, I know as much as my curiosity requires. Fainall, are you for the Mall?

Fain. Ay, I'll take a turn before dinner.

Wit. Ay, we'll all walk in the Park ; the ladies talk'd
of being there.

Mir. I thought you were oblig'd to watch for your brother Sir Wilfull's arrival.

Wit. No, no; he comes to my aunt's, my Lady Wifh-fort; pox on him, I fhall be troubled with him too; what fhall I do with the fool?

Pet. Beg him for his eftate, that I may beg you afterwards: and fo have but one trouble with you both.

Wit. O rare Petulant; thou art as quick as fire in a frofty morning; thou fhalt to the Mall with us, and we'll be very fevere.

Pet. Enough, I'm in a humour to be fevere.

Mir. Are you? pray then walk by yourfelves—let not us be accefary to your putting the ladies out of countenance with your fenfelefs ribaldry, which you roar out aloud as often as they pafs by you; and when you have made a handfome woman blufh, then you think you have been fevere.

Pet. What, what? then let 'em either fhew their innocence by not underftanding what they hear, or elfe fhew their difcretion by not hearing what they wou'd not be thought to underftand.

Mir. But haft not thou then fenfe enough to know that thou ought'ft to be moft afhamed thyfelf, when thou haft put another out of countenance?

Pet. Not I, by this hand—I always take blufhing either for a fign of guilt, or ill-breeding.

Mir. I confefs you ought to think fo. You are in the right, that you may plead the error of your judgment in defence of your practice.

Where modefty's ill-manners, 'tis but fit
That impudence and malice pafs for wit.

ACT II. SCENE I.

St James's Park.

Mrs FAINALL, *and* Mrs MARWOOD,

Mrs FAINALL.

AY, ay, dear Marwood, if we will be happy, we muſt find the means in ourſelves, and among ourſelves. Men are ever in extremes; either doating or averſe. While they are lovers, if they have fire and ſenſe, their jealouſies are unſupportable; and when they ceaſe to love, (we ought to think at leaſt) they lothe; they look upon us with horror and diſtaſte; they meet us like the ghoſts of what we were, and as from ſuch, fly from us.

Mrs *Mar.* True, 'tis an unhappy circumſtance of life, that love ſhou'd ever die before us; and that the man ſo often ſhou'd out-live the lover. But ſay what you will, 'tis better to be left, than never to have been lov'd. To paſs our youth in dull indifference, to refuſe the ſweets of life becauſe they once muſt leave us, is as prepoſterous as to wiſh to have been born old, becauſe we one day muſt be old. For my part, my youth may wear and waſte, but it ſhall never ruſt in my poſſeſſion.

Mrs *Fain.* Then it ſeems you diſſemble an averſion to mankind, only in compliance to my mother's humour.

Mrs *Mar.* Certainly. To be free; I have no taſte of thoſe inſipid dry diſcourſes, with which our ſex of force muſt entertain themſelves, apart from men. We may affect endearments to each other, profeſs eternal friendſhips, and ſeem to doat like lovers; but 'tis not in our natures long to perſevere. Love will reſume his empire in our

breasts, and every heart, soon or late, receive and re-
admit him as its lawful tyrant.

Mrs *Fain.* Bless me, how have I been deceiv'd! why
you profess a libertine.

Mrs *Mar.* You see my friendship by my freedom.
Come, be as sincere, acknowledge that your sentiments
agree with mine.

Mrs *Fain.* Never.

Mrs *Mar.* You hate mankind?

Mrs *Fain.* Heartily, inveterately.

Mrs *Mar.* Your husband?

Mrs *Fain.* Most transcendently; ay, tho' I say it, meri-
toriously.

Mrs *Mar.* Give me your hand upon it.

Mrs *Fain.* There.

Mrs *Mar.* I join with you; what I have said has been
to try you.

Mrs *Fain.* Is it possible? dost thou hate those vipers
men?

Mrs *Mar.* I have done hating 'em, and am now come
to despise 'em; the next thing I have to do, is eternally
to forget 'em.

Mrs *Fain.* There spoke the spirit of an Amazon, a
Penthesilea.

Mrs *Mar.* And yet I am thinking sometimes to carry
my aversion further.

Mrs *Fain.* How?

Mrs *Mar.* Faith by marrying; if I cou'd but find one
that lov'd me very well, and would be throughly sensible
of ill usage, I think I should do myself the violence of
undergoing the ceremony.

Mrs *Fain.* You would not make him a cuckold?

Mrs *Mar.* No; but I'd make him believe I did, and
that's as bad.

Mrs *Fain.* Why, had not you as good do it?

Mrs *Mar.* O if he shou'd ever discover it, he wou'd
then know the worst, and be out of his pain; but I wou'd

have him ever to continue upon the rack of fear and jealoufy.

Mrs *Fain.* Ingenious mifchief! wou'd thou wert married to Mirabell.

Mrs *Mar.* Wou'd I were.

Mrs *Fain.* You change colour.

Mrs *Mar.* Becaufe I hate him.

Mrs *Fain.* So do I; but I can hear him nam'd. But
what reafon have you to hate him in particular?

Mrs *Mar.* I never lov'd him; he is, and always was
infufferable proud.

Mrs *Fain.* By the reafon you give for your averfion,
one wou'd think it diffembled; for you have laid a fault
to his charge, of which his enemies muft acquit him.

Mrs *Mar.* O then it feems you are one of his favourable enemies. Methinks you look a little pale, and now
you flufh again.

Mrs *Fain.* Do I? I think I am a little fick o'the
fudden.

Mrs *Mar.* What ails you?

Mrs *Fain.* My hufband. Don't you fee him? He
turn'd fhort upon me unawares, and has almoft overcome
me.

S C E N E II.

[*To them*] F A I N A L L *and* M I R A B E L L.

Mrs *Mar.* Ha, ha, ha! he comes opportunely for you.

Mrs *Fain.* For you, for he has brought Mirabell with
him.

Fain. My dear.

Mrs *Fain.* My foul.

Fain. You don't look well to-day, child.

Mrs *Fain.* D'ye think fo?

Mira. He is the only man that does, Madam.

Mrs *Fain.* The only man that wou'd tell me fo at

leaft; and the only man from whom I cou'd hear it without mortification.

Fain. O my dear, I am fatisfy'd of your tendernefs; I know you cannot refent any thing from me; efpecially what is an effect of concern.

Mrs *Fain.* Mr Mirabell, my mother interrupted you in a pleafant relation laft night, I wou'd fain hear it out.

Mir. The perfons concern'd in that affair, have yet a tolerable reputation.————I am afraid Mr Fainall will be cenforious.

Mrs *Fain.* He has a humour more prevailing than his curiofity, and will willingly difpenfe with the hearing of one fcandalous ftory, to avoid giving an occafion to make another by being feen to walk with his wife. This way, Mr Mirabell, and I dare promife you will oblige us both.

SCENE III.

FAINALL, Mrs MARWOOD.

Fain. Excellent creature! well, fure if I fhou'd live to be rid of my wife, I fhou'd be a miferable man.

Mrs *Mar.* Ay!

Fain. For having only that one hope, the accomplifhment of it, of confequence, muft put an end to all my hopes; and what a wretch is he who muft furvive his hopes! Nothing remains when that day comes, but to fit down and weep like Alexander, when he wanted other worlds to conquer.

Mrs *Mar.* Will you not follow 'em?

Fain. Faith, I think not.

Mrs *Mar.* Pray let us; I have a reafon.

Fain. You are not jealous?

Mrs *Mar.* Of whom?

Fain. Of Mirabell.

Mrs *Mar.* If I am, is it inconfiftent with my love to you that I am tender of your honour?

Fain. You wou'd intimate then, as if there were a fellow-feeling between my wife and him.

Mrs *Mar.* I think she does not hate him to that degree she wou'd be thought.

Fain. But he, I fear, is too insensible.

Mrs *Mar.* It may be you are deceiv'd.

Fain. It may be so. I do now begin to apprehend it.

Mrs *Mar.* What?

Fain. That I have been deceiv'd, Madam, and you are false.

Mrs *Mar.* That I am false! what mean you?

Fain. To let you know I see through all your little arts ———come, you both love him; and both have equally dissembled your aversion. Your mutual jealousies of one another, have made you clash 'till you have both struck fire. I have seen the warm confession redning on your cheeks, and sparkling from your eyes.

Mrs *Mar.* You do me wrong.

Fain. I do not—'twas for my case to oversee and wilfully neglect the grofs advances made him by my wife; that by permitting her to be engag'd, I might continue unsuspected in my pleasures; and take you oftner to my arms in full security. But cou'd you think, because the nodding husband wou'd not wake, that e'er the watchful lover slept?

Mrs *Mar.* And wherewithal can you reproach me?

Fain. With infidelity, with loving another, with love of Mirabell.

Mrs *Mar.* 'Tis false. I challenge you to shew an instance that can confirm your groundless accusation. I hate him.

Fain. And wherefore do you hate him? he is insensible, and your resentment follows his neglect. An instance! the injuries you have done him are a proof: your interposing in his love. What cause had you to make discoveries of his pretended passion? To undeceive the credulous aunt, and be the officious obstacle of his match with Millamant?

Mrs Mar. My obligations to my Lady urg'd me; I had profefs'd a friendfhip to her; and cou'd not fee her eafy nature fo abus'd by that diffembler.

Fain. What, was it confcience then? Profefs'd a friend-fhip! O the pious friendfhips of the female fex?

Mrs Mar. More tender, more fincere, and more endur-ing, than all the vain and empty vows of men, whether profeffing love to us, or mutual faith to one another.

Fain. Ha, ha, ha! you are my wife's friend too.

Mrs Mar. Shame and ingratitude! do you reproach me? You, you upbraid me! Have I been falfe to her, thro' ftrict fidelity to you, and facrific'd my friendfhip to keep my love inviolate? And have you the bafenefs to charge me with the guilt, unmindful of the merit? to you it fhou'd be meritorious, that I have been vicious: and do you reflect that guilt upon me, which fhou'd ly buried in your bofom?

Fain. You mifinterpret my reproof. I meant but to remind you of the flight account you once cou'd make of ftricteft ties, when fet in competition with your love to me.

Mrs Mar. 'Tis falfe, you urg'd it with deliberate malice —'twas fpoken in fcorn, and I never will forgive it.

Fain. Your guilt, not your refentment, begets your rage. If you yet lov'd, you cou'd forgive a jealoufy: but you are ftung to find you are difcover'd.

Mrs Mar. It fhall be all difcover'd. You too fhall be difcover'd; be fure you fhall. I can but be expos'd—— If I do it myfelf I fhall prevent your bafenefs.

Fain. Why, what will you do?

Mrs Mar. Difclofe it to your wife; own what has paft between us.

Fain. Frenzy!

Mrs Mar. By all my wrongs I'll do't—I'll publifh to the world the injuries you have done me, both in my fame and fortune; with both I trufted you, you bankrupt in honour, as indigent of wealth.

Fain. Your fame I have preferv'd: Your fortune has been beftow'd as the prodigality of your love wou'd have it, in pleafures which we both have fbar'd. Yet, had not you been falfe, I had ere this repaid it——'tis true—— had you permitted Mirabell with Millamant to have ftol'n their marriage, my Lady had been incens'd beyond all means of reconcilement: Millamant had forfeited the moiety of her fortune; which then wou'd have defcended to my wife;————and wherefore did I marry, but to make lawful prize of a rich widow's wealth, and fquander it on love and you?

Mrs *Mar.* Deceit and frivolous pretence!

Fain. Death, am I not married? What's pretence? Am I not imprifon'd, fetter'd? Have I not a wife? Nay a wife that was a widow, a young widow, a handfome widow; and wou'd be again a widow, but that I have a heart of proof, and fomething of a conftitution to buftle thro' the ways of wedlock and this world! Will you yet be reconcil'd to truth and me?

Mrs *Mar.* Impoffible. Truth and you are inconfiftent ——I hate you, and fhall for ever.

Fain. For loving you?

Mrs *Mar.* I loath the name of love after fuch ufage; and next to the guilt with which you would afperfe me, I fcorn you moft. Farewel.

Fain. Nay, we muft not part thus.

Mrs *Mar.* Let me go.

Fain. Come, I'm forry.

Mrs *Mar.* I care not—let me go——break my hands, do——I'd leave 'em to get loofe.

Fain. I wou'd not hurt you for the world. Have I no other hold to keep you here?

Mrs *Mar.* Well, I have deferv'd it all.

Fain. You know I love you.

Mrs *Mar.* Poor diffembling!————O that——well, is it not yet——

K 2

Fain. What? What is it not? What is it not yet? is it not yet too late——

Mrs *Mar.* No, it is not yet too late——I have that comfort.

Fain. It is, to love another.

Mrs *Mar.* But not to loath, deteſt, abhor mankind, myſelf, and the whole treacherous world.

Fain. Nay, this is extravagance——come, I aſk your pardon—no tears—I was to blame, I cou'd not love you and be eaſy in my doubts—pray forbear—I believe you; I'm convinc'd I've done you wrong; and any way, ev'ry way will make amends ;——I'll hate my wife yet more, damn her, I'll part with her, rob her of all ſhe's worth, and will retire ſomewhere, any where, to another world. I'll marry thee————be pacified————'ſdeath, they come, hide your face, your tears————you have a maſk, wear it a moment. This way, this way, be perſuaded.

SCENE IV.

MIRABELL *and* Mrs FAINALL.

Mrs *Fain.* They are here yet.

Mir. They are turning into the other walk.

Mrs *Fain.* While I only hated my huſband, I cou'd bear to ſee him ; but ſince I have deſpis'd him, he's too offenſive.

Mir. O you ſhou'd hate with prudence.

Mrs *Fain.* Yes, for I have lov'd with indiſcretion.

Mir. You ſhou'd have juſt ſo much diſguſt for your huſband, as may be ſufficient to make you reliſh your lover.

Mrs *Fain.* You have been the cauſe that I have lov'd without bounds, and wou'd you ſet limits to that averſion of which you have been the occaſion ? why did you make me marry this man ?

Mir. Why do we daily commit difagreeable and dangerous actions? to fave that idol reputation. If the familiarities of our loves had produc'd that confequence of which you were apprehenfive, where cou'd you have fix'd a father's name with credit, but on a hufband? I knew Fainall to be a man lavifh of his morals, an interefted and profeffing friend, a falfe and defigning lover; yet one whofe wit and outward fair behaviour, have gain'd a reputation with the town, enough to make that woman ftand excus'd, who has fuffer'd herfelf to be won by his addreffes. A better man ought not to have been facrific'd to the occafion; a worfe had not anfwer'd the purpofe. When you are weary of him, you know your remedy.

Mrs *Fain.* I ought to ftand in fome degree of credit with you, Mirabell.

Mir. In juftice to you, I have made you privy to my whole defign, and put it in your power to ruin or advance my fortune.

Mrs *Fain.* Whom have you inftructed to reprefent your pretended uncle?

Mir. Waitwell, my fervant.

Mrs *Fain.* He is an humble fervant to Foible my mother's woman, and may win her to your intereft.

Mir. Care is taken for that—fhe is won and worn by this time. They were married this morning.

Mrs *Fain.* Who?

Mir. Waitwell and Foible: I wou'd not tempt my fervant to betray me by trufting him too far. If your mother, in hopes to ruin me, fhou'd confent to marry my pretended uncle, he might, like Mofca in the Fox, ftand upon terms; fo I made him fure beforehand.

Mrs *Fain.* So, if my poor mother is caught in a contract, you will-difcover the impofture betimes; and releafe her by producing a certificate of her gallant's former marriage?

Mir. Yes, upon condition that fhe confent to my marriage with her niece, and furrender the moiety of her fortune in her poffeffion.

K 3

Mrs Fain. She talk'd laſt night of endeavouring at a match between Millamant and your uncle.

Mir. That was by Foible's direction, and my inſtruction, that ſhe might ſeem to carry it more privately.

Mrs Fain. Well, I have an opinion of your ſucceſs; for I believe my Lady will do any thing to get an huſband; and when ſhe has this, which you have provided for her, I ſuppoſe ſhe will ſubmit to any thing to get rid of him.

Mir. Yes, I think the good lady wou'd marry any thing that reſembled a man, though 'twere no more than what a butler could pinch out of a napkin.

Mrs Fain. Female frailty! we muſt all come to it, if we live to be old, and feel the craving of a falſe appetite when the true is decay'd.

Mir. An old woman's appetite is depraved like that of a girl—'tis the green ſickneſs of a ſecond childhood; and like the faint offer of a latter ſpring, ſerves but to uſher in the fall, and withers in an ineffectual bloom.

Mrs Fain. Here's your miſtreſs.

S C E N E V.

[*To them*] Mrs M I L L A M A N T, W I T W O U D, M I N-
C I N G.

Mir. Here ſhe comes, i'faith, full ſail, with her-fan ſpread and ſtreamers out, and a ſhoal of fools for tenders; ha, no, I cry her mercy.

Mrs Fain. I ſee but one poor empty ſculler; and he tows her woman after him.

Mir. You ſeem to be unattended, Madam——you us'd to have the beau monde throng after you; and a flock of gay ſine perukes hovering round you.

Wit. Like moths about a candle——I had like to have loſt my compariſon for want of breath.

Mil. O I have denied myſelf airs to-day, I have walk'd as faſt through the croud——

Wit. As a favourite juſt diſgraced; and with as few followers.

Mil. Dear Mr Witwoud, truce with your ſimilitudes; for I am as ſick of 'em——

Wit. As a phyſician of a good air—I cannot help it, Madam, though 'tis againſt myſelf.

Mil. Yet again! Mincing, ſtand between me and his wit.

Wit. Do, Mrs Mincing, like a ſcreen before a great fire. I confeſs I do blaze to-day, I am too bright.

Mrs *Fain.* But, dear Millamant, why were you ſo long?

Mil. Long! Lord, have I not made violent haſte? I have aſk'd every living thing I met for you; I have enquir'd after you, as after a new faſhion.

Wit. Madam, truce with your ſimilitudes—no, you met her huſband, and did not aſk him for her.

Mir. By your leave, Witwoud, that were like enquiring after an old faſhion, to aſk a huſband for his wife.

Wit. Hum, a hit, a hit, a palpable hit, I confeſs it.

Mrs *Fain.* You were dreſs'd before I came abroad.

Mil. Ay, that's true——O but then I had——Mincing, what had I? why was I ſo long?

Min. O mem, your Laſhip ſtaid to peruſe a pacquet of letters.

Mil. O ay, letters—I had letters—I am perſecuted with letters—I hate letters——no body knows how to write letters, and yet one has 'em, one does not know why—they ſerve one to pin up one's hair.

Wit. Is that the way? Pray, Madam, do you pin up your hair with all your letters? I find I muſt keep copies.

Mil. Only with thoſe in verſe, Mr Witwoud, I never pin up my hair with proſe. I think I try'd once, Mincing.

Mir. O mem, I ſhall never forget it.

Mill. Ay, poor Mincing tift and tift all the morning.

I

Min. 'Till I had the cramp in my fingers, I'll vow, mem: And all to no purpose. But when your Lafhip pins it up with poetry, it fits fo pleafant the next day as any thing, and is fo pure and fo crips.

Wit. Indeed, fo crips?

Min. You're fuch a critic, Mr Witwoud.

Mil. Mirabell, did you take exceptions laft night? O ay, and went away——now I think on't, I'm angry——no, now I think on't I'm pleas'd——for I believe I gave you fome pain.

Mir. Does that pleafe you?

Mil. Infinitely; I love to give pain.

Mir. You wou'd affect a cruelty which is not in your nature; your true vanity is in the power of pleafing.

Mil. O I afk your pardon for that——one's cruelty is in one's power; and when one parts with one's cruelty, one parts with one's power; and when one has parted with that, I fancy one's old and ugly.

Mir. Ay, ay, fuffer your cruelty to ruin the object of your power, to deftroy your lover——and then how vain, how loft a thing you'll be! nay, 'tis true: you are no longer handfome when you've loft your lover; your beauty dies upon the inftant; for beauty is the lover's gift; 'tis he beftows your charms——your glafs is all a cheat. The ugly and the old, whom the looking-glafs mortifies, yet after commendation can be flatter'd by it, and difcover beauties in it; for that reflects our praifes, rather than our face.

Mil. O the vanity of thefe men! Fainall, d'ye hear him? If they did not commend us, we were not handfome! now you muft know they cou'd not commend one, if one was not handfome. Beauty the lover's gift——Lord, what is a lover, that it can give? Why, one makes lovers as faft as one pleafes, and they live as long as one pleafes, and they die as foon as one pleafes; and then if one pleafes, one makes more.

Wit. Very pretty. Why, you make no more of making of lovers, Madam, than of making so many card-matches.

Mil. One no more owes one's beauty to a lover, than one's wit to an echo; they can but reflect what we look and say; vain empty things if we are silent or unseen, and want a being.

Mir. Yet to those two vain empty things, you owe two the greatest pleasures of your life.

Mil. How so?

Mir. To your lover you owe the pleasure of hearing yourselves prais'd; and to an echo the pleasure of hearing yourselves talk.

Wit. But I know a lady that loves talking so incessantly, she won't give an echo fair play; she has that everlasting rotation of tongue, that an echo must wait 'till she dies, before it can catch her last words.

Mil. O fiction; Fainall, let us leave these men.

Mir. Draw off Witwoud.   [*Aside to* Mrs Fain.

Mrs *Fain.* Immediately; I have a word or two for Mr Witwoud.

SCENE VI.

MILLAMANT, MIRABELL, MINCING.

Mir. I wou'd beg a little private audience too——you had the tyranny to deny me last night; though you knew I came to impart a secret to you that concern'd my love.

Mil. You saw I was engag'd.

Mir. Unkind. You had the leisure to entertain a herd of fools; things who visit you from their excessive idleness; bestowing on your easiness that time, which is the incumbrance of their lives. How can you find delight in such society? It is impossible they shou'd admire you, they are not capable: or if they were, it shou'd be to you as a mortification; for sure to please a fool is some degree of folly.

Mil. I pleafe myfelf——befides, fometimes to converfe with fools is for my health.

Mir. Your health! is there a worfe difeafe than the converfation of fools?

Mil. Yes, the vapours; fools are phyfic for it, next to affa foetida.

Mir. You are not in a courfe of fools?

* *Mil.* Mirabell, if you perfift in this offenfive freedom——you'll difpleafe me—I think I muft refolve after all, not to have you—we fhan't agree.

Mir. Not in our phyfic, it may be.

Mil. And yet our diftemper, in all likelihood, will be the fame; for we fhall be fick of one another. I fhan't endure to be reprimanded, nor inftructed; 'tis fo dull to act always by advice, and fo tedious to be told of one's faults——I can't bear it. Well, I won't have you, Mirabell——I'm refolv'd——I think——you may go—ha, ha, ha! what would you give, that you could help loving me?

Mir. I wou'd give fomething that you did not know I cou'd not help it.

Mil. Come, don't look grave then. Well, what do you fay to me?

Mir. I fay that a man may as foon make a friend by his wit, or a fortune by his honefty, as win a woman with plain-dealing, and fincerity.

Mil. Sententious Mirabell!—Pr'ythee, don't look with that violent and inflexible wife face, like Solomon at the dividing of the child in an old tapeftry hanging.

Mir. You are merry, Madam, but I would perfuade you for a moment to be ferious.

Mil. What, with that face? No, if you keep your countenance, 'tis impoffible I fhou'd hold mine. Well, after all, there is fomething very moving in a love-fick face. Ha, ha, ha!——well, I won't laugh, don't be peevifh ——heigho! now I'll be melancholy, as melancholy as a watch-light. Well, Mirabell, if ever you will win me

woo me now—nay, if you are fo tedious, fare you well;—
I fee you are walking away.

Mir. Can you not find in the variety of your difpofition
one moment———

Mil. To hear you tell me Foible's marry'd, and your
plot like to fpeed——no.

Mir. But how you came to know it——

Mil. Without the help of the devil, you can't imagine;
unlefs fhe fhou'd tell me herfelf. Which of the two it
may have been, I will leave you to confider; and when
you have done thinking of that, think of me.

S C E N E VII.

MIRABELL *alone.*

Mir. I have fomething more—gone—think of you? to
think of a whirlwind, tho' 'twere in a whirlwind, were a
cafe of more fteady contemplation; a very tranquillity of
mind and manfion A fellow that lives in a windmill,
has not a more whimfical dwelling than the heart of a
man that is lodg'd in a woman. There is no point of the
compafs to which they cannot turn, and by which they
are not turn'd; and by one as well as another; for motion,
not method, is their occupation. To know this, and yet
continue to be in love, is to be made wife from the dic-
tates of reafon, and yet perfevere to play the fool by the
force of inftinct.——O here come my pair of turtles,——
what, billing fo fweetly! is not Valentine's day over with
you yet?

S C E N E VIII.

[*To him*] WAITWELL, FOIBLE.

Mir. Sirrah, Waitwell, why fure you think you were
marry'd for your own recreation, and not for my conve-
niency.

Wait. Your pardon, Sir. With fubmiffion, we have indeed been folacing in lawful delights; but ftill with an eye to bufinefs, Sir. I have inftructed her as well as I could. If fhe can take your directions as readily as my inftructions, Sir, your affairs are in a profperous way.

Mir. Give you joy, Mrs Foible.

Foib. O-las, Sir, I'm fo afham'd—I'm afraid my Lady has been in a thoufand inquietudes for me. But I proteft, Sir, I made as much hafte as I could.

Wait. That fhe did indeed, Sir. It was my fault that fhe did not make more.

Mir. That I believe. -

Foib. But I told my Lady as you inftructed me, Sir, that I had a profpect of feeing Sir Rowland your uncle; and that I wou'd put her Ladyfhip's picture in my pocket to fhew him; which I'll be fure to fay has made him fo enamour'd of her beauty, that he burns with impatience to ly at her Ladyfhip's feet, and worfhip the original.

Mir. Excellent Foible! matrimony has made you eloquent in love.

Wait. I think fhe has profited, Sir, I think fo.

Foib. You have feen Madam Millamant, Sir?

Mir. Yes.

Foib. I told her, Sir, becaufe I did not know that you might find an opportunity; fhe had fo much company laft night.

Mir. Your diligence will merit more——in the mean time——   [*Gives money.*

Foib. O dear Sir, your humble fervant.

Wait. Spoufe.

Mir. Stand off, Sir, not a penny—go on and profper, Foible—the leafe fhall be made good, and the farm ftock'd, if we fucceed.

Foib. I don't queftion your generofity, Sir: and you need not doubt of fuccefs. If you have no more commands, Sir, I'll be gone; I'm fure my Lady is at her toilet, and can't drefs 'till I come.——O dear, I'm fure that [*Looking out.*] was Mrs Marwood that went by in a mafk;

If she has seen me with you I'm sure she'll tell my Lady.
I'll make haste home and prevent her. Your servant, Sir.
B'w'y, Waitwell.

SCENE IX.

MIRABELL, WAITWELL.

Wait. Sir Rowland, if you please. The jade's so pert
upon her preferment she forgets herself.

Mir. Come, Sir, will you endeavour to forget yourself
——and transform into Sir Rowland?

Wait. Why, Sir, it will be impossible I shou'd remember myself——marry'd, knighted and attended all in one
day! 'tis enough to make any man forget himself. The
difficulty will be how to recover my acquaintance and familiarity with my former self; and fall from my transfor-
mation to a reformation into Waitwell. Nay, I shan't
be quite the same Waitwell neither—for now I remember
me, I'm marry'd, and can't be my own man again.

Ay there's my grief; that's the sad change of life;
To lose my title, and yet keep my wife.

ACT III. SCENE I.

A Room in Lady Wishfort's *House.*

Lady WISHFORT *at her toilet,* PEG *waiting.*

LADY,

MERCIFUL! no news of Foible yet?
    Peg. No, Madam.

Lady. I have no more patience——if I have not fretted
myself, 'till I am pale again, there's no veracity in me.
Fetch me the red——the red, do you hear, sweet-heart?
An errant ash colour, as I am a person. Look you how
this wench stirs! why dost thou not fetch me a little red?
Didst thou not hear me, Mopus?

Peg. The red Ratafia does your Ladyfhip mean, or the cherry-brandy?

Lady. Ratafia, fool! no, fool. Not the Ratafia, fool ———grant me patience! I mean the Spanifh paper, idiot, complexion, darling. Paint, paint, paint, doft thou underftand that, changeling, dangling thy hands like bobbins before thee? why doft thou not ftart, puppet? thou wooden thing upon wires.

Peg. Lord, Madam, your Ladyfhip is fo impatient—— I cannot come at the paint, Madam, Mrs Foible has lock'd it up, and carry'd the key with her.

Lady. A pox take you both——fetch me the cherry-brandy then.

S C E N E II.

Lady WISHFORT.

I'm as pale and as faint, I look like Mrs Qualmfick the curate's wife, that's always breeding———wench, come, come, wench, what art thou doing? fipping? tafting? Save thee, doft thou not know the bottle?

S C E N E III.

Lady WISHFORT, PEG *with a bottle and China cup.*

Peg. Madam, I was looking for a cup.

Lady. A cup, fave thee, and what a cup haft thou brought! doft thou take me for a fairy, to drink out of an acorn? Why didft thou not bring thy thimble? Haft thou ne'er a brafs thimble clinking in thy pocket with a bit of nutmeg? I warrant thee. Come, fill, fill.——— ——So——— again. See who that is———[*One knocks.*] Set down the bottle firft———here, here, under the table———what, woud'ft thou go with the bottle in thy hand like a tapfter? As I am a perfon, this wench has liv'd in an inn upon the road, before fhe came to me, like Maritornes the Auftrian in Don Quixote. No Foible yet?

Peg. No, Madam, Mrs Marwood.

Lady. O Marwood, let her come in. Come in, good Marwood.

SCENE IV.

[*To them*] Mrs MARWOOD.

Mrs Mar. I'm furpriz'd to find your Ladyfhip in difhabille at this time of day.

Lady. Foible's a loft thing; has been abroad fince morning, and never heard of fince.

Mrs Mar. I faw her but now, as I came mafk'd thro' the park, in conference with Mirabell.

Lady. With Mirabell! you call my blood into my face, with mentioning that traitor. She durft not have the confidence. I fent her to negotiate an affair, in which if I'm detected, I'm undone. If that wheedling villain has wrought upon Foible to detect me, I'm ruin'd. O my dear friend, I'm a wretch of wretches if I'm detected.

Mrs Mar. O Madam, you cannot fufpect Mrs Foible's integrity.

Lady. O, he carries poifon in his tongue that wou'd corrupt integrity itfelf. If fhe has giv'n him an opportunity, fhe has as good as put her integrity into his hands. Ah dear Marwood, what's integrity to an opportunity?—— Hark! I hear her——dear friend, retire into my clofet, that I may examine her with more freedom——you'll pardon me, dear friend, I can make bold with you——there are books over the chimney——Quarles and Pryn, and The fhort View of the Stage, with Bunyan's works, to entertain you.——Go, you thing, and fead her in. [*To* Peg.

SCENE V.

Lady WISHFORT, FOIBLE.

Lady. O Foible, where haſt thou been ? what haſt thou been doing ?

Foib. Madam, I have ſeen the party.

Lady. But what haſt thou done ?

Foib. Nay, 'tis your Ladyſhip has done, and are to do; I have only promiſed. But a man ſo enamour'd—ſo tranſported! well, if worſhipping of pictures be a ſin——poor Sir Rowland, I ſay.

Lady. The miniature has been counted like—but haſt thou not betray'd me, Foible ? Haſt thou not detected me to that faithleſs Mirabell ?——What hadſt thou to do with him in the park ? Anſwer me, has he got nothing out of thee ?

Foib. So, the devil has been beforehand with me. What ſhall I ſay ?——Alas, Madam, could I help it, if I met that confident thing ? Was I in fault ? If you had heard how he us'd me, and all upon your Ladyſhip's account, I'm ſure you would not ſuſpect my fidelity. Nay, if that had been the worſt, I could have borne: but he had a fling at your Ladyſhip too; and then I could not hold; but i'faith I gave him his own.

Lady. Me ? what did the filthy fellow ſay?

Foib. O Madam, 'tis a ſhame to ſay what he ſaid—— with his taunts and his fleers, toſſing up his noſe. Humph (ſays he) what, you are a hatching ſome plot (ſays he) you are ſo early abroad, or catering (ſays he) ferreting for ſome diſbanded officer, I warrant——half pay is but thin ſubſiſtence (ſays he)—well, what penſion does your lady propoſe ? Let me ſee (ſays he) what, ſhe muſt come down pretty deep now, ſhe's ſuperannuated (ſays he) and——

Lady. Odds my life, I'll have him, I'll have him murder'd. I'll have him poiſon'd. Where does he eat ? I'll marry a drawer to have him poison'd in his wine. I'll send for Robin from Locket's—immediately.

Foib. Poison him! poisoning's too good for him. Starve him, Madam, starve him; marry Sir Rowland, and get him disinherited. O you wou'd bless yourself to hear what he said.

Lady. A villain! superannuated!

Foib. Humph (says he) I hear you are laying designs against me too (says he) and Mrs Millamant is to marry my uncle; (he does not suspect a word of your Ladyship;) but (says he) I'll fit you for that. I warrant you (says he) I'll hamper you for that (says he) you and your old frippery too (says he) I'll handle you——

Lady. Audacious villain! handle me, wou'd he durst— frippery? old frippery! was there ever such a foul-mouth'd fellow? I'll be married to-morrow, I'll be contracted to-night.

Foib. The sooner the better, Madam.

Lady. Will Sir Rowland be here, say'st thou? when, Foible?

Foib. Incontinently, Madam. No new sheriff's wife expects the return of her husband after knighthood, with that impatience in which Sir Rowland burns for the dear hour of kissing your Ladyship's hand after dinner.

Lady. Frippery? superannuated frippery! I'll frippery the villain; I'll reduce him to frippery and rags: a tatterdemalion———I hope to see him hung with tatters, like a Long-Lane pent-house, or a gibbet thief. A slandermouth'd railer: I warrant the spendthrift prodigal's in debt as much as the million lottery, or the whole court upon a birth-day. I'll spoil his credit with his tailor. Yes, he shall have my niece with her fortune, he shall.

Foib. He! I hope to see him lodge in Ludgate first, and angle into Black-friars for brass farthings, with an old mitten.

Lady. Ay, dear Foible; thank thee for that, dear Foible. He has put me out of all patience. I shall never recompose my features, to receive Sir Rowland with an œconomy of face. This wretch has fretted me that I am abfolutely decay'd. Look, Foible.

Foib. Your Ladyfhip has frown'd a little too rafhly, indeed, Madam. There are fome cracks difcernible in the white varnifh.

Lady. Let me fee the glafs————cracks fay'ft thou ? Why, I am errantly flea'd————I look like an old peel'd wall. Thou muft repair me, Foible, before Sir Rowland, comes ; or I fhall never keep up to my picture.

Foib. I warrant you, Madam; a little art once made your picture like you ; and now a little of the fame art muft make you like your picture. Your picture muft fit for you, Madam.

Lady. But art thou fure Sir Rowland will not fail to come ? Or will he not fail when he does come ? Will he be importunate, Foible, and pufh ? For if he fhould not be importunate—I fhall never break decorums—I fhall die with confufion, if I'm forc'd to advance.—Oh no, I can never advance————I fhall fwoon if he fhould expect advances. No, I hope Sir Rowland is better bred, than to put a lady to the neceffity of breaking her forms. I won't be too coy neither.———I won't give him defpair————but a little difdain is not amifs ; a little fcorn is alluring.

Foib. A little fcorn becomes your Ladyfhip.

Lady. Yes, but tendernefs becomes me beft————a fort of a dyingnefs—you fee that picture has a fort of a ——ha, Foible ! a fwimmingnefs in the eyes—yes, I'll look fo —— my niece affects it ; but fhe wants features. Is Sir Rowland handfome ? Let my toilet be remov'd————I'll drefs above. I'll receive Sir Rowland here. Is he handfome ? Don't anfwer me. I won't know : I'll be furpriz'd, I'll be taken by furprize.

Foib. By ftorm, Madam. Sir Rowland's a brifk man.

Lady. Is he ! O then he'll importune, if he's a brifk man. I fhall fave decorums if Sir Rowland importunes. I have a mortal terror at the apprehenfion of offending againft decorums. O I'm glad he's a brifk man. Let my things be remov'd, good Foible.

SCENE VI.

Mrs FAINALL, FOIBLE.

Mrs Fain. O Foible, I have been in a fright, left I fhou'd come too late. That devil Marwood, fay you, in the park with Mirabell? and I'm afraid will difcover it to my Lady.

Foib. Difcover what, Madam?

Mrs Fain Nay, nay, put not on that ftrange face, I am privy to the whole defign, and know that Waitwell, to whom thou wert this morning married, is to perfonate Mirabell's uncle, and as fuch, winning my Lady, to involve her in thofe difficulties from which Mirabell only muft re-leafe her, by his making his conditions to have my coufin and her fortune left to her own difpofal.

Foib. O dear Madam, I beg your pardon. It was not my confidence in your Ladyfhip that was deficient; but I thought the former good correfpondence between your Ladyfhip and Mr Mirabell, might have hindered his com-municating this fecret.

Mrs Fain. Dear Foible, forget that.

Foib. O dear Madam, Mr Mirabell is fuch a fweet winning gentleman—but your Ladyfhip is the pattern of generofity.——Sweet Lady, to be fo good! Mr Mirabell cannot choofe but be grateful. I find your Ladyfhip has his heart ftill. Now, Madam, I can fafely tell your Lady-fhip our fuccefs; Mrs Marwood had told my Lady; but I warrant I manag'd myfelf. I turn'd it all for the better. I told my Lady that Mr Mirabell railed at her; I laid horrid things to his charge, I'll vow; and my Lady is fo incens'd that fhe'll be contracted to Sir Rowland to-night, fhe fays;——I warrant I work'd her up, that he may have her for afking for, as they fay of a Welfh maiden-head.

Mrs Fain. O rare Foible!

Foib. Madam, I beg your Ladyfhip to acquaint Mr Mi-

rabell of his fuccefs. I wou'd be feen as little as poffible
to fpeak to him——befides, I believe, Madam Marwood
watches me.——She has a month's mind; but I know
Mr Mirabell can't abide her.——[*Cails*] John——
remove my Lady's toilet. Madam, your fervant. My
Lady is fo impatient, I fear fhe'll come for me if I ftay.

Mrs *Fain.* I'll go with you up the back-ftairs, left I
fhou'd meet her.

S C E N E VII.

Mrs MARWOOD *alone.*

Indeed, Mrs Engine, is it thus with you? Are you
become a go-between of this importance? yes, I fhall
watch you. Why this wench is the Pafs-par-toute, a very
mafter-key to every body's ftrong box. My friend Fainall, have you carried it fo fwimmingly? I thought there
was fomething in it; but it feems 'tis over with .you.
Your loathing is not from a want of appetite then, but
from a furfeit. Elfe you could never be fo cool to fail
from a principal to be an affiftant; to procure for him!
a pattern of generofity, that, I confefs. Well, Mr Fainall, you have met with your match.——O man, man!
woman, woman! the devil's an afs: if I were a painter,
I would draw him like an ideot, a driveler with a bib and
bells. A man fhou'd have his head and horns, and woman
the reft of him. Poor fimple fiend! Madam Marwood
has a month's mind, but he cannot abide her——'twere
better for him you had not been his confeffor in that affair; without you could have kept his counfel clofer. I
fhall not prove another pattern of generofity—he has not
obliged me to that with thofe exceffes of himfelf; and now
I'll have none of him. Here comes the good Lady, panting ripe; with a heart full of hope, and a head full of care,
like any chymift upon the day of projection.

SCENE VIII.

[*To her*] Lady WISHFORT.

Lady. O dear Marwood, what fhall I fay for this rude forgetfulnefs——but my dear friend is all goodnefs.

Mrs Mar. No apologies, dear Madam, I have been very well entertained.

Lady. As I'm a perfon, I am in a very chaos to think I fhould fo forget myfelf——but I have fuch an olio of affairs, really I know not what to do——[*Calls.*]—Foible—— I expect my nephew Sir Wilfull ev'ry moment too :—— Why, Foible—he means to travel for improvement.

Mrs Mar. Methinks Sir Willful fhould rather think of marrying than travelling at his years. I hear he is turn'd of forty.

Lady. O he's in lefs danger of being fpoil'd by his travels——I am againft my nephew's marrying too young. It will be time enough when he comes back, and has acquir'd difcretion to choofe for himfelf.

Mrs Mar. Methinks Mrs Millamant and he would make a very fit match. He may travel afterwards. 'Tis a thing very ufual with young gentlemen.

Lady. I promife you I have thought on't—and fince 'tis your judgment, I think on't again. I affure you I will; I value your judgment extremely. On my word, I'll propofe it.

SCENE IX.

[*To them*] FOIBLE.

Lady. Come, come, Foible——I had forgot my nephew will be here before dinner——I muft make hafte.

Foib. Mr Witwoud and Mr Petulant are come to dine with your Ladyfhip.

Lady. O dear, I can't appear 'till I'm dress'd. Dear Marwood, shall I be free with you again, and beg you to entertain 'em. I'll make all imaginable haste. Dear friend, excuse me.

SCENE X.

Mrs MARWOOD, Mrs MILLAMANT, MINCING.

Mil. Sure never any thing was so unbred as that odious man——Marwood, your servant.

Mrs Mar. You have a colour; what's the matter?

Mil. That horrid fellow, Petulant, has provok'd me into a flame——I have broken my fan——Mincing, lend me yours; is not all the powder out of my hair?

Mrs Mar. No, what has he done?

Mil. Nay, he has done nothing; he has only talked—nay, he has said nothing neither; but he has contradicted ev'ry thing that has been said. For my part, I thought Witwoud and he would have quarrel'd.

Min. I vow, Mem, I thought once they would have fit.

Mil. Well, 'tis a lamentable thing, I swear, that one has not the liberty of choosing one's acquaintance as one does one's clothes.

Mrs Mar. If we had that liberty, we should be as weary of one set of acquaintance, tho' never so good, as we are of one suit, tho' never so fine. A fool and a doily stuff would now and then find days of grace, and be worn for variety.

Mil. I could consent to wear 'em, if they would wear alike; but fools never wear out——they are such drapdeberry things! without one could give 'em to one's chamber-maid after a day or two.

Mrs Mar. 'Twere better so indeed. Or what think you of the play-house? A fine gay glossy fool shou'd be given there, like a new masking habit, after the masquerade is over, and we have done with the disguise. For

a fool's viſit is always a diſguiſe; and never admitted by a
woman of wit, but to blind her affair with a lover of
ſenſe. If you would appear barefac'd now, and own Mirabell; you might as eaſily put off Petulant and Witwoud
as your hood and ſcarf. And indeed, 'tis time, for the
town has found it : the ſecret is grown too big for the pretence. 'Tis like Mrs Primly's great belly; ſhe may lace
it down before, but it burniſhes on her hips. Indeed,
Millamant, you can no more conceal it, than my Lady
Strammel can her face, that goodly face, which in defiance
of her Rheniſh wine tea, will not be comprehended in a
maſk.

Mil. I'll take my death, Marwood, you are more
cenſorious than a decay'd beauty, or a diſcarded toaſt.
Mincing, tell the men they may come up. My aunt is
not dreſſing here ; their folly is leſs provoking than your
malice.

S C E N E   XI.

MILLAMANT, MARWOOD.

Mil. The town has found it ! what has it found:
That Mirabell loves me is no more a ſecret, than it is a ſecret that you diſcovered it to my aunt, or than the reaſon
why you diſcovered it is a ſecret.

Mrs *Mar.* You are nettled.

Mil. You're miſtaken. Ridiculous !

Mrs *Mar.* Indeed, my dear, you'll tear another fan, if
you don't mitigate thoſe violent airs.

Mil. O ſilly ! ha, ha, ha ! I could laugh immoderately. Poor Mirabell! his conſtancy to me has quite de-
ſtroyed his complaiſance for all the world beſide. I ſwear,
I never enjoin'd it him to be ſo coy——If I had the vanity to think he would obey me, I would command him to
ſhew more gallantry——'tis hardly well bred to be ſo
particular on one hand, and ſo inſenſible on the other.
But I deſpair to prevail, and ſo let him follow his own

way. Ha, ha, ha! pardon me, dear creature, I muſt laugh, ha, ha, ha! tho' I grant you 'tis a little barbarous, ha, ha, ha!

Mrs Mar. What pity 'tis ſo much fine raillery, and delivered with ſo ſignificant geſture, ſhould be ſo unhappily directed to miſcarry!

Mil. Ha! dear creature, I aſk your pardon——I ſwear I did not mind you.

Mrs Mar. Mr Mirabell and you both may think it a thing impoſſible, when I ſhall tell him by telling you——

Mil. O dear, what? for it is the ſame thing if I hear it ——ha, ha, ha!

Mrs Mar. That I deteſt him, hate him, Madam.

Mil. O, Madam, why ſo do I——and yet the creature loves me, ha, ha, ha! how can one forbear laughing to think of it——I am a Sybil if I am not amaz'd to think what he can ſee in me. I'll take my death, I think you are handſomer—and within a year or two as young—if you could but ſtay for me, I ſhould overtake you——but that cannot be.—Well, that thought makes me melancholic.—Now, I'll be ſad.

Mrs Mar. Your merry note may be chang'd ſooner than you think.

Mil. D'ye ſay ſo? Then I'm reſolv'd I'll have a ſong to keep up my ſpirits.

SCENE XII.

[*To them*] MINCING.

Minc. The gentlemen ſtay but to comb, Madam, and will wait on you.

Mil. Deſire Mrs——that is in the next room to ſing the ſong I would have learn'd yeſterday. You ſhall hear it, Madam——not that there's any great matter in't—but 'tis agreeable to my humour.

S O N G.

Set by Mr John Eccles.

I.

LOVE's but the frailty of the mind,
When 'tis not with ambition join'd;
A sickly flame, which, if not fed, expires,
And feeding, wastes in self-consuming fires.

II.

'Tis not to wound a wanton boy,
Or am'rous youth, that gives the joy;
But 'tis the glory to have pierc'd a swain,
For whom inferior beauties sigh'd in vain.

III.

Then I alone the conquest prize,
When I insult a rival's eyes:
If there's delight in love, 'tis when I see
That heart, which others bleed for, bleed for me.

S C E N E   XIII.

[*To them*] PETULANT, WITWOUD.

Mil. Is your animosity compos'd, gentlemen ?

Wit. Rallery, rallery, Madam; we have no animosity ——we hit off a little wit now and then, but no animosity——the falling out of wits is like the falling out of lovers——we agree in the main, like treble and base. Ha, Petulant ?

Pet. Ay, in the main——but when I have the humour to contradict——

Wit. Ay, when he has a humour to contradict, then I contradict too What, I know my cue. Then we contradict one another like two battle-dores ; for contradictions beget one another like Jews.

Pet. If he fays black's black——if I have a humour to fay 'tis blue——let that pafs——all's one for that. If I have a humour to prove it, it muft be granted.

Wit. Not pofitively muft———but it may———it may.

Pet. Yes, it pofitively muft, upon proof pofitive.

Wit. Ay, upon proof pofitive it muft; but upon proof prefumptive it only may. That's a logical diftinction now, Madam.

Mrs *Mar.* I perceive your debates are of importance, and very learnedly handled.

Pet. Importance is one thing, and learning's another; but a debate's a debate, that I affert.

Wit. Petulant's an enemy to learning; he relies altogether on his parts.

Pet. No, I'm no enemy to learning; it hurts not me.

Mrs *Mar.* That's a fign indeed 'tis no enemy to you.

Pet. No, no, 'tis no enemy to any body, but them that have it.

Mil. Well, an illiterate man's my averfion : I wonder at the impudence of an illiterate man, to offer to make love.

Wit. That I confefs I wonder at too.

Mil. Ah ! to marry an ignorant ! that can hardly read or write

Pet. Why fhould a man be any further from being marry'd, though he can't read, than he is from being hang'd. The ordinary's paid for fetting the pfalm, and the parifh-prieft for reading the ceremony. And for the reft which is to follow in both cafes, a man may do it without book ———fo all's one for that.

Mil. D'ye hear the creature ? Lord, here's company, I'll be gone.

SCENE XIV.

Sir WILFULL WITWOUD *in a riding dress*, Mrs
MARWOOD, PETULANT, WITWOUD, FOOT-
MAN.

Wit. In the name of Bartlemew and his fair, what have
we here ?

Mrs Mar. 'Tis your brother, I fancy. Don't you know
him ?

Wit. Not I————Yes, I think it is he————I've almoſt forgot him; I have not ſeen him ſince the revolution.

Foot. Sir, my Lady's dreſſing. Here's company; if you
pleaſe to walk in, in the mean time.

Sir Wilf. Dreſſing ! what, 'tis but morning here, I warrant, with you in London; we ſhou'd count it towards af-
ternoon in our parts, down in Shropſhire————why then,
belike, my aunt han't din'd yet————ha, friend ?

Foot. Your aunt, Sir ?

Sir Wilf. My aunt, Sir; yes, my aunt, Sir, and your
Lady, Sir ; your Lady is my aunt, Sir————why, what
doſt thou not know me, friend ? Why then ſend ſome-
body hither that does. How long haſt thou liv'd with thy
Lady, fellow, ha ?

Foot. A week, Sir; longer than any body in the houſe,
except my Lady's woman.

Sir Wilf. Why then belike thou doſt not know thy Lady,
if thou ſee'ſt her, ha, friend ?

Foot. Why truly, ſir, I cannot ſafely ſwear to her face
in a morning, before ſhe is dreſs'd. 'Tis like I may give
a ſhrewd gueſs at her by this time.

Sir Wilf. Well, pr'ythee try what thou can'ſt do; if
thou canſt not gueſs, enquire her out, doſt hear, fellow ?
and tell her, her nephew, Sir Wilfull Witwoud, is in the
houſe.

Foot. I ſhall, Sir.

Sir *Wilf.* Hold ye, hear me, friend; a word with you in your ear; pr'ythee who are thefe gallants?

Fool. Really, Sir, I can't tell; here come fo many here, 'tis hard to know 'em all.

S C E N E XV.

Sir WILFULL WITWOUD, PETULANT, WIT-WOUD, Mrs MARWOOD.

Sir *Wilf.* Oons, this fellow knows lefs than a ftarling; I don't think a' knows his own name.

Mrs *Mar.* Mr Witwoud, your brother is not behind-hand in forgetfulnefs———I fancy he has forgot you too.

Wit. I hope fo———the 'devil take him that remembers firft, I fay.

Sir *Wilf.* Save you, gentlemen and lady.

Mrs *Mar.* For fhame, Mr Witwoud; why won't you fpeak to him?———And you, Sir.

Wit. Petulant, fpeak.

Pet. And you, Sir.

Sir *Wilf.* No offence, I hope.   [*Salutes* Marwood.

Mrs *Mar.* No fure, Sir.

Wit. This is a vile dog, I fee that already. No offence! ha, ha, ha! to him; to him, Petulant, fmoke him.

Pet. It feems as if you had come a journey, Sir; hem, hem.   [*Surveying him round.*

Sir *Wilf.* Very likely, Sir, that it may feem fo.

Pet. No offence, I hope, Sir.

Wit. Smoke the boots, the boots; Petulant, the boots; ha, ha, ha!

Sir *Wilf.* May be not, Sir; thereafter as 'tis meant, Sir.

Pet. Sir, I prefume upon the information of your boots.

Sir *Wilf.* Why, 'tis like you may, Sir: if you are not fatisfy'd with the information of my boots, Sir, if you will ftep to the ftable, you may enquire further of my horfe, Sir.

Pet. Your horfe, Sir! your horfe is an afs, Sir!

Sir Wilf. Do you fpeak by way of offence, Sir ?

Mrs Mar. The gentleman's merry, that's all, Sir——
S'life, we fhall have a quarrel betwixt an horfe and an afs
before they find one another out. You muft not take any
thing amifs from your friends, Sir. You are among your
friends here, tho' it may be you don't know it——If I am
not miftaken, you are Sir Wilfull Witwoud.

Sir Wilf. Right, Lady; I am Sir Wilfull Witwoud, fo I
write myfelf; no offence to any body, I hope; and nephew to the Lady Wifhfort of this manfion.

Mrs Mar. Don't you know this gentleman, Sir?

Sir Wilf. Hum! what, fure 'tis not—yea by'r Lady, but
'tis——'Sheart, I know not whether 'tis or no——yea,
but 'tis, by the Rekin. Brother Antony! what, Tony,
i'faith! what, doft thou not know me? By'r Lady, nor I
thee, thou art fo becravated, and fo beperiwig'd————
'Sheart, why doft thou not fpeak? art thou overjoy'd ?

Wit. Odfo, brother, is it you? your fervant, brother.

Sir Wilf. Your fervant! why yours, Sir. Your fervant
again—'Sheart, and your friend and fervant to that—and
a—[*puff*] and a flap dragon for your fervice, Sir: and a
hare's foot, and a hare's fcut for your fervice, Sir; and
you be fo cold and fo courtly.

Wit. No offence, I hope, brother.

Sir Wilf. 'Sheart, Sir, but there is, and much offence
——a pox, is this your inns o' court breeding, not to
know your friends and your relations, your elders and
your betters!

Wit. Why, brother Wilfull of Salop, you may be as
fhort as a Shrewfbury-cake, if you pleafe. But I tell you
'tis not modifh to know relations in town: you think
you're in the country, where great lubberly brothers flab-
ber and kifs one another when they meet, like a call of
ferjeants——'tis not the fafhion here; 'tis not indeed,
dear brother.

Sir Wilf. The fafhion's a fool; and you're a fop, dear
brother. 'Sheart, I've fufpected this——by'r lady, I con-

jectur'd you were a fop, since you began to change the style
of your letters, and write in a scrap of paper gilt round
the edges, no bigger than a subpoena. I might expect this
when you left off, " honour'd brother;" and " hoping
" you are in good health," and so forth——to begin with
a " rat me, knight, I'm so sick of a last night's debauch"—
'ods heart, and then tell a familiar tale of a cock and a
bull, and a whore and a bottle, and so conclude——
you could write news before you were out of your time.
When you liv'd with honest Pumple Nose the attorney of
Furnival's inn——you cou'd intreat to be remember'd then
to your friends round the Rekin. We could have gazettes,
then, and Dawks's letter, and the weekly bill, 'till of late
days.

Pet. 'Slife, Witwoud, were you ever an attorney's clerk?
of the family of the Furnivals. Ha, ha, ha!

Wit. Ay, ay, but that was but for a while : not long,
not long; pshaw, I was not in my own power then. An
orphan, and this fellow was my guardian; ay, ay, I was
glad to consent to that, man, to come to London. He had
the disposal of me then. If I had not agreed to that, I
might have been bound 'prentice to a felt-maker in Shrews-
bury; this fellow would have bound me to a maker of
felts.

Sir *Wilf.* 'Sheart, and better than to be bound to a maker
of fops; where, I suppose, you have serv'd your time;
and now you may set up for yourself.

Mrs *Mar.* You intend to travel, Sir, as I'm inform'd.

Sir *Wilf.* Belike I may, Madam. I may chance to sail
upon the salt-seas, if my mind hold.

Pet. And the wind serve.

Sir *Wilf.* Serve or not serve, I shan't ask license of you,
Sir; nor the weather-cock your companion. I direct my
discourse to the Lady, Sir; 'tis like my aunt may have
told you, Madam——yes, I have settled my concerns, I
may say now, and am minded to see foreign parts. If an
how that the peace holds, whereby that is taxes abate.

Mrs *Mar.* I thought you had defign'd for France at all adventures.

Sir *Wilf.* I can't tell that; 'tis like I may, and 'tis like I may not. I am fomewhat dainty in making a refolution ——becaufe when I make it I keep it. I don't ftand ftill I, fhall I, then; if I fay't I'll do't; but I have thoughts to tarry a finall matter in town, to learn fomewhat of your lingo firft, before I crofs the feas. I'd gladly have a fpice of your French as they fay, whereby to hold difcourfe in foreign countries.

Mrs *Mar.* Here's an academy in town for that ufe.

Sir *Wilf.* There is? 'Tis like there may.

Mrs *Mar.* No doubt you will return very much improv'd.

Wit. Yes, refin'd like a Dutch fkipper from a whale-fifhing.

S C E N E XVI.

[To them] Lady W I S H F O R T, *and* F A I N A L L.

Lady. Nephew, you are welcome.

Sir *Wilf.* Aunt, your fervant.

Fain. Sir Wilfull, your moft humble fervant.

Sir *Wilf.* Coufin Fainall, give me your hand.

Lady. Coufin Witwoud, your fervant; Mr Petulant, your fervant—nephew, you are welcome again. Will you drink any thing after your journey, nephew, before you eat? Dinner's almoft ready.

Sir *Wilf.* I'm very well, I thank you, aunt——however, I thank you for your courteous offer. 'Sheart, I was afraid you wou'd have been in the fafhion too, and have remember'd to have forgot your relations. Here's your Coufin Tony, belike, I mayn't call him brother for fear of offence.

Lady. O he's a railer, nephew——my coufin's a wit: and your great wits always rally their beft friends to chufe.

When you have been abroad, nephew, you'll underſtand
raillery better.

[Fain. *and* Mrs Mar. *talk apart.*

Sir *Wilf.* Why then let him hold his tongue in the mean
time; and rail when that day comes.

S C E N E XVII.

[*To them*] M I N C I N G.

Min. Mem, I come to acquaint your Laſhip that dinner
is impatient.

Sir *Wilf.* Impatient! Why then belike it won't ſtay till
I pull off my boots. Sweet-heart, can you help me to
a pair of ſlippers?———My man's with his horſes, I
warrant.

Lady. Fy, fy, nephew, you would not pull off your boots
here—go down into the hall—dinner ſhall ſtay for you—
my nephew's a little unbred, you'll pardon him, Madam—
gentlemen, will you walk? Marwood?

Mrs *Mar.* I'll follow you, Madam—before Sir Wilfull's
ready.

S C E N E XVIII.

MARWOOD, FAINALL.

Fain. Why then Foible's a bawd, an errant, rank, match-
making bawd. And I it ſeems am a huſband, a rank huſband; and my wife a very errant, rank wife——all in the
Way of the World. 'Sdeath, to be a cuckold by anticipa-
tion, a cuckold in embryo! ſure I was born with budding
antlers, like a young ſatyr, or a citizen's child. 'Sdeath to
be out-witted, to be out-jilted—out-matrimony'd—if I had
kept my ſpeed like a ſtag, 'twere ſomewhat,—but to crawl
after, with my horns, like a ſnail, and be outſtripped by
my wife——'tis ſcurvy wedleck.

Mrs *Mar.* Then ſhake it off; you have often wiſh'd

for an opportunity to part——and now you have it.   But firſt prevent their plot————the half of Millamant's fortune is too confiderable to be parted with, to a foe, to Mirabell.

Fain. Damn him, that had been mine——had you not made that fond difcovery—that had been forfeited, had they been married.   My wife had added luſtre to my horns, by that increafe of fortune, I cou'd have worn 'em tipt with gold, though my forehead had been furnifh'd like a deputy-lieutenant's hall.

Mrs *Mar.* They may prove a cap of maintenance to you ſtill, if you can away with your wife.   And ſhe's no worfe than when you had her——I dare fwear ſhe had given up her game, before ſhe was married.

Fain. Hum! that may be——

Mrs *Mar.* You married her to keep you; and if you can contrive to have her keep you better than you expected, why ſhould you not keep her longer than you intended?

Fain. The means, the means.

Mrs *Mar.* Difcover to my Lady your wife's conduct; threaten to part with her—my Lady loves her, and will come to any compofition to fave her reputation.   Take the opportunity of breaking it, juſt upon the difcovery of this impoſture.   My Lady will be enrag'd beyond bounds, and facrifice niece, and fortune, and all at that conjuncture.   And let me alone to keep her warm; if ſhe ſhould flag in her part, I will not fail to prompt her.

Fain. Faith, this has an appearance.

Mrs *Mar.* I'm forry I hinted to my Lady to endeavour a match between Millamant and Sir Wilfull: that may be an obſtacle.

Fain. O, for that matter, leave me to manage him; I'll difable him for that; he will drink like a Dane; after dinner, I'll fet his hand in.

Mrs *Mar.* Well, how do you ſtand affected towards your Lady?

Fain. Why, faith, I'm thinking of it—Let me see—I am married already, so that's over—my wife has play'd the jade with me—well, that's over too—I never lov'd her, or if I had, why that wou'd have been over too by this time—jealous of her I cannot be, for I am certain; so there's an end of jealousy. Weary of her I am, and shall be——no, there's no end of that? no, no, that were too much to hope. Thus far concerning my repose. Now for my reputation——As to my own, I married not for it, so that's out of the question—and as to my part in my wife's—why, she had parted with hers before; so bringing none to me, she can take none from me; 'tis against all the rule of play, that I should lose to one, who has not wherewithal to stake.

Mrs *Mar.* Besides, you forget, marriage is honourable.

Fain. Hum, faith, and that's well thought on; marriage is honourable as you say; and if so, wherefore should cuckoldom be a discredit, being derived from so honourable a root?

Mrs *Mar.* Nay, I know not; if the root be honourable, why not the branches?

Fain. So, so, why this point's clear——well, how do we proceed?

Mrs *Mar.* I will contrive a letter which shall be deliver'd to my Lady at the time when that rascal who is to act Sir Rowland is with her. It shall come as from an unknown hand——for the less I appear to know of the truth, the better I can play the incendiary. Besides, I would not have Foible provok'd if I could help it—because you know she knows some passages—nay, I expect all will come out—but let the mine be sprung first, and then I care not if I am discover'd.

Fain. If the worst come to the worst—I'll turn my wife to grass—I have already a deed of settlement of the best part of her estate; which I wheedled out of her; and that you shall partake at least.

Mrs *Mar.* I hope you are convinced that I hate Mirabell now: you'll be no more jealous?

Fain. Jealous, no——by this kiſs——let huſbands be jealous; but let the lover ſtill believe; or if he doubt, let it
be only to endear his pleaſure, and prepare the joy that
follows, when he proves his miſtreſs true. But let huſbands doubts convert to endleſs jealouſy; or if they have
belief, let it corrupt to ſuperſtition, and blind credulity. - I
am ſingle, and will herd no more with 'em. True, I wear
the badge, but I'll diſown the order. And ſince I take my
leave of 'em, I care not if I leave 'em a common motto to
their common creſt.

All huſbands muſt or pain or ſhame endure;
The wife too jealous are, fools too ſecure.

ACT IV.   SCENE I.

SCENE *continues.*

Lady WISHFORT *and* FOIBLE.

LADY.

IS Sir Rowland coming, ſay'ſt thou, Foible? and are
things in order?

Foib. Yes, Madam. I have put wax lights in the ſconces,
and plac'd the footmen in a row in the hall, in their beſt
liveries, with the coachman and poſtilion to fill up the e-
quipage.

Lady. Have you pulvill'd the coachman and poſtilion,
that they may not ſtink of the ſtable, when Sir Rowland
comes by?

Foib. Yes, Madam.

Lady. And are the dancers and the muſic ready, that he
may be entertain'd in all points with correſpondence to
his paſſion?

Foib. All is ready, Madam.

Lady. And—well—and how do I look, Foible?

Foib. Moſt killing well, Madam.

Lady. Well, and how ſhall I receive him? in what fi-gure ſhall I give his heart the firſt impreſſion? There is a great deal in the firſt impreſſion: ſhall I ſit?—No, I won't ſit—I'll walk—ay, I'll walk from the door upon his en-trance; and then turn full upon him——no, that will be too ſudden. I'll ly——ay, I'll ly down——I'll receive him in my little dreſſing-room, there's a couch——yes, yes, I'll give the firſt impreſſion on a couch——I won't ly neither, but loll and lean upon one elbow: with one foot a little dangling off, jogging in a thoughtful way——yes——and then as ſoon as he appears, ſtart, ay, ſtart and be ſurpriz'd, and riſe to meet him in a pretty diſorder ——yes——O, nothing is more alluring than a levee from a couch, in ſome confuſion——it ſhews the foot to advan-tage, and furniſhes with bluſhes, and recompoſing airs be-yond compariſon. Hark! there's a coach.

Foib. 'Tis he, Madam.

Lady. O dear, has my nephew made his addreſſes to Millamant? I order'd him.

Foib. Sir Wilfull is ſet in to drinking, Madam, in the parlour.

Lady. Odds my life, I'll ſend him to her. Call her down, Foible; bring her hither. I'll ſend him as I go— when they are together, then come to me, Foible, that I may not be too long alone with Sir Rowland.

S C E N E II.

Mrs MILLAMANT, Mrs FAINALL, FOIBLE.

Foib. Madam, I ſtay'd here, to tell your Ladyſhip that Mr Mirabell has waited this half hour, for an opportunity to talk with you; though my Lady's orders were to leave you and Sir Wilfull together. Shall I tell Mr Mirabell that you are at leiſure?

Mil. No,——what would the dear man have ? I am
thoughtful, and would amufe myfelf——bid him come
another time.

> *There never yet was woman made,*
> *Nor fhall but to be curs'd.*

                              [*Repeating, and walking about.*

That's hard !

Mrs *Fain.* You are very fond of Sir John Suckling to-
day, Millamant, and the poets.

Mil He ? Ay, and filthy verfes——fo I am.

Foib. Sir Wilfull is coming, Madam. Shall I fend Mr
Mirabell away ?

Mil. Ay, if you pleafe, Foible, fend him away——
or fend him hither—juft as you will, dear Foible.—I think
I'll fee him—fhall I ? Ay, let the wretch come.

> *Thyrfis, a youth of the infpired train.*

                                 [*Repeating.*

Dear Fainall, entertain Sir Wilfull——thou haft philofophy to undergo a fool, thou art marry'd and haft patience
——I would confer with my own thoughts.

Mrs *Fain.* I am oblig'd to you, that you would make
me your proxy in this affair ; but I have bufinefs of my
own.

S C E N E   III.

[*To them*] Sir W I L F U L L.

Mrs *Fain.* O Sir Wilfull ; you are come at the critical
inftant.   There's your miftrefs up to the ears in love and
contemplation ; purfue your point, now or never.

Sir *Wilf.* Yes ; my aunt would have it fo—I would gladly have been encouraged with a bottle or two, becaufe I'm
fomewhat wary at firft, before I am acquainted ;——
[*This while* Millamant *walks about repeating to herfelf.*]———
But I hope, after a time, I fhall break my mind——tha

is, upon further acquaintance—so for the present, cousin, I'll take my leave——if so be you'll be so kind to make my excuse, I'll return to my company——

Mrs *Fain.* O fy, Sir Wilfull! what, you must not be daunted.

Sir *Wilf.* Daunted, no, that's not it, it is not so much for that——for if so be that I set on't, I'll do't. But only for the present, 'tis sufficient 'till further acquaintance, that's all——your servant.

Mrs *Fain.* Nay, I'll swear you shall never lose so favourable an oppportunity, if I can help it. I'll leave you together, and lock the door,

S C E N E IV.

Sir WILFULL, MILLAMANT.

Sir *Wilf.* Nay, nay, cousin—I have forgot my gloves—what d'ye do? 'Sheart, a'has lock'd the door indeed, I think—nay, cousin Fainall, open the door—p'shaw, what a vixon trick is this?—nay, now a'has seen me too—cousin, I made bold to pass thro' as it were——I think this door's inchanted——

Mil. repeating.]
　　　　I pr'ythee spare me, gentle boy,
　　　　Press me no more for that slight toy.

Sir *Wilf.* Anan? Cousin, your servant.

Mil. ——— *That foolish trifle of a heart* ———————Sir Wilfull!

Sir *Wilf.* Yes———your servant. No offence, I hope, cousin.

Mil. repeating.]
　　　　I swear it will not do it's part,
　　　　Tho' thou dost thine, employ'st thy power and art.
Natural, easy Suckling!

Sir *Wilf.* Anan? Suckling? No such suckling, neither, cousin, nor stripling: I thank Heav'n, I'm no minor.

Mil. Ah rustic, ruder than Gothic!

Sir Wilf. Well, well, I fhall underftand your lingo one of thefe days, coufin, in the mean while I muft anfwer in plain Englifh.

Mil. Have you any bufinefs with me, Sir Wilfull?

Sir Wilf. Not at prefent, coufin——yes, I make bold to fee, to come and know if that how you were difpofed to fetch a walk this evening, if fo be that I might not be troublefome, I would have fought a walk with you.

Mil. A walk? What then?

Sir Wilf. Nay, nothing——only for the walk's fake, that's all——

Mil. I naufeate walking; 'tis a country diverfion; I loath the country, and every thing that relates to it.

Sir Wilf. Indeed! hah! look ye, look ye, you do? nay, 'tis like you may——here are choice of paftimes here in town, as plays, and the like, that muft be confeffed indeed——

Mil. Ah, l'etourdie! I hate the town too.

Sir Wilf. Dear heart, that's much——hah! that you fhould hate 'em both! hah! 'tis like you may; there are fome can't relifh the town, and others can't away with the country——'tis like you may be one of thofe, coufin.

Mil. Ha, ha, ha! yes, 'tis like I may.——You have nothing further to fay to me?

Sir Wilf. Not at prefent, coufin——'Tis like when I have an opportunity to be more private—I may break my mind in fome meafure—I conjecture you partly guefs——however, that's as time fhall try—but fpare to fpeak and fpare to fpeed, as they fay.

Mil. If it is of no great importance, Sir Wilfull, you will oblige me to leave me; I have juft now a little bufinefs——

Sir Wilf. Enough, enough, coufin: yes, yes, all a cafe ——when you're difpos'd: Now's as well as another time; and another time as well as now. All's one for that——yes, yes, if your concerns call you, there's no

hafte; it will keep cold, as they fay—coufin, your fervant
——I think this door's lock'd.

Mil. You may go this way, Sir.

Sir Wilf. Your fervant, then with your leave I'll return
to my company.

Mil. Ay, ay; ha, ha, ha!

　　Like Phœbus *fung the no lefs am'rous boy.*

S C E N E V.

MILLAMANT, MIRABELL.

Mir. ——*Like* Daphne *fhe, as lovely and as coy.*
Do you lock yourfelf up from me, to make my fearch
more curious ? Or is this pretty artifice contriv'd. to fignify
that here the chace muft end, and my purfuit be crown'd?
For you can fly no further.——

Mil. Vanity ! no——I'll fly, and be follow'd to the
laft moment. Tho' I am upon the very verge of matrimony,
I expect you fhould folicit me as much as if I were waver-
ing at the grate of a monaftery, with one foot over the
threfhold. I'll be folicited to the very laft, nay, and afterwards.

Mir. What, after the laft ?

Mil. O, I fhould think I was poor and had nothing to
beftow, if I were reduc'd to an inglorious eafe, and freed
frcm the agreeable fatigues of folicitation.

Mir. But do you not know, that when favours are conferr'd upon inftant and tedious folicitation, that they dimi-
nifh in their value, and that both the giver lofes the grace,
and the receiver leffens his pleafure.

Mil. It may be in things of common application ;
but never fure in love. O, I hate a lover that can dare
to think he draws a moment's air, independent on the
bounty of his miftrefs. There is not fo impudent a thing
in nature, as the faucy look of an affured man. confident
of fuccefs. The pedantic arrogance of a very hufband

has not ſo pragmatical an air. Ah! I'll never marry, unleſs I am firſt made ſure of my will and pleaſure.

Mir. Wou'd you have 'em both before marriage? Or
will you be contented with the firſt now, and ſtay for the
other 'till after grace?

Mil. Ah! don't be impertinent———my dear liberty,
ſhall I leave thee? my faithful ſolitude, my darling contemplation, muſt I bid you then adieu? Ay-h adieu—my
morning thoughts, agreeable wakings, indolent ſlumbers,
ye *douceurs,* ye *ſommeils du matin,* adieu.———I can't
do't, 'tis more than impoſſible——poſitively, Mirabell, I'll
ly a-bed in a morning as long as I pleaſe.

Mir. Then I'll get up in a morning as early as I
pleaſe.

Mil. Ah! idle creature, get up when you will——and
d'ye hear, I won't be call'd names after I'm married; poſitively I won't be call'd names.

Mir. Names!

Mil. Ay, as wife, ſpouſe, my dear, joy, jewel, love,
ſweet-heart, and the reſt of that nauſeous cant, in which
men and their wives are ſo fulſomely familiar——I ſhall
never bear that—good Mirabell, don't let us be familiar or
fond, nor kiſs before folks, like my Lady Fadler, and Sir
Francis: nor go to Hyde-Park together the firſt Sunday
in a new chariot, to provoke eyes and whiſpers, and then
never be ſeen there together again; as if we were proud
of one another the firſt week, and aſham'd of one another
ever after. Let us never viſit together, nor go to a play
together; but let us be very ſtrange and well-bred: let
us be as ſtrange as if we had been married a great while;
and as well bred as if we were not married at all.

Mir. Have you any more conditions to offer? Hitherto
your demands are pretty reaſonable.

Mil. Trifles———as liberty to pay and receive viſits to
and from whom I pleaſe; to write and receive letters,
without interrogatories or wry faces on your part; to wear
what I pleaſe; and chooſe converſation with regard only
to my own taſte; to have no obligation upon me to con-

verfe with wits that I don't like, becaufe they are your acquaintance; or to be intimate with fools, becaufe they may be your relations. Come to dinner when I pleafe; dine in my dreffing-room when I'm out of humour, without giving a reafon To have my clofet inviolate; to be fole emprefs of my tea-table, which you muft never prefume to approach without firft afking leave. And, laftly, where-ever I am, you fhall always knock at the door before you come in. Thefe articles fubfcrib'd, if I continue to endure you a little longer, I may by degrees dwindle into a wife.

Mir. Your bill of fare is fomething advanc'd in this latter account. Well, have I liberty to offer conditions—that when you are dwindled into a wife, I may not be beyond meafure enlarg'd into a hufband.

Mil. You have free leave; propofe your utmoft, fpeak and fpare not.

Mir. I thank you. *Imprimis* then, I covenant, that your acquaintance be general; that you admit no fworn confident, or intimate of your own fex; no fhe friend to fkreen her affairs under your countenance, and tempt you to make trial of a mutual fecrecy. No decoy-duck to wheedle you a fop-fcrambling to the play in a mafk—then bring you home in a pretended fright, when you think you fhall be found out——and rail at me for miffing the play, and difappointing the frolic which you had to pick me up, and prove my conftancy.

Mil. Deteftible *imprimis!* I go to the play in a mafk!

Mir. Item, I article, that you continue to like your own face, as long as I fhall: and while it paffes current with me, that you endeavour not to new-coin it. To which end, together with all vizards for the day, I prohibit all mafks for the night, made of oil'd-fkins, and I know not what——hogs bones, hares gall, pig-water, and the marrow of a roafted cat. In fhort, I forbid all commerce with the gentlewoman in what-d'ye-call-it court. Item, I fhut my doors againft all bawds with bafkets, and penny-

worths of muſlin, china, fans, atlaſſes, etc.——Item, when
you ſhall be breeding——

Mil. Ah! name it not.

Mir. Which may be preſum'd with a bleſſing on our
endeavours——

Mil. Odious endeavours!

Mir. I denounce againſt all ſtrait lacing, ſqueezing for
a ſhape, 'till you mould my boy's head like a ſugar-loaf,
and inſtead of a man-child, make me father to a crooked
billet. Laſtly, to the dominion of the tea-table I ſubmit.
—But with proviſo, that you exceed not in your province;
but reſtrain yourſelf to native and ſimple tea-table drinks,
as tea, chocolate, and coffee. As likewiſe to genuine and
authoriz'd tea-table talk——ſuch as mending of faſhions,
ſpoiling reputations, railing at abſent friends, and ſo forth
——but that on no account you encroach upon the mens
prerogative, and preſume to drink healths, or toaſt fellows;
for prevention of which I baniſh all foreign forces, all
auxiliaries to the tea-table, as orange-brandy, all anniſeed,
cinnamon, citron and Barbadoes-waters, together with
Ratafia, and the moſt noble ſpirit of clary———————
but for couſlip wine, poppy water, and all dormitives,
thoſe I allow.——Theſe proviſo's admitted, in other things
I may prove a tractable and complying huſband.

Mil. O horrid proviſo's! filthy ſtrong-waters! I toaſt
fellows! odious men! I hate your odious proviſo's.

Mir. Then we're agreed. Shall I kiſs your hand upon
the contract? And here comes one to be a witneſs to the
ſealing of the deed.

S C E N E VI.

[To them] Mrs F A I N A L L.

Mil. Fainall, what ſhall I do? ſhall I have him? I think
I muſt have him.

Mrs Fain. Ay, ay, take him, take him, what fhou'd
you do?

Mil. Well then———I'll take my death I'm in a horrid
fright———Fainall, I fhall never fay it———well
———I think———I'll endure you.

Mrs Fain. Fy, fy, have him, have him, and tell him fo
in plain terms : for I am fure you have a mind to him.

Mil. Are you ? I think I have——and the horrid man
looks as if he thought fo too———well, you ridiculous
thing you, I'll have you———I won't be kifs'd, nor I
won't be thank'd———here kifs my hand tho'———fo,
hold your tongue now, don't fay a word.

Mrs Fain. Mirabell, there's a neceffity for your obedience;———you have neither time to talk nor ftay.   My
mother is coming; and in my confcience if fhe fhou'd fee
you, wou'd fall into fits, and may be not recover time
enough to return to Sir Rowland, who, as Foible tells me,
is in a fair way to fucceed.   Therefore fpare your extafies
for another occafion, and flip down the back-ftairs, where
Foible waits to confult you.

Mil. Ay, go, go.   In the mean time I fuppofe you
have faid fomething to pleafe me.

Mir. I am all obedience.

S C E N E VII.

MILLAMANT, Mrs FAINALL.

Mrs Fain. Yonder Sir Wilfull's drunk, and fo noify that
my mother has been forc'd to leave Sir Rowland to ap-
peafe him; but he anfwers her only with finging and
drinking———what they may have done by this time I
know not; but Petulant and he were upon quarrelling as
I came by.

Mil. Well, if Mirabell fhou'd not make a good hufband, I am a loft thing———for I find I love him
violently.

Mrs Fain. So it feems; for you mind not what's faid

tô you————If you doubt him, you had beſt take up with Sir Wilfull.

Mil. How can you name that ſuperannuated lubber ? Foh !

S C E N E VIII.

[To them] W I T W O U D *from drinking.*

Mrs *Fain.* So, is the fray made up, that you have left 'em ?

Wit. Left 'em ? I cou'd ſtay no longer————I have laugh'd like ten Chriſtnings————I am tipſy with laughing ————if I had ſtaid any longer I ſhou'd have burſt,————I muſt have been let out and piec'd in the ſides like an un-ſiz'd camlet————Yes, yes, the fray is compos'd; my Lady came in like a *noli proſequi*, and ſtopp'd the proceedings.

Mil. What was the diſpute?

Wit. That's the jeſt; there was no diſpute. They cou'd neither of 'em ſpeak for rage, and ſo fell a ſputt'ring at one another like two roaſted apples.

S C E N E IX.

[To them] P E T U L A N T, *drunk.*

Wit. Now, Petulant, all's over, all's well. Gad my head begins to whim it about————why doſt thou not ſpeak? thou art both as drunk and as mute as a fiſh.

Pet. Look you, Mrs Millamant————if you can love me, dear nymph—ſay it—and that's the concluſion————paſs on, or paſs off————that's all.

Wit. Thou haſt utter'd volumes, folios, in leſs than *decimo ſexto*, my dear Lacedemonian. Sirrah, Petulant, thou art an epitomizer of words.

Pet. Witwoud————you art an annihilator of ſenſe.

Wit. Thou art a retailer of phraſes; and doſt deal in

remnants of remnants, like a maker of pincushions—thou art in truth (metaphorically speaking) a speaker of short-hand.

Pet. Thou art (without a figure) just one half of an ass, and Baldwin yonder, thy half-brother, is the rest.—A gemini of asses split wou'd make just four of you.

Wit. Thou dost bite, my dear mustard-seed; kiss me for that.

Pet. tand off———I'll kiss no more males———I have kiss'd your twin yonder in a humour of reconciliation, 'till he [*hiccup*] rises upon my stomach like a radish.

Mil. Eh! filthy creature————what was the quarrel?

Pet. There was no quarrel———there might have been a quarrel.

Wit. If there had been words enow between 'em to have express'd provocation, they had gone together by the ears like a pair of castanets.

Pet. You were the quarrel.

Mil. Me!

Pet. If I have a humour to quarrel, I can make less matters conclude the premises.—If you are not handsome, what then, if I have a humour to prove it? if I shall have my reward, say so; if not, fight for your face the next time yourself—I'll go sleep.

Wit. Do, wrap thyself up like a wood-louse, and dream revenge—and hear me, if thou canst learn to write by to-morrow morning, pen me a challenge———I'll carry it for thee.

Pet. Carry your mistress's monkey a spider———go flea dogs, and read romances———I'll go to bed to my maid.

Mrs Fain. He's horridly drunk——how came you all in this pickle?

Wit. A plot, a plot, to get rid of the knight——your husband's advice; but he sneak'd off.

SCENE X.

Sir WILFULL *drunk*, Lady WISHFORT, WIT-
WOUD, MILLAMANT, Mrs FAINALL.

Lady. Out upon't, out upon't, at years of difcretion and
comport yourfelf at this rantipole rate!

Sir *Wilf.* No offence, aunt.

Lady. Offence! as I'm a perfon, I'm afham'd of you
———fogh! how you ftink of wine! d'ye think my niece
will ever endure fuch a Borachio! you're an abfolute Borachio.

Sir *Wilf.* Borachio?

Lady. At a time when you fhou'd commence an amour,
and put your beft foot foremoft———

Sir *Wilf.* 'Sheart, an you grutch me your liquor, make a
bill—give me more drink, and take my purfe.

[Sings.] *Pr'ythee fill me the glafs*
    'Till it laugh in my face,
  With ale that is potent and mellow;
    He that whines for a lafs
    Is an ignorant afs,
  For a bumper has not it's fellow.

But if you wou'd have me marry my coufin———fay the
word, and I'll do't——— Wilfull will do't, that's the word
———Wilfull will do't, that's my creft———my motto I
have forgot.

Lady. My nephew's a little overtaken, coufin———but
'tis with drinking your health ———O' my word you are
oblig'd to him.

Sir *Wilf. In vino veritas*, aunt:———If I drunk your
health to-day, coufin———I am a Borachio. But if you
have a mind to be marry'd, fay the word, and fend for the
piper; Wilfull will do't. If not, duft it away, and let's
have t'other round———Tony, odds heart, where's

'Tony?——Tony's an honeſt fellow; but he ſpits after a bumper, and that's a fault.

[Sings.] *We'll drink, and we'll never have done, boys,*
   Put the glaſs then round with the ſun, boys.
   Let Apollo's example invite us;
   For he's drunk ev'ry night,
   And that makes him ſo bright,
   That he's able next morning to light us.

The ſun's a good pimple, an honeſt ſoaker; he has a cellar at your Antipodes. If I travel, aunt, I touch at your Antipodes——Your Antipodes are a good raſcally ſort of topſy-turvy fellows——If I had a bumper, I'd ſtand upon my head and drink a health to 'em.—A match, or no match, couſin, with the hard name——aunt, Wilfull will do't. If ſhe has her maidenhead, let her look to't; if ſhe has not, let her keep her own counſel in the mean time, and cry out at the nine month's end.

Mil. Your pardon, Madam, I can ſtay no longer—— Sir Wilfull grows very powerful. Egh! how he ſmells! I ſhall be overcome, if I ſtay. Come, couſin.

S C E N E XI.

Lady WISHFORT, Sir WILFULL WITWOUD, Mr WITWOUD, FOIBLE.

Lady. Smells! he would poiſon a tallow-chandler and his family. Beaſtly creature, I know not what to do with him——travel, quoth-a; ay, travel, travel, get thee gone, get thee gone, get thee but far enough, to the Saracens, or the Tartars, or the Turks—for thou art not fit to live in a Chriſtian commonwealth, thou beaſtly Pagan.

Sir *Wilf.* Turks, no; no Turks, aunt: your Turks are infidels, and believe not in the grape. Your Mahometan, your Muſſulman, is a dry ſtinkard——no offence, aunt. My map ſays, that your Turk is not ſo honeſt a

2

man as your Chriſtian——I cannot find by the map that your Mufti is orthodox—whereby it is a plain caſe, that orthodox is a hard word, aunt, and [hiccup] Greek for claret.

[Sings.]   To drink is a Chriſtian diverſion,
             Unknown to the Turk or the Perſian:
                 Let Mahometan fools
                 Live by Heatheniſh rules,
             And be damn'd over tea-cups and coffee.
                 But let Britiſh lads ſing,
                 Crown a health to the King,
             And a fig for the Sultan and Sophy.

Ah, Tony!   [Foible whiſpers Lady Wiſhfort.
 Lady. Sir Rowland impatient? Good lack! what ſhall I do with this beaſtly tumbril?—Go ly down and ſleep, you ſot——or as I'm a perſon, I'll have you baſtinado'd with broom-ſticks. Call up the wenches with broom-ſticks.
 Sir Wilf. Ahey! wenches, where are the wenches?
 Lady. Dear couſin Witwoud, get him away, and you will bind me to you inviolably. I have an affair of moment that invades me with ſome precipitation——you will oblige me to all futurity.
 Wit. Come, knight—pox on him, I don't know what to ſay to him——will you go to a cock-match?
 Sir Wilf. With a wench, Tony! Is ſhe a ſhake-bag, ſirrah? Let me bite your cheek for that.
 Wit. Horrible! he has a breath like a bag-pipe—ay, ay, come, will you march, my Salopian?
 Sir Wilf. Lead on, little Tony——I'll follow thee, my Anthony, my Tantony. Sirrah, thou ſhalt be my Tantony, and I'll be thy pig.

         ——And a fig for the Sultan and Sophy.

 Lady. This will never do. It will never make a match ——at leaſt before he has been abroad.

S C E N E XII.

Lady WISHFORT, WAITWELL *disguised as for*
Sir Rowland.

*La*ty. Dear Sir Rowland, I am confounded with confusion at the retrospection of my own rudeness——I have
more pardons to ask than the Pope distributes in the year
of Jubilee. But I hope where there is likely to be so near
an alliance,—we may unbend the severity of decorums—
and dispense with a little ceremony.

Wait. My impatience, Madam, is the effect of my tranfport;——and 'till I have the possession of your adorable
person, I am tantalized on the rack; and do but hang,
Madam, on the tenter of expectation.

Lady. You have excess of gallantry, Sir Rowland, and
press things to a conclusion with a most prevailing vehemence.——But a day or two for decency of marriage—

Wait. For decency of funeral, Madam. The delay will
break my heart ——or, if that should fail, I shall be
poison'd. My nephew will get an inkling of my designs, and poison me,——and I would willingly starve him
before I die—I would gladly go out of the world with that
satisfaction————That would be some comfort to me,
if I could but live so long as to be revenged on that unnatural viper.

Lady. Is he so unnatural, say you? Truly I would contribute much both to the saving of your life, and the ac-
complishment of your revenge——Not that I respect myfelf, tho' he has been a perfidious wretch to me.

Wait. Perfidious to you!

Lady. O Sir Rowland, the hours that he has died away
at my feet, the tears that he has shed, the oaths that he
has sworn, the palpitations that he has felt, the trances
and tremblings, the ardours and the ecstasies, the kneel-
ings and the risings, the heart-heavings and the hand-grip-

ings, the pangs and the pathetic regards of his protesting eyes! Oh no memory can register.

Wait. What, my rival! is the rebel my rival? a'dies.

Lady. No, don't kill him at once, Sir Rowland, starve him gradually, inch by inch.

Wait. I'll do't. In three weeks he shall be barefoot; in a month out at knees with begging alms——he shall starve upward and upward, 'till he has nothing living but his head, and then go out in a stink like a candle's end upon a save-all.

Lady. Well, Sir Rowland, you have the way——you are no novice in the labyrinth of love—you have the clue —but as I am a person, Sir Rowland, you must not attribute my yielding to any sinister appetite, or indigestion of widowhood; nor impute my complacency to any lethargy of continence—I hope you do not think me prone to any iteration of nuptials——

Wait. Far be it from me—

Lady. If you do, I protest I must recede—or think that I have made a prostitution of decorums ; but in the vehemence of compassion, and to save the life of a person of so much importance—

Wait. I esteem it so——

Lady. Or else you wrong my condescension—

Wait. I do not, I do not——

Lady. Indeed you do.

Wait. I do not, fair shrine of virtue.

Lady. If you think the least scruple of carnality was an ingredient——

Wait. Dear Madam, no. You are all camphire and frankincense, all chastity and odour.

Lady. Or that——

SCENE XIII.

[*To them*] FOIBLE.

Foib. Madam, the dancers are ready, and there's one with a letter, who muft deliver it into your own hands.

Lady. Sir Rowland, will you give me leave! Think favourably, judge candidly, and conclude you have found a perfon who would fuffer racks in honour's caufe, dear Sir Rowland, and will wait on you inceffantly.

SCENE XIV.

WAITWELL, FOIBLE.

Wait. Fy, fy,———What a flavery have I undergone? Spoufe, haft thou any cordial? I want fpirits.

Foib. What a wafhy rogue art thou, to pant thus for a quarter of an hour's lying and fwearing to a fine lady?

Wait. O, fhe is the antidote to defire. Spoufe, thou wilt fare the worfe for't—I fhall have no appetite to iteration of nuptials—this eight-and-forty hours.—By this hand I'd rather be a chairman in the dog-days———than act Sir Rowland 'till this time to-morrow.

SCENE. V.

[*To them*] LADY, *with a letter.*

Lady. Call in the dancers ;———Sir Rowland, we'll fit, if you pleafe, and fee the entertainment.   [*Dance.*

Now, with your permiffion, Sir Rowland, I will perufe my letter———I would open it in your prefence, becaufe I would not make you uneafy. If it fhould make you uneafy, I would burn it—fpeak if it does—but you may fee the fuperfcription is like a woman's hand.

Foib. By Heav'n! Mrs Marwood's, I know it,——my heart akes——get it from her——   [*To him.*

Wait. A woman's hand? No, Madam, that's no woman's hand, I fee already. That's fomebody whofe throat muft be cut.

Lady. Nay, Sir Rowland, fince you give me a proof of your paffion by your jealoufy, I promife you I'll make a return, by a frank communication——you fhall fee it ———we'll open it together——look you here.

Reads——" Madam, tho' unknown to you," [Look you there, 'tis from no body that I know.]——" I have that " honour for your character, that I think myfelf oblig'd to " let you know you are abus'd. He who pretends to be " Sir Rowland, is a cheat and a rafcal"———

Oh Heav'ns! what's this?

Foib. Unfortunate! all's ruin'd.

Wait. How, how; let me fee, let me fee,——[*Reading,*] " A rafcal, and difguis'd and fuborn'd for that impofture," ——O villainy! O villainy!—" by the contrivance of "——

Lady. I fhall faint, I fhall die, oh!

Foib. Say 'tis your nephew's hand———quickly, his plot, fwear it, fwear it.——   [*To him.*

Wait. Here's a villain! Madam, don't you perceive it, don't you fee it?

Lady. Too well, too well. I have feen too much.

Wait. I told you at firft I knew the hand.———A woman's hand? The rafcal writes a fort of a large hand; your Roman hand——I faw there was a throat to be cut prefently. If he were my fon, as he is my nephew, I'd piftol him——

Foib. O treachery! But are you fure, Sir Rowland, it is his writing?

Wait. Sure! am I here? do I live? do I love this pearl of India? I have twenty letters in my pocket from him in the fame character.

Lady. How!

Foib. O what luck it is, Sir Rowland, that you were prefent at this juncture! this was the bufinefs that brought

Mr Mirabell difguis'd to Madam Millamant this after-
noon. I thought fomething was contriving, when he ftole
by me and would have hid his face.

Lady. How, how!———I heard the villain was in the
houfe indeed; and now I remember, my niece went away
abruptly, when Sir Wilfull was to have made his addreffes.

Foib. Then, then, Madam, Mr Mirabell waited for
her in her chamber; but I would not tell your Ladyfhip
to difcompofe you when you were to receive Sir Rowland.

Wait. Enough, his date is fhort.

Foib. No, good Sir Rowland, don't incur the law.

Wait. Law! I care not for law. I can but die, and
'tis in a good caufe———My Lady fhall be fatisfied of my
truth and innocence, tho' it coft me my life.

Lady. No, dear Sir Rowland, don't fight, if you fhould
be kill'd I muft never fhew my face; or hang'd—O confider my reputation, Sir Rowland,———No, you fhan't
fight,———I'll go in and examine my niece; I'll make
her confefs. I conjure you, Sir Rowland, by all your
love not to fight.

Wait. I am charm'd, Madam, I obey. But fome proof
you muft let me give you; I'll go for a black box, which
contains the writings of my whole eftate, and deliver that
into your hands.

Lady. Ay, dear Sir Rowland, that will be fome comfort, bring the black box.

Wait. And may I prefume to bring a contract to be
fign'd this night? May I hope fo far?

Lady. Bring what you will; but come alive, pray come
alive. O this is a happy difcovery!

Wait. Dead or alive I'll come———and married we will
be in fpite of treachery; ay, and get an heir that fhall
defeat the laft remaining glimpfe of hope in my abandon'd
nephew. Come, my buxom widow:

Ere long you fhall fubftantial proof receive,
That I'm an errant knight———

Foib. Or errant knave.

ACT V. SCENE I.

SCENE *continues.*

Lady WISHFORT, *and* FOIBLE.

LADY.

OUT of my houfe, out of my houfe, thou viper, thou
ferpent, that I have fefter'd; thou bofom traitrefs,
that I rais'd from nothing———Begone, begone, begone,
go, go———That I took from wafhing of old gaufe and
weaving dead hair, with a bleak blue nofe over a chaf-
fing-difh of ftarv'd embers, and dining behind a traverfe
rag, in a fhop no bigger than a bird-cage,———go, go,
ftarve again, do, do.

Foib. Dear Madam, I'll beg pardon on my knees.

Lady. Away, out, out, go, fet up for yourfelf again———
do, drive a trade, do, with your three penny-worth of
fmall ware, flaunting upon a packthread, under a brandy-
feller's bulk, or againft a dead wall by a ballad-monger.
Go, hang out an old Frifoneer gorget, with a yard of
yellow Colberteen again; do; an old gnaw'd mafk, two
rows of pins, and a child's fiddle; a glafs necklace with
the beads broken, and a quilted night-cape with one ear.
Go, go, drive a trade——Thefe were your commodities,
you treacherous trull, this was the merchandife you dealt
in, when I took you into my houfe, plac'd you next myfelf, and made you governante of my whole family. You
have forgot this, have you, now you have feather'd your
neft?

Foib. No, no, dear Madam. Do but hear me, have
but a moment's patience———I'll confefs all. Mr Mirabell feduc'd me; I am not the firft that he has wheedled
with his diffembling tongue; your Ladyfhip's own wifdom
has been deluded by him; then how fhould I, a poor ignorant, defend myfelf? O Madam, if you knew but what
he promis'd me, and how he affur'd me your Ladyfhip

. ſhould come to no damage————Or elſe the wealth of
the Indies ſhould not have brib'd me to conſpire againſt
ſo good, ſo ſweet, ſo kind a Lady as you have been to
me.

Lady. No damage? What, to betray me, to marry me
to a caſt-ſervingman; to make me a receptacle, an ho-
ſpital for a decay'd pimp? No damage? O thou frontleſs
impudence, more than a big-belly'd actreſs.

Foib. Pray, do but hear me, Madam, he could not marry
your Ladyſhip, Madam——No indeed his marriage was
to have been void in law, for he was married to me firſt,
to ſecure your Ladyſhip. He could not have bedded your
Ladyſhip; for if he had conſummated with your Ladyſhip
he muſt have run the riſque of the law, and been put upon the clergy————Yes indeed, I inquir'd of the law in
that caſe before I would meddle or make.

Lady. What then, I have been your property, have I?
I have been convenient to you, it ſeems,——while you
were catering for Mirabell, I have been broker for you?
What, have you made a paſſive bawd of me?——this ex-
ceeds all precedent; I am brought to fine uſes, to become
a botcher of ſecond-hand marriages between Abigails and
Andrews! I'll couple you. Yes, I'll baſte you together,
you and your Philander. I'll Duke♥-place you, as I'm a
perſon. Your turtle is in cuſtody already: you ſhall coo
in the ſame cage, if there be a conſtable or warrant in the
pariſh.

Foib. O that I ever was born, O that I was ever
marry'd,————a birde, ay I ſhall be a Bridewell-birde.
Oh!

S C E N E II.

Mrs F I N A L L, F O I B L E.

Mrs *Fain.* Poor Foible, what's the matter?

Foib. O Madam, my Lady's gone for a conſtable; I ſhall
be had to juſtice, and put to Bridewell to beat hemp; poor
Waitwell's gone to priſon already.

Mrs *Fain.* Have a good heart, Foible, Mirabell's gone to give fecurity for him. This is all Marwood's and my hufband's doing.

Foib. Yes, yes: I know it, Madam: fhe was in my Lady's clofet, and overheard all that you faid to me before dinner. She fent the letter to my Lady; and that miffing effect, Mr Fainall laid this plot to arreft Waitwell, when he pretended to go for the papers; and in the mean time Mrs Marwood declar'd all to my Lady.

Mrs *Fain.* Was there no mention made of me in the letter———My mother does not fufpect me being in the confederacy: I fancy Marwood has not told her, tho' fhe has told my hufband.

Foib. Yes, Madam : but my Lady did not fee that part : we ftifled the letter before fhe read fo far. Has that mifchievous devil told Mrs Fainall of your Ladyfhip then?

Mrs *Fain.* Ay, all's out, my affair with Mirabell, every thing difcover'd. This is the laft day of our living together, that's my comfort.

Foib. Indeed, Madam, and fo 'tis a comfort if you knew all———he has been even with your Ladyfhip; which I cou'd have told you long enough fince, but I love to keep peace and quietnefs by my good will: I had rather bring friends together, than fet them at diftance. But Mrs Marwood and he are nearer related than ever their parents thought for.

Mrs *Fain.* Say'ft thou fo, Foible? Canft thou prove this?

Foib. I can take my oath of it, Madam, fo can Mrs Mincing; we have had many a fair word from Madam Marwood, to conceal fomething that paffed in our chamber one evening when you were at Hide-park;———and we were thought to have gone a walking; but we went up unawares,———tho' we were fworn to fecrecy too; Madam Marwood took a book and fwore us upon it; but it was but a book of poems.——— So long as it was not a bible oath, we may break it with a fafe confcience.

Mrs Fain. This difcovery is the moft opportune thing I cou'd wifh. Now, Mincing?

SCENE III.

[*To them*] MINCING.

Min. My Lady would fpeak to Mrs Foible, Mem   Mr Mirabell is with her; he has fet your fpoufe at liberty, Mrs Foible, and would have you hide yourfelf in my Lady's clofet, 'till my old Lady's anger is abated. O, my old Lady is in a perilous paffion at fomething Mr Fainall has faid; he fwears, and my old Lady cries. There's a fearful hurricane, I vow. He fays, Mem, how that he'll have my Lady's fortune made over to him, or he'll be divorced.

Mrs Fain. Does your Lady or Mirabell know that ?

Min. Yes, Mem, they have fent me to fee if Sir Wilfull be fober, and to bring him to them. My Lady is refolved to have him, I think, rather than lofe fuch a vaft fum as fix thoufand pound. O come, Mrs Foible, I hear my old Lady.

Mrs Fain. Foible, you muft tell Mincing, that fhe muft prepare to vouch when I call her.

Foib. Yes, yes, Madam.

Min. O yes, Mem, I will vouch any thing for your Ladyfhip's fervice, be what it will.

SCENE IV.

Mrs FAINALL, Lady WISHFORT, MARWOOD.

Lady. O my dear friend, how can I enumerate the benefits that I have received from your goodnefs ? To you I owe the timely difcovery of the falfe vows of Mirabell; to you I owe the detection of the impoftor Sir Rowland. And now you are become an interceffor with my fon-in-law, to fave the honour of my houfe, and compound for the frailties of my daughter. Well, friend, you are enough to reconcile me to the bad world, or elfe I would retire to defarts and folitudes; and feed harmlefs fheep by groves and purling ftreams. Dear Marwood, let us leave the world, and retire by ourfelves and be fhepherdeffes.

Mrs *Mar.* Let us firft difpatch the affair in hand, Madam. We fhall have leifure to think of retirement afterwards. Here is one who is concerned in the treaty.

Lady. O daughter, daughter, is it poffible thou fhould'ft be my child, bone of my bone, and flefh of my flefh, and as I may fay, another me, and yet tranfgrefs the moft minute particle of fevere virtue? Is it poffible you fhould lean afide to iniquity, who have been caft in the direct mold of virtue? I have not only been a mold but a pattern for you, and a model for you, after you were brought into the world.

Mrs *Fain.* I don't underftand your Ladyfhip.

Lady. Not underftand? Why, have you not been naught? have you not been fophifticated? Not underftand? here I'm ruin'd to compound for your caprices and your cuckoldoms. I muft pawn my plate and my jewels, and ruin my niece, and all little enough——

Mrs *Fain.* I am wrong'd and abus'd, and fo are you. 'Tis a falfe accufation, as falfe as hell, as falfe as your friend there, ay, or your friend's friend, my falfe hufband.

Mrs *Mar.* My friend, Mrs Fainall? your hufband my friend, what do you mean?

Mrs *Fain.* I know what I mean, Madam, and fo do you; and fo fhall all the world at a time convenient.

Mrs *Mar.* I am forry to fee you fo paffionate, Madam. More temper would look more like innocence. But I have done. I am forry my zeal to ferve your Ladyfhip and family fhould admit of mifconftruction, or make me liable to affronts. You will pardon me, Madam, if I meddle no

more with an affair in which I am not perfonally concerned.

Lady. O dear friend, I am fo afhamed that you fhould
meet with fuch returns;——you ought to afk pardon on
your knees, ungrateful creature; fhe deferves more from
you than all your life can accomplifh——O don't leave
me deftitute in this perplexity——no, ftick to me, my good
genius.

Mrs *Fain.* I tell you, Madam, you're abus'd——ftick to
you ? ay, like a leach, to fuck your beft blood—fhe'll drop
off when fhe's·full. Madam, you fhan't pawn a bodkin,
nor part with a brafs counter,- in compofition for me. I
defy 'em all. Let 'em prove their afperfions·; I know my
own innocence, and dare ftand a trial.

S C E N E V.

Lady WISHFORT, MARWOOD.

Lady. Why, if fhe fhould be innocent, if fhe fhould be
wrong'd after all, ha ?——I don't know what to think,—
and I promife you her education has been very unexcep-
tionable—I may fay it; for I chiefly made it my own care
to initiate her very fancy in the rudiments of virtue, and
to imprefs upon her tender years a young odium and averfion to the very fight of men——ay, friend, fhe wou'd ha'
fhriek'd if fhe had but feen a man, 'till fhe was in her
teens. As I am a perfon 'tis true——fhe was never fuffer'd to play with a male child, though but in coats; nay,
her very babies were of the feminine gender——O, fhe
never look'd a man in the face but her own father, or the
chaplain, and him we made a fhift to put upon her for a
woman,- by the help of his long garments, and his fleek
face, 'till fhe was going in her fifteen.

Mrs *Mar.* 'Twas much fhe fhould be deceived fo
long.

Lady. I warrant you, or fhe would never have borne to
have been catechiz'd by him; and have heard his long

lectures againſt ſinging and dancing, and ſuch debauch-
eries ; and going to filthy plays, and profane muſic-meet-
ings, where the lewd trebles ſqueak nothing but bawdy,
and the baſes roar blaſphemy. O, ſhe wou'd have ſwoon'd
at the ſight or name of an obſcene play-book——and can
I think, after all this, that my daughter can be naught?
What, a whore? and thought it excommunication to ſet
her foot, within the door of a play-houſe? O dear friend, I
can't believe it, no, no; as ſhe ſays, let him prove it, let
him prove it.

Mrs Mar. Prove it, Madam? What, and have your
name proſtituted in a public court; yours and your daughter's reputation worried at the bar by a pack of brawling
lawyers? To be uſher'd in with an Oyes of ſcandal; and
have your caſe opened by an old fumbling lecher in a
quoif like a man-midwife, to bring your daughter's infamy
to light; to be a theme for legal punſters, and quibblers
by the ſtatute; and become a jeſt againſt a rule of court,
where there is no precedent for a jeſt in any record; not
even in doomſday-book : to diſcompoſe the gravity of the
bench, and provoke naughty interrogatories in more
naughty law Latin; while the good judge, tickled with
the proceeding, ſimpers under a grey beard, and ſidges off
and on his cuſhion as if he had ſwallowed cantharides, or
ſat upon *cow-itch.*

Lady. O, 'tis very hard!

Mrs Mar. And then to have my young revellers of the
Temple take notes, like prentices at a conventicle; and
after talk it over again in commons, or before drawers in
an eating-houſe.

Lady. Worſe and worſe.

Mrs Mar. Nay, this is nothing; if it would end here
'twere well. But it muſt, after this, be conſign'd by the
ſhort-hand-writers to the public preſs; and from thence
be transferred to the hands, nay, into the throats and
lungs of hawkers, with voices more licentious than the
loud flounder-man's : and this you muſt hear 'till you are
ſtunn'd; nay, you muſt hear nothing elſe for ſome days.

Lady. O, 'tis infupportable. No, no, dear friend, make it up, make it up; ay, ay, I'll compound. I'll give up all, myfelf and my all, my niece and her all———any thing, every thing for compofition.

Mrs *Mar.* Nay, Madam, I advife nothing, I only lay before you, as a friend, the inconveniences which perhaps you have overfeen. Here comes Mr Fainall; if he will be fatisfied to huddle up all in filence, I fhall be glad. You muft think I would rather congratulate than condole with you.

S C E N E VI.

FAINALL, Lady WISHFORT, Mrs MARWOOD.

Lady. Ay, ay, I do not doubt it, dear Marwood: no, no, I do not doubt it.

Fain. Well, Madam; I have fuffer'd myfelf to be overcome by the importunity of this Lady your friend; and am content you fhall enjoy your own proper eftate during life, on condition you oblige yourfelf never to marry, under fuch penalty as I think convenient.

Lady. Never to marry?

Fain. No more Sir Rowlands,—the next impofture may not be fo timely detected.

Mrs *Mar.* That condition, I dare anfwer, my Lady will confent to, without difficulty; fhe has already but too much experienc'd the perfidioufnefs of men. Befides, Madam, when we retire to our paftoral folitude we fhall bid adieu to all other thoughts.

Lady. Ay, that's true; but in cafe of neceffity, as of health, or fome fuch emergency———

Fain. O, if you are prefcrib'd marriage, you fhall be confider'd; I will only referve to myfelf the power to chufe for you. If your phyfic be wholefome, it matters not who is your apothecary. Next, my wife fhall fettle on me the remainder of my fortune, not made over already; and for her maintenance depend entirely on my diſcretion.

Lady. This is moſt inhumanly ſavage; exceeding the barbarity of a Muſcovite huſband.

Fain. I learn'd it from his Czariſh Majeſty's retinue, in a winter's evening's conference over brandy and pepper, amongſt other ſecrets of matrimony and policy, as they are at preſent practis'd in the northern hemiſphere. But this muſt be agreed unto, and that poſitively. Laſtly, I will be endow'd, in right of my wife, with that ſix thou-ſand pound, which is the moiety of Mrs Millamant's for-tune in your poſſeſſion; and which ſhe has forfeited (as will appear by the laſt will and teſtament of your deceas'd huſband, Sir Jonathan Wiſhfort) by her obedience in con-tracting herſelf againſt your conſent or knowledge; and by refuſing the offer'd match with Sir Wilfull Witwoud, which you, like a careful aunt, had provided for her.

Lady. My nephew was *non compos,* and could not make his addreſſes.

Fain. I come to make demands——I'll hear no objec-tions.

Lady. You will grant me time to conſider?

Fain. Yes, while the inſtrument is drawing, to which you muſt ſet your hand 'till more ſufficient deeds can be perfected: which I will take care ſhall be done with all poſſible ſpeed. In the mean while I'll go for the ſaid in-ſtrument, and 'till my return you may balance this matter in your own diſcretion.

SCENE VII.

Lady WISHFORT, Mrs MARWOOD.

Lady. This inſolence is beyond all precedent, all parallel; muſt I be ſubject to this mercileſs villain?

Mrs Mar. 'Tis ſevere indeed, Madam, that you ſhou'd ſmart for your daughter's wantonneſs.

Lady. 'I was againſt my conſent that ſhe marry'd this

Barbarian, but she wou'd have him, tho' her year was not out.———Ah! her first husband, my son Languish, wou'd not have carry'd it thus. Well, that was my choice, this is hers; she is match'd now with a witness——I shall be mad, dear friend, is there no comfort for me? must I live to be confiscated at this rebel-rate?—Here come two more of my Egyptian plagues too.

S C E N E   VIII.

[*To them*] M I L L A M A N T, Sir W I L F U L L.

Sir *Wilf.* Aunt, your servant.

Lady. Out caterpillar, call not me aunt; I know thee not.

Sir *Wilf.* I confess I have been a little in disguise, as they say,——'Sheart! and I'm sorry for't. What wou'd you have? I hope I committed no offence, aunt——and if I did I am willing to make satisfaction; and what can a man say fairer? If I have broke any thing I'll pay for't, an it cost a pound. And so let that content for what's past, and make no more words. For what's to come, to pleasure you I'm willing to marry my cousin. So pray let's all be friends, she and I are agreed upon the matter before a witness.

Lady. How's this, dear niece? have I any comfort? can this be true?

Mil. I am content to be a sacrifice to your repose, Madam; and to convince you that I had no hand in the plot, as you were misinform'd, I have laid my commands on Mirabell to come in person, and be a witness that I give my hand to this flower of knight-hood: and for the contract that passed between Mirabell and me, I have oblig'd him to make a resignation of it in your Ladyship's presence;—he is without, and waits your leave for admittance.

Lady. Well, I swear I am something reviv'd at this testimony of your obedience; but I cannot admit that traitor.——I fear I cannot fortify myfelf to fupport his appearance. He is as terrible to me as a gorgon; if I fee him I fear I fhall turn to ftone, petrify inceffantly.

Mil. If you difoblige him, he may refent your refufal, and infift upon the contract ftill. Then 'tis the laft time he will be offenfive to you.

Lady. Are you fure it will be the laft time?——If I were fure of that——fhall I never fee him again?

Mil. Sir Wilfull, you and he are to travel together, are you not?

Sir *Wilf.* 'Sheart, the gentleman's a civil gentleman, aunt, let him come in; why, we are fworn brothers and fellow-travellers.——We are to be Pylades and Oreftes, he and I —He is to be my interpreter in foreign parts. He has been over-feas once already; and with provifo that I marry my coufin, will crofs 'em once again, only to bear me company. ——'Sheart, I'll call him in,——an I fet on't once, he fhall come in; and fee who'll hinder him.

[*Goes to the door and hems.*

Mrs *Mar.* This is precious fooling, if it wou'd pafs; but I'll know the bottom of it.

Lady. O dear Marwood, you are not going?

Mrs *Mar.* Not far, Madam; I'll return immediately.

SCENE IX.

Lady WISHFORT, MILLAMANT, Sir WILFULL, MIRABELL.

Sir *Wilf.* Look up, man, I'll ftand by you; 'fbud an fhe do frown, fhe can't kill you;——befides——harkee, fhe dare not frown defperately, becaufe her face is none of her own; 'Sheart, and fhe fhou'd, her forehead wou'd wrinkle like the coat of a cream-cheefe; but mum for that, fellow-traveller.

Mir. If a deep fenfe of the many injuries I have offer'd to fo good a lady, with a fincere remorfe, and a

hearty contrition, can but obtain the leaſt glance of compaſſion, I am happy.———Ah, Madam, there was a time
———But let it be forgotten———I confeſs I have deſervedly
forfeited the high place I once held of ſighing at your feet.
Nay, kill me not, by turning from me in diſdain.—I come
not to plead for favour;—nay, not for pardon; I am a
ſuppliant only for pity—I am going where I never ſhall
behold you more——.

Sir Wilf. How, fellow-traveller! you ſhall go by yourſelf then.

Mir. Let me be pitied firſt, and afterwards forgotten.
—I aſk no more.

Sir Wilf. By'r lady, a very reaſonable requeſt, and will
coſt you nothing, aunt—Come, come, forgive and forget,
aunt; why you muſt an you are a Chriſtian.

Mir. Conſider, Madam, in reality, you could not receive much prejudice; it was an innocent device; though
I confeſs it had a face of guiltineſs,———it was at moſt an
artifice which love contriv'd———— And errors which
love produces have ever been accounted venial. At leaſt
think it is puniſhment enough, that I have loſt what in
my heart I hold moſt dear, that to your cruel indignation
I have offered up this beauty, and with her my peace and
quiet; nay, all my hopes of future comfort.

Sir Wilf. An he does not move me, would I may never
be o' the quorum ;———an it were not as good a deed as
to drink, to give her to him again,———I would I might
never take ſhipping——Aunt, if you don't forgive quickly, I ſhall melt, I can tell you that. My contract went
no farther than a little mouth-glue, and that's hardly dry ;
———one doleful ſigh more from my fellow-traveller, and
'tis diſſolved.

Lady. Well, nephew, upon your account ———Ah, he
has a falſe inſinuating tongue—well, Sir, I will ſtiſle my
juſt reſentment at my nephew's requeſt.——I will endeavour what I can to forget,—but on proviſo that you re-
ſign the contract with my niece immediately.

Mir. It is in writing, and with papers of concern ;

but I have fent my fervant for it, and will deliver it to you, with all the acknowledgments for your tranfcendant goodnefs.

Lady. Oh, he has witchcraft in his eyes and tongue; ——When I did not fee him, I could have bribed a villain to his affaffination ; but his appearance rakes the embers which have fo long lain fmother'd in my breaft— [*Afide.*

S C E N E   X.

[*To them*] F A I N A L L, Mrs M A R W O O D.

Fain. Your date of deliberation, Madam, is expir'd. Here is the inftrument; are you prepar'd to fign ?

Lady. If I were prepar'd, I am not impower'd. My niece exerts a lawful claim, having match'd herfelf by my direction to Sir Wilfull.

Fain. That fham is too grofs to pafs on me——tho' 'tis impos'd on you, Madam.

Mil. Sir, I have given my confent.

Mir. And, Sir, I have refign'd my pretenfions.

Sir *Wilf.* And, Sir, I affert my right; and will maintain it in defiance of you, Sir, and of your inftrument. 'sheart, an you talk of an inftrument, Sir, I have an old fox by my thigh fhall hack your inftrument of Ram vellum to fhreds, Sir. It fhall not be fufficient for a mittimus or a tailor's meafure; therefore withdraw your inftrument, Sir, or, by'r lady, I fhall draw mine.

Lady. Hold, nephew, hold.

Mil. Good Sir Wilfull, refpite your valour.

Fain. Indeed ! Are you provided of your guard, with your fingle beef-eater there ? but I'm prepar'd for you, and infift upon my firft propofal. You fhall fubmit your own eftate to my management, and abfolutely make over my wife's to my fole ufe, as purfuant to the purport and tenor of this other covenant——I fuppofe, Madam, your confent is not requifite in this cafe; nor, Mr Mirabell, your refignation; nor, Sir Wilfull, your right.——You may draw your fox if you pleafe, Sir, and make a beargarden flourifh fomewhere elfe : for here it will not avail. This, my Lady Wifhfort, muft be fubfcribed, or your darling daughter's turn'd adrift, like a leaky hulk, to fink or fwim, as fhe and the current of this lewd town can agree.

Lady. Is there no means, no remedy to ftop my ruin? Ungrateful wretch! doft thou not owe thy being, thy fubfiftence, to my daughter's fortune?

Fain. I'll anfwer you when I have the reft of it in my poffeffion.

Mir. But that you would not accept of a remedy from my hands—I own I have not deferved you fhould owe any obligation to me; or elfe perhaps I cou'd advife——

Lady. O what? what? to fave me and my child from ruin, from want, I'll forgive all that's paft; nay, I'll confent to any thing to come, to be delivered from this tyranny.

Mir. Ay, Madam; but that is too late, my reward is intercepted. You have difpofed of her, who only could have made a compenfation for all my fervices——but be it as it may, I am refolv'd I'll ferve you; you fhall not be wrong'd in this favage manner.

Lady. How! dear Mr Mirabell, can you be fo generous at laft! But it is not poffible. Harkee, I'll break my nephew's match; you fhall have my niece yet, and all her fortune, if you can but fave me from this imminent danger.

Mir. Will you? I take you at your word. I afk no more. I muft have leave for two criminals to appear.

Lady. Ay, ay, any body, any body.

Mir. Foible is one, and a penitent.

SCENE XI.

[*To them*] Mrs FAINALL, FOIBLE, MINCING.

Mrs Mar. O my fhame! [Mirabell *and* Lady *go to Mrs* Fainwell *and* Foible.] Thefe corrupt things are brought hither to expofe me.   [*To* Fain.

Fain. If it muft all come out, why let 'em know it; 'tis but the Way of the World. That fhall not urge me to relinquifh or abate one tittle of my terms; no, I will infift the more.

Foib. Yes indeed, Madam, I'll take my bible oath of it.

Min. And fo will I, Mem.

Lady. O Marwood, Marwood, art thou falfe? my friend deceive me! haft thou been a wicked accomplice with that profligate man?

Mrs Mar. Have you fo much ingratitude and injuftice to give credit againft your friend, to the afperfions of two fuch mercenary trulls?

Min. Mercenary, Mem? I fcorn your words. 'Tis true we found you and Mr Fainall in the blue garret; by the fame token, you fwore us to fecrecy upon Meffalina's poems. Mercenary? No, if we wou'd have been mercenary, we fhou'd have held our tongues; you wou'd have brib'd us fufficiently.

Fain. Go, you are an infignificant thing.——Well, what are you the better for this? is this Mr Mirabell's expedient? I'll be put off no longer——You thing, that was a wife, fhall fmart for this. I will not leave thee wherewithal to hide thy fhame; your body fhall be naked as your reputation.

Mrs Fain. I defpife you, and defy your malice——you have afpers'd me wrongfully——I have prov'd your falfehood——go you and your treacherous——I will not name it, but ftarve together——perifh.

Fain. Not while you are worth a groat, indeed, my dear. Madam, I'll be fool'd no longer,

Lady. Ah, Mr Mirabell, this is small comfort, the detection of this affair.

Mir. O in good time—your leave for the other offender and penitent to appear, Madam.

S C E N E XII.

[*To them*] W A I T W E L L, *with a box of writings.*

Lady. O Sir Rowland——well, rascal.

Wait. What your Ladyship pleases. I have brought the black box at last, Madam.

Mir. Give it me; Madam, you remember your promise.

Lady. Ay, dear Sir.

Mir. Where are the gentlemen?

Wait. At hand, Sir, rubbing their eyes——just risen from sleep.

Fain. 'Sdeath, what's this to me? I'll not wait your private concerns.

S C E N E XIII.

[*To them*] P E T U L A N T, W I T W O U D.

Pet. How now? What's the matter? Whose hand's out?

Wit. Hey-day! what, are you all got together, like players at the end of the last act?

Mir. You may remember, gentlemen, I once requested your hands as witnesses to a certain parchment.

Wit. Ay, I do, my hand I remember——Petulant set his mark.

Mir. You wrong him, his name is fairly written, as shall appear——You do not remember, gentlemen, any thing of what that parchment contain'd——

[*Undoing the box.*

Wit. No.

Pet. Not I, I write, I read nothing.

Mir. Very well, now you fhall know—Madam, your promife.

Lady. Ay, ay, Sir, upon my honour.

Mir. Mr Fainall, it is now time that you fhou'd know, that your Lady, while fhe was at her own difpofal, and before you had by your infinuations wheedled her out of a pretended fettlement of the greateft part of her fortune—

Fain. Sir! pretended?

Mir. Yes, Sir. I fay that this lady while a widow, having it feems received fome cautions refpecting your inconftancy and tyranny of temper, which from her own partial opinion and fondnefs of you fhe cou'd never have fufpected—fhe did, I fay, by the wholfome advice of friends and of fages learned in the laws of this land, deliver this fame as her act and deed to me in truft, and to the ufes within mentioned. You may read if you pleafe—[*Holding out the parchment.*] though perhaps what is written on the back may ferve your occafions.

Fain. Very likely, Sir. What's here? Damnation!

[*Reads.*] " A deed of conveyance of the whole eftate real of " Arabella Anguifh, widow, in truft to Edward " Mirabell."

Confufion!

Mir. Even fo, Sir, 'tis the Way of the World, Sir; of the widows of the world. I fuppofe this deed may bear an elder date than what you have obtain'd from your Lady.

Fain. Perfidious fiend! then thus I'll be reveng'd.
[*Offers to run at Mrs* Fain.

Sir Wilf. Hold, Sir, now you may make your bear-garden flourifh fomewhere elfe, Sir.

Fain. Mirabell, you fhall hear of this, Sir, be fure you fhall——Let me pafs, oaf.

Mrs Fain. Madam, you feem to ftifle your refentment: you had better give it vent.

2

Mrs *Mar.* Yes, it muſt have vent—and to your confuſion, or I'll periſh in the attempt.

S C E N E *the Laſt.*

Lady WISHFORT, MII AMANT, MIRABELL,
Mrs FAINALL,   Sir WILFULL, PETULANT,
WITWOUD, FOIBLE, MINCING, WAITWELL.

Lady. O daughter, daughter, 'tis plain thou haſt inherit-
ed thy mother's prudence.

Mrs *Fain.* Thank Mr Mirabell, a cautious friend, to
whoſe advice all is owing.

Lady. Well, Mr Mirabell, you have kept your promiſe—
and I muſt perform mine—-—Firſt, I pardon, for your ſake,
Sir Rowland there, and Foible—the next thing is to break
the matter to my nephew—and how to do that——

Mir. For that, Madam, give yourſelf no trouble—let
me have your conſent—Sir Wilfull is my friend; he has
had compaſſion upon lovers, and generouſly engaged a vo-
lunteer in this action, for our ſervice; and now deſigns to
proſecute his travels.

Sir *Wilf.* 'Sheart, aunt, I have no mind to marry. My
couſin's a fine lady, and the gentleman loves her, and ſhe
loves him, and they deſerve one another; my reſolution is
to ſee foreign parts—I have ſet on't—and when I'm ſet
on't I muſt do't. And if theſe two gentlemen would travel too, I think they may be ſpar'd.

Pet. For my part, I ſay little—I think things are beſt off
or on.

Wit. I'gad I underſtand nothing of the matter—I'm in a
maze yet, like a dog in a dancing-ſchool.

Lady. Well, Sir, take her, and with her all the joy I can
give you.

Mil. Why does not the man take me? wou'd you have
me give myſelf to you over again?

Mir. Ay, and over and over again; [*Kiſſes her hard.*] I
wou'd have you as often as poſſibly I can. Well, Heaven
grant I love you not too well, that's all my fear.

Sir Wilf. 'Sheart, you'll have time enough to toy after you're married; or if you will toy now, let us have a dance in the mean time, that we who are not lovers may have some other employment besides looking on.

Mir. With all my heart, dear Sir Wilfull. What shall we do for mufic?

Foib. O Sir, some that were provided for Sir Rowland's entertainment are yet within call.   [*A Dance.*

Lady. As I am a person I can hold out no longer;——I have wasted my spirits so to-day already, that I am ready to sink under the fatigue; and I cannot but have some fears upon me yet, that my son Fainall will pursue some desperate course.

Mir. Madam, disquiet not yourself on that account; to my knowledge his circumstances are such, he must of force comply. For my part, I will contribute all that in me lyes to a reunion; in the mean time, Madam, [*To Mrs* Fain.] let me before these witnesses restore to you this deed of trust; it may be a means, well-manag'd, to make you live easily together.

From hence let those be warn'd, who mean to wed;
Lest mutual falsehood stain the bridal bed;
For each deceiver to his cost may find,
That marriage-frauds too oft are paid in kind.

                    [*Exeunt omnes.*

EPILOGUE.

AFTER our Epilogue this croud difmiffes,
   I'm thinking how this play'll be pull'd to pieces.
But pray confider, e'er you doom its fall,
How hard a thing 'twou'd be to pleafe you all.
There are fome critics fo with fpleen difeas'd,
They fcarcely come inclining to be pleas'd :
And fure he muft have more than mortal fkill,
That pleafes any one againft his will.
Then all bad poets we are fure are foes,
And how their number fwells, the town well knows :
In fhoals I've mark'd 'em judging in the pit ;
Though they're, on no pretence, for judgment fit,
But that they have been damn'd for want of wit.
Since when, they by their own-offences taught,
Set up for fpies on plays, and finding fault.
Others there are whofe malice we'd prevent ;
Such who watch plays with fcurrilous intent
To mark out who by characters are meant.
And though no perfect likenefs they can trace,
Yet each pretends to know the copy'd face.
Thefe with falfe gloffes, feed their own ill nature,
And turn to libel what was meant a fatire.
May fuch malicious fops this fortune find,
To think themfelves alone the fools defign'd :
If any are fo arrogantly vain,
To think they fingly can fupport a fcene,
And furnifh fool enough to entertain.
For well the learn'd and the judicious know
That fatire fcorns to ftoop fo meanly low,
As any one abftracted fop to fhow.
For, as when painters form a matchlefs face,
They from each fair one catch fome different grace ;
And fhining features in one portrait blend,
To which no fingle beauty muft pretend ;
So poets oft do in one piece expofe
Whole belles-affemblees of coquets and beaux.

THE

JUDGMENT

OF

PARIS:

A

MASQUE.

———————"Vincit utramque Venus."
Ov. Art. Am. l. 1.

Q 2

JUDGMENT OF PARIS.

The SCENE is a landscape of a beautiful pasture suppo-
sed on mount Ida. The shepherd Paris is seen seated
under a tree, and playing on his pipe; his crook and
scrip, &c. lying by him. While a symphony is playing,
Mercury descends with his caduceus in one hand, and
an apple of gold in the other; after the symphony he
sings.

MERCURY.

FROM high Olympus, and the realms above,
    Behold I come the messenger of Jove ;
       His dread commands I bear :
       Shepherd, arise and hear ;
    Arise, and leave a while thy rural care;
Forbear thy woolly flock to feed,
And lay aside thy tuneful reed ;
For thou to greater honours art decreed.
  Par. O Hermes, I thy godhead know,
    By thy winged heels and head,
    By thy rod that wakes the dead,
    And guides the shades below.
Say wherefore dost thou seek this humble plain,
    To greet a lowly swain ?
What does the mighty thunderer ordain ?
  Mer. This radiant fruit behold,
More bright than burnish'd gold ;

Three Goddesses for this contend ;

    See now they descend,

    · And this way they bend.

Shepherd, take the golden prize,

Yield it to the brightest eyes.

[*Juno, Pallas, and* Venus *are seen at a distance descending in several machines.*

Par. O ravishing delight !

What mortal can support the sight ?

    Alas ! too weak is human brain,

    So much rapture to sustain.

I faint, I fall ! O take me hence,

Ere ecstacy invades my aking sense.

    Help me, Hermes, or I die,

    Save me from excess of joy.

Mer. Fear not, mortal, none shall harm thee ;

With my sacred rod I'll charm thee.

    Freely view and gaze all over,

    Thou may'st ev'ry grace discover.

Though a thousand darts fly round thee,

Fear not, mortal, none shall wound thee.

In two ⎧ Happy thou of human race,

parts. ⎪ Gods with thee would change their place,

Paris. ⎨ With no God I'd change my place,

    ⎩ Happy I of human race.   [*Mer. ascends.*

[*While a symphony is playing,* Juno *descends from her machine ; after the symphony she sings.*

Juno. Saturnia, wife of thundering Jove am I,

Belov'd by him, and empress of the sky ;

Shepherd, fix on me thy wond'ring sight,

Beware, and view me well, and judge aright.

[*Symphony for* Pallas.

Pal. This way, mortal, bend thy eyes,

Pallas claims the golden prize :

A virgin goddess free from stain,

And Queen of arts and arms I reign.

[*Symphony for* Venus.

Ven. Hither turn thee, gentle swain,
Let not Venus sue in vain;
Venus rules the Gods above,
Love rules them, and she rules Love.
    Hither turn thee, gentle swain.
Pal. Hither turn to me again.
Juno. Turn to me, for I am she.
All three. To me, to me, for I am she.
Ven. Hither turn thee, gentle swain.
Juno and Pal. She will deceive thee.
Ven. They will deceive thee, I'll never leave thee.

Chorus of all three.
{ Hither turn to me again,
{ To me, to me, for I am she;
{ Hither turn thee, gentle swain.

P A R I S.

I.

Distracted I turn, but I cannot decide;
So equal a title sure never was try'd.
United, your beauties so dazzle the sight,
    That lost in amaze,
    I giddily gaze.
Confus'd and o'erwhelm'd with a torrent of light.

II.

Apart let me view then each heav'nly fair,
For three at a time there's no mortal can bear;
And since a gay robe an ill shape may disguise,
    When each is undrest,
    I'll judge of the best,
For 'tis not a face that must carry the prize.

J U N O *sings alone.*

I.

Let ambition fire thy mind,
Thou wert born o'er men to reign,
Not to follow flocks design'd;
Scorn thy crook, and leave the plain.

II.

Crowns I'll throw beneath thy feet,
Thou on necks of kings shall tread,

Joys in circles joys shall meet,
Which way e're thy fancies lead.

III.

Let not toils of empire fright,
Toils of empire pleasures are;
Thou shalt only know delight,
All the joy, but not the care.

IV.

Shepherd, if thou'lt yield the prize,
For the blessings I bestow,
Joyful I'll ascend the skies,
Happy thou shalt reign below.

CHORUS.

Let Ambition fire thy mind,
Thou wert born o'er men to reign,
Not to follow flocks design'd;
Scorn thy crook, and leave the plain.

PALLAS *sings alone.*

I.

Awake, awake, thy spirits raise,
Waste not thus thy youthful days,
 Piping, toying,
 Nymphs decoying,
Lost in wanton and inglorious ease.

II.

Hark, hark! the glorious voice of war
Calls aloud, for arms prepare:
 Drums are beating,
 Rocks repeating,
Martial music charms the joyful air.   [*Symphony.*

PALLAS *sings.*

O what joys does conquest yield!
When returning from the field,
 O how glorious 'tis to see
The godlike hero crown'd with victory!
  Laurel wreaths his head surrounding,
  Banners waving in the wind,
Fame her golden trumpet sounding,
  Ev'ry voice in chorus join'd.

To me, kind fwain, the prize refign,
And fame and conqueft fhall be thine.

CHORUS.

O how glorious 'tis to fee
The godlike hero crown'd with victory!   [*Symphony.*

VENUS *fings alone.*

Stay, lovely youth, delay thy choice;
Take heed left empty names enthral thee ;
Attend to Cytherea's voice ;
Lo! I who am Love's mother call thee.

Far from thee be anxious care,
And racking thoughts that vex the great :
Empire's but a gilded fnare,
And fickle is the warrior's fate :
One only joy mankind can know,
And love alone can that beftow.

CHORUS.

One only joy, &c.

VENUS *fings.*
I.

Nature fram'd thee fure for loving,
Thus adorn'd with ev'ry grace ;
Venus' felf thy form approving,
Looks with pleafure on thy face.

II.

Happy nymph who fhall enfold thee,
Circled in her yielding arms !
Should bright Helen once behold thee,
She'd furrender all her charms.

III.

Faireft fhe, all nymphs tranfcending,
That the fun himfelf has feen,
Were fhe for the crown contending,
Thou wou'd own her beauty's Queen.

IV.

Gentle fhepherd, if my pleading
Can from thee the prize obtain,

Love himſelf thy conqueſt aiding,
Thou that matchleſs fair ſhalt gain.

Par. I yield, I yield, O take the prize,
And ceaſe, O ceaſe, th' inchanting ſong;
All Love's darts are in thy eyes,
And harmony falls from thy tongue.

Forbear, O Goddeſs of deſire,
Thus my raviſh'd ſoul to move;
Forbear to fan the raging fire,
And be propitious to my love.

[Here Paris gives to Venus the golden apple. Several Cu-
pids deſcend, the three Graces alight from the chariot of
Venus, they call the Hours, who aſſemble, with all the
attendants on Venus. All join in a circle round her,
and ſing the laſt grand chorus, while Juno and Pallas
aſcend.]

GRAND CHORUS.

Hither all ye Graces, all ye loves,
Hither all ye Hours reſort;
Billing ſparrows, cooing doves;
Come all the train of Venus' court.
Sing all the great Cytherea's name;
Over empire, over fame,
Her victory proclaim.
Sing, ſing and ſpread the joyful news around,
The Queen of Love, is Queen of Glory crown'd.

S E M E L E.

A N

O P E R A.

" A natura difcedimus; populo nos damus, nullius rei
" bono auctori, et in hac re, ficut in omnibus, incon-
" ftantiffimo." .

Seneca, Ep. 99.

ARGUMENT

OPERA of SEMELE.

AFTER Jupiter's amour with Europa, the daughter of Agenor King of Phœnicia, he again incenses Juno by a new affair in the same family; viz. with Semele, niece to Europa, and daughter to Cadmus King of Thebes. Semele is on the point of marriage with Athamas; which marriage is about to be solemniz'd in the Temple of Juno goddess of marriages, when Jupiter by ill omens interrupts the ceremony; and afterwards transports Semele to a private abode prepared for her. Juno, after many circumstances, at length assumes the shape and voice of Ino, sister to Semele; by help of which disguise and artful insinuations, she prevails with her to make a request to Jupiter, which being granted, must end in her utter ruin.

This fable is related in Ovid. Metam. l. iii. but there Juno is said to impose on Semele in the shape of an old woman, her nurse. It is hoped, the liberty taken in substituting Ino instead of the old woman will be excused: it was done, because Ino is interwoven in the design by her love of Athamas; to whom she was married, according to Ovid; and, because

her character bears a proportion with the dignity of
the other perfons reprefented. This reafon, it is pre-
fumed, may be allowed in a thing entirely fictitious;
and more efpecially being reprefented under the title
of an Opera, where greater abfurdities are every
day excufed.

It was not thought requifite to have any regard
either to rhyme or equality of meafure, in the lines of
the dialogue which was defign'd for the recitative
ftyle in mufic. For as that ftyle in mufic is not con-
fined to the ftrict obfervation of time and meafure,
which is required in the compofitions of airs and fo-
natas, fo neither is it neceffary that the fame exact-
nefs in numbers, rhymes or meafure, fhould be ob-
ferved in words defign'd to be fet in that manner,
which muft ever be obferved in the formation of odes
and fonnets. For what they call recitative in mufic,
is only a more tuneable fpeaking, it is a kind of profe
in mufic; its beauty confifts in coming nearer nature,
and in improving the natural accents of words by
more pathetic or emphatical tones.

Persons Reprefented.

JUPITER.
CADMUS, King of Thebes.
ATHAMAS, a prince of Bœotia, in love with, and defigned
   to marry Semele.
SOMNUS.
APOLLO.
CUPID.
ZEPHYRS.
LOVES.
Shepherds.
Satyrs.

JUNO.
IRIS.
SEMELE, daughter to Cadmus, beloved by, and in love
   with Jupiter.
INO, fifter to Semele, in love with Athamas.
Shepherdeffes.

Chief Priefts of Juno, other Priefts and Augurs.

SCENE, BOEOTIA.

S E M E L E.

ACT I. SCENE I.

The SCENE is the Temple of JUNO, near the altar is
a golden image of the goddefs. Priefts are in their fo-
lemnities, as after a facrifice newly offer'd : flames arife
from the altar, and the ftatue of JUNO is feen to bow.

CADMUS, ATHAMAS, SEMELE, and INO.

FIRST PRIEST.

BEHOLD! aufpicious flafhes rife;.
   Juno accepts our facrifice ;
   The grateful odour fwift afcends,
   And fee, the golden image bends.

FIRST and SECOND PRIEST.

Lucky omens blefs our rites,
And fure fuccefs fhall crown your loves;
   Peaceful days and fruitful nights
   Attend the pair that fhe approves.

Cad. Daughter, obey,
   Hear, and obey.
   With kind confenting
   Eafe a parent's care ;
   Invent no new delay.

Atha. O hear a faithful lover's pray'r ;
   On this aufpicious day
Invent no new delay.

CADMUS and ATHAMAS.

Hear, and obey;
Invent no new delay
On this auspicious day.

Seme. apart.] Ah me!
What refuge now is left me?
How various, how tormenting,
Are my miseries!
O Jove assist me.
Can Semele forego thy love,
And to a mortal's passion yield?
Thy vengeance will o'ertake
Such perfidy.
If I deny, my father's wrath I fear.
O Jove, in pity teach me which to chuse,
Incline me to comply, or help me to refuse.

Atha. See, she blushing turns her eyes;
See, with sighs her bosom panting:
If from love those sighs arise,
Nothing to my bliss is wanting.
Hymen haste, thy torch prepare,
Love already his has lighted,
One soft sigh has cur'd despair,
And more than my past pains requited.

Ino. Alas! she yields,
And has undone me:
I can no longer hide my passion;
It must have vent———
Or inward burning
Will consume me.
O Athamas———
I cannot utter it———

Atha. On me fair Ino calls
With mournful accent,
Her colour fading,
And her eyes o'erflowing!

Ino. O Semele!

Seme. On me she calls,

Yet feems to fhun me !
What would my fifter ?
Speak————————

Ino. Thou haft undone me.

Cad. Why doft thou thus untimely grieve,
And all our folemn rites prophane ?
Can he, or fhe, thy woes relieve ?
Or I ? of whom doft thou complain ?

Ino. Of all ? but all, I fear, in vain.

Atha. Can I thy woes relieve ?

Seme. Can I affwage thy pain ?

CADMUS, ATHAMAS, *and* SEMELE.
Of whom doft thou complain ?

Ino. Of all ; but all, I fear, in vain.

[*It lightens, and thunder is heard at a diftance ; then a noife of
rain ; the fire is fuddenly extinguifhed on the altar : the Chief
Prieft comes forward.*

1ft *Prieft.* Avert thefe omens, all ye pow'rs !
Some God averfe our holy rites controls,
O'erwhelm'd with fudden night, the day expires !
Ill-boding thunder on the right hand rolls,
And Jove himfelf defcends in fhow'rs,
To quench our late propitious fires.

CHORUS *of* PRIESTS.
Avert thefe omens all ye pow'rs !

2d *Prieft.* Again aufpicious flafhes rife,
Juno accepts our facrifice.

[*Flames are again kindled on the altar, and the Statue nods.*

3d *Prieft.* Again the fickly flame decaying dies :
Juno affents, but angry Jove denies.

[*The fire is again extinguifh'd.*

ATHAMAS [*Apart.*]
Thy aid, connubial Juno, Athamas implores.

SEMELE [*Apart.*]
Thee Jove, and thee alone, thy Semele adores.

[*A loud clap of thunder ; the altar finks.*

1ft *Prieft.* Ceafe, ceafe your vows, 'tis impious to proceed;
Be gone, and fly this holy place with fpeed.

R 3

This dreadful conflict is of dire presage;
Be gone, and fly from Jove's impending rage.

[*All but the Priests come forward. The scene closes on the
Priests, and shews to view the front and outside of the Temple,
Cadmus leads off* Semele, *Attendants follow.* Athamas
and Ino *remain.*

S C E N E II.

ATHAMAS, INO.

ATHAMAS.

O Athamas, what torture hast thou borne!
And O, what hast thou yet to bear!
From love, from hope, from near possession torn,
And plung'd at once in deep despair.

Ino. Turn, hopeless lover, turn thy eyes,
And see a maid bemoan,
In flowing tears and aking sighs,
Thy woes too like her own.

Atha. She weeps!
The gentle maid, in tender pity,
Weeps to behold my misery!
So Semele wou'd melt
To see another mourn.

Such unavailing mercy is in beauty found,
Each nymph bemoans the smart
Of every bleeding heart,
But that where she herself inflicts the wound.

Ino. Ah me, too much inflicted!

Atha. Can pity for another's pain
Cause such anxiety!

Ino. Cou'dst thou but guess
What I endure!
Or could I tell thee————
Thou, Athamas,
Wouldst for a while

Thy forrows ceafe, a little ceafe,
And liften for a while
To my lamenting.
Atha. Of grief too fenfible
I know your tender nature.
Well I remember,
When I oft have fu'd
To cold, difdainful Semele;
When I with fcorn have been rejected;
Your tuneful voice my tale would tell,
In pity of my fad defpair;
And with fweet melody, compel
Attention from the flying fair.
Ino. Too well I fee
Thou wilt not underftand me.
Whence cou'd proceed fuch tendernefs?
Whence fuch compaffion?
Infenfible! ingrate!
Ah no, I cannot blame thee:
For by effects unknown before
Who could the hidden caufe explore?
Or think that love could act fo ftrange a part,
To plead for pity in a rival's heart?
Atha. Ah me, what have I heard!
She does her paffion own.
Ino. What, had I not defpair'd,
You never fhou'd have known.
You've undone me;
Look not on me;
Guilt upbraiding,
Shame invading;
Look not on me;
You've undone me;
Atha. With my life I wou'd atone
Pains you've borne, to me unknown.
Ceafe, ceafe to fhun me.
Ino. Look not on me,
You've undone me.
Atha. Ceafe ceafe to fhun me:

Love, love alone
Has both undone.
Ino, Alba. Love, love alone
Has both undone.

S C E N E III.

[To them] Enter C A D M U S *attended.*

C A D M U S.

Ah wretched Prince, doom'd to difaftrous love!
Ah me, of parents moft forlorn!
Prepare, O Athamas, to prove
    The fharpeft pangs that e'er were born:
    Prepare with me our common lofs to mourn.
Alba. Can fate, or Semele invent
    Another, yet another punifhment?
Cad. Wing'd with our fears, and pious hafte,
    From Juno's fan we fled;
    Scarce we the brazen gates had pafs'd,
    When Semele around her head
        With azure flames was grac'd,
Whofe lambent glories in her treffes play'd.
    While thus we faw with dread furprize,
Swifter than lightning downwards tending
    An eagle ftoop'd, of mighty fize,
        On purple wings defcending;
Like gold his beak, like ftars fhone forth his eyes,
His filver plumy breaft with fnow contending:
        Sudden he fnatch'd the trembling maid,
        And foaring from our fight convey'd;
Diffufing ever as he leffening flew
Celeftial odour, and ambrofial dew.
    Alba. O prodigy, to me of dire portent!
    Ino. To me, I hope, of fortunate event.

S C E N E IV.

Enter to them the CHIEF-PRIEST, *with* AUGURS *and other* PRIESTS.

CADMUS.

See, fee Jove's Priefts, and holy Augurs come :
Speak, fpeak, of Semele and me declare the doom.
1ft *Aug.* Hail Cadmus, hail! Jove falutes the Theban king.
  Ceafe your mourning,
  Joys returning,
Songs of mirth and triumph fing.
2d *Aug.* Endlefs pleafure, endlefs love
  Semele enjoys above ;
  On her bofom Jove reclining,
  Ufelefs now his thunder lyes ;
  To her arms his bolts refigning,
  And his lightning to her eyes.
  Endlefs pleafure, endlefs love
  Semele enjoys above ;
1ft *Prieft.* Hafte, hafte, hafte, to facrifice prepare,
  Once to the thunderer, once to the fair,
  - Jove and Semele implore :
  Jove and Semele like honours fhare ;
  Whom gods admire, let men adore.
  Hafte, hafte, hafte, to facrifice prepare.

CHORUS *of* Priefts *and* Augurs.

Hail, Cadmus, hail! Jove falutes the Theban king.
  Ceafe your mourning,
  Joys returning,
Songs of mirth and triumph fing.   [Exeunt omnes.

A C T II: S C E N E I.

The SCENE is a pleasant country, the prospect is terminated by a beautiful mountain adorn'd with woods and water-falls. JUNO and IRIS descend in different machines. JUNO in a chariot drawn by peacocks; IRIS on a rain-bow; they alight and meet.

JUNO.

IRIS, impatient of thy stay,
  From Samos have I wing'd my way,
    To meet thy slow return;
      Thou know'st what cares infest
        My anxious breast;
And how with rage and jealousy I burn:
      Then why this long delay?
Iris. With all his speed not yet the sun
      Through half his race has run,
Since I to execute thy dread command
      Have thrice encompass'd seas and land,
  Juno. Say, where is Semele's abode?
      'Till that I know,
      Though thou hadst on lightning rode,
      Still thou tedious art and slow.
  Iris. Look where Citheron proudly stands,
      Bœotia parting from Cecropian lands:
High on the summit of that hill,
Beyond the reach of mortal eyes,
By Jove's command, and Vulcan's skill,
Behold a new-erected palace rise.

There from mortal cares retiring,
  She resides in sweet retreat;
On her pleasure, Jove requiring,
  All the loves and graces wait.

Thither Flora the fair
With her train muſt repair,
Her amorous Zephyr attending,
All her ſweets ſhe muſt bring
To continue the ſpring,
Which never muſt there know an ending.

Bright Aurorà, 'tis ſaid,
From her old lover's bed
No more the grey orient adorning,
For the future muſt rife
From fair Semele's eyes,
And wait 'till ſhe wakes for the morning.

Juno. No more————I'll hear no more.
How long muſt I endure ?————
How long muſt indignation burning,
From impious mortals
Bear this infolence !
Awake Saturnia from thy lethargy ;
Seize, deſtroy the curſt adultrefs.
Scale proud Citherion's top ;
Snatch her, tear her in thy fury,
And down, down to the flood of Acheron
Let her fall, let her fall, fall, fall ;
Rolling down the depths of night,
Never more to behold the light.
    If I am own'd above,
     Siſter and wife of Jove ;
   (Siſter at leaſt I ſure may claim,
    Tho' wife be a neglected name.)
If I th' imperial ſcepter ſway——I ſwear
By hell————
Tremble thou univerſe this oath to hear,
Not one of curſt Agenor's race to ſpare.
  Iris. Hear, mighty queen, while I recount
   What obſtacles you muſt ſurmount ;

With adamant the gates are barr'd,
  Whose entrance two fierce dragons guard;
At each approach they lash their forky stings,
  And clap their brazen wings:
And as their scaly horrors rise,
  They all at once disclose
  A thousand fiery eyes,
  Which never know repose.

Juno. Hence Iris, hence away,
  Far from the realms of day;
O'er Scythian hills to the Meotian lake
  A speedy flight we'll take:
  There Somnus I'll compell
His downy bed to leave and silent cell:
With noise and light I will his peace molest,
Nor shall he sink again to downy rest,
'Till to my vow'd revenge he grants supplies,
And seals with sleep the wakeful dragons eyes. [*They ascend.*

S C E N E II.

The SCENE changes to an apartment in the palace of SEMELE; she is sleeping; LOVES and ZEPHYRS waiting.

Cup. See, after the toils of an amorous fight,
Where weary and pleas'd, still panting she lyes;
While yet in her mind she repeats the delight,
  How sweet is the slumber that steals on her eyes!
  Come Zephyrs, come, while Cupid sings,
  Fan her with your silky wings;
    New desire
    I'll inspire,
  And revive the dying flames;
    Dance around her
    While I wound her,
  And with pleasure fill her dreams.

A dance of Zephyrs, after which Semele awakes, and rises.

Seme. O sleep, why dost thou leave me ?
 Why thy visionary joys remove ?
 O sleep again deceive me,
 To my arms restore my wand'ring love.

S C E N E   III.

Two Loves *lead in* Jupiter. *While he meets and*
embraces Semele, Cupid *sings.*

Cup. Sleep forsaking,
 Seize him waking ;
 Love has fought him,
 Back has brought him ;
 Mighty Jove tho' he be,
 And tho' Love cannot see,
 Yet by feeling about
 He has found him out,
 And has caught him.
Seme. Let me not another moment
Bear the pangs of absence.
Since you have form'd my soul for loving,
No more afflict me
With doubts and fears, and cruel jealousies.
 Jupi. Lay your doubts and fears aside,
 And for joys alone provide ;
 Tho' this human form I wear,
 Think not I man's falsehood bear.
You are mortal, and require
Time to rest and to respire.
 Nor was I absent,
 Tho' a while withdrawn,
 To take petitions
 From the needy world.
 While love was with thee

I was prefent;
Love and I are one.

Seme. If chearful hopes
  And chilling fears,
  Alternate fmiles,
  Alternate tears,
  Eager panting,
  Fond defiring,
With grief now fainting,
Now with blifs expiring;
If this be love, not you alone,
But love and I are one.

Both. If this be love, not you alone,
But love and I are one.

Seme. Ah me!

Jupi. Why fighs my Semele?
  What gentle forrow
  Swells thy foft bofom?
  Why tremble thofe fair eyes
  With interrupted light?
  Where hov'ring for a vent,
  Amidft their humid fires,
  Some new-form'd wifh appears:
  Speak, and obtain.

Seme. At my own happinefs
  I figh and tremble;
  Mortals whom gods affect
  Have narrow limits fet to life,
  And cannot long be blefs'd.
  Or if they could——
  A god may prove inconftant.

Jupi. Beware of jealoufy;
  Had Juno not been jealous,
  I ne'er had left Olympus,
  Nor wander'd in my love.

Seme. With my frailty don't upbraid me,
  I am a woman as you made me,

Caufelefs doubting or defpairing,
Rafhly trufting, idly fearing.
If obtaining
Still complaining;
If confenting
Still repenting;
Moft complying
When denying,
And to be follow'd only flying.
With my frailty don't upbraid me,
I am a woman as you made me.

Jupi. Thy fex of Jove's the mafter-piece,
Thou of thy fex art moft excelling.
Frailty in thee is ornament,
In thee perfection.
Giv'n to agitate the mind,
And keep awake men's paffions;
To banifh indolence,
And dull repofe,
The foes of tranfport
And of pleafure.

Seme. Still I am mortal,
Still a woman;
And ever when you leave me,
Tho' compafs'd round with deities
Of loves and graces,
A fear invades me,
And confcious of a nature
Far inferior,
I feek for folitude,
And fhun fociety.

Jupi. apart.] Too well I read her meaning,
But muft not underftand her.
Aiming at immortality
With dangerous ambition,
She wou'd dethrone Saturnia;
And reigning in my heart

Would reign in Heav'n.
　　Left she too much explain,
　　I must with speed amuse her;
It gives the lover double pain,
　　Who hears his nymph complain,
　　And hearing must refuse her.

Seme. Why do you cease to gaze upon me?
　　Why musing turn away?
　　Some other object
　　Seems more pleasing.

Jupi. Thy needless fears remove,
　　My fairest, latest, only love.
　　By my command,
　　Now at this instant,
　　Two winged Zephyrs
　　From her downy bed
　　Thy much-lov'd Ino bear;
　　And both together
　　Waft her hither.
　　Thro' the balmy air.

Seme. Shall I my sister see!
　　The dear companion
　　Of my tender years.

Jupi. See, she appears,
　　But sees not me;
　　For I am visible
　　Alone to thee.

While I retire, rise and meet her,
And with welcomes greet her.
Now all this scene shall to Arcadia turn,
　　The seat of happy nymphs and swains;
There without the rage of jealousy they burn,
And taste the sweets of love without its pains.

Jupiter retires. Semele and Ino meet and embrace.
The SCENE is totally changed, and ſhews an open
country. Several Shepherds and Shepherdeſſes enter.
Semele and Ino having entertained each other in
dumb ſhew, ſit and obſerve the rural ſports, which end
the ſecond Act.

ACT III. SCENE I.

The SCENE is the cave of Sleep. The god of Sleep lying on his bed. A ſoft ſymphony is heard. Then the
muſic changes to a different movement.

JUNO and IRIS.

JUNO.

SOMNUS, awake.
  Raiſe thy declining head;
Iris. Thyſelf forſake,
  And lift up thy heavy lids of lead.
Som. waking.] Leave me, loathſome light;
Receive me, ſilent night.
Lethe, why does thy ling'ring current ceaſe?
O murmur, murmur me again to peace.

                     [*Sinks down again.*

Iris. Dull God, canſt thou attend the waters' fall,
  And not hear Saturnia call!
Juno. Peace, Iris, peace, I know how to charm him:
  Paſithea's name alone can warm him.

JUNO, IRIS.

  Only Love on ſleep has pow'r;
    O'er gods and men
    Tho' Somnus reign,
  Love alternate has his hour.

Juno. Somnus, arife,
  Difclofe thy tender eyes;
  For Pafithea's fight
   Endure the light :
   Somnus, arife.

Som. rifing.] More fweet is that name
  Than a foft purling ftream;
  With pleafure repofe I'll forfake,
  If you'll grant me but her to foothe me awake.

Juno. My will obey,
  She fhall be thine.
  Thou with thy fofter pow'rs
  Firft Jove fhall captivate :
  To Morpheus then give order,
  Thy various minifter,
  That with a dream in fhape of Semele,
  But far more beautiful,
  And more alluring,
  He may invade the fleeping deity;
  And more to agitate
  His kindling fire,
  Still let the fantom feem
  To fly before him,
  That he may wake impetuous,
  Furious in defire;
  Unable to refufe whatever boon
  Her coynefs fhall require.

Som. I tremble to comply.

Juno. To me thy leaden rod refign,
  To charm the fentinels
  On mount Citheron ;
  Then caft a fleep on mortal Ino,
  That I may feem her form to wear
  When I to Semele appear.
  Obey my will, thy rod refign,
  And Pafithea fhall be thine.

Som. All I muft grant, for all is due
  To Pafithea, love and you.

Juno. Away let us hafte,
 Let neither have reft,
'Till the fweeteft of pleafures we prove;
 'Till of vengeance poffefs'd
 I doubly am blefs'd,
And thou art made happy in love.

       [*Ex.* Juno *and* Iris.

  [Somnus *retires within his cave, the fcene changes to*
  Semele's *apartment.*

S C E N E II.

S E M E L E , *alone.*

S E M E L E.

I love, and am lov'd, yet more I defire;
Ah, how foolifh a thing is fruition!
As one paffion cools, fome other takes fire,
And I'm ftill in a longing condition.
  Whate'er I poffefs
  Soon feems an excefs.
For fomething untry'd I petition;
  Tho' daily I prove
  The pleafures of love,
I die for the joys of ambition.

S C E N E III.

Enter J U N O *as* Ino, *with a mirrour in her hand.*

J U N O [*apart.*]

  Thus fhaped like Ino,
  With eafe I fhall deceive her,
  And in this mirrour fhe fhall fee
  Herfelf as much transform'd as me.
  Do I fome goddefs fee!
  Or is it Semele?

Seme. Dear fifter, fpeak,
  Whence this aftonifhment?

Juno. Your charms improving
  To divine perfection,
  Shew you were late admitted
  Among celeftial beauties.
  Has Jove confented?
  And are you made immortal?

Seme. Ah no, I ftill am mortal;
  Nor am I fenfible
  Of any change or new perfection.

   J U N O.   *[Giving her the glafs.*
  Behold in this mirrour
  Whence comes my furprize;
  Such luftre and terrour
  Unite in your eyes,
That mine cannot fix on a radiance fo bright;
'Tis unfafe for the fenfe, and too flippery for fight.

   S E M E L E.   *[Looking in tee glafs.*
O ecftacy of happinefs!
Celeftial graces
I difcover in each feature!
  Myfelf I fhall adore,
  If I perfift in gazing;
  No object fure before
  Was ever half fo pleafing.
How did that glance become me?
But take this flattering mirrour from me.
  Yet once again let me view me.
   Ah charming all o'er.
   [Offering the glafs, withdraws her hand again.
Here———hold, I'll have one look more,
Tho' that look I were fure would undo me.

   J U N O.   *[Taking the glafs from her.*
Be wife as you are beautiful,
Nor lofe this opportunity.
When Jove appears,
All ardent with defire,

Refuse his proffer'd flame
'Till you obtain a boon without a name.

Seme. Can that avail me?

Juno. Unknowing your intent,
 And eager for poſſeſſing,
 He unawares will grant
 The nameleſs bleſſing.
 But bind him by the Stygian lake,
 Leſt lover-like his word he break.

Seme. But how ſhall I attain
 To immortality?

Juno. Conjure him by his oath
 Not to approach your bed
 In likeneſs of a mortal,
 But like himſelf the mighty thunderer,
 In pomp of majeſty,
 And heav'nly attire;
As when he proud Saturnia charms,
 And with ineffable delights
 Fills her encircling arms,
And pays the nuptial rites.
 By this conjunction
 With entire divinity
 You ſhall partake of heav'nly eſſence,
 And thenceforth leave this mortal ſtate
  To reign above,
   Ador'd by Jove,
 In ſpite of jealous Juno's hate.

Seme. Thus let my thanks be paid,
 Thus let my arms embrace thee;
 And when I'm a goddeſs made,
 With charms like mine I'll grace thee.

Juno. Rich odours fill the fragrant air,
 And Jove's approach declare.
 I muſt retire————

Seme. Adieu————Your counſel I'll purſue.

Juno. apart.] And ſure deſtruction will enſue.
Vain, wretched fool——[*To her.*] Adieu. [*Exit,*

S C E N E   IV.

JUPITER *enters, offers to embrace* SEMELE; *she looks kindly on him, but retires a little from him.*

JUPITER.

Come to my arms, my lovely fair,
Soothe my uneasy care :
In my dream late I woo'd thee,
And in vain I pursu'd thee, -
'For you fled from my pray'r,
And bid me despair.
Come to my arms, my lovely fair.

Seme. 'Tho' 'tis easy to please ye,
And hard to deny ;
Tho' possessing's a blessing
For which I could die,
I dare not, I cannot comply.

Jupi. When I languish with anguish,
And tenderly sigh,
Can you leave me, deceive me,
And scornfully fly ?
Ah, fear not; you must not deny.

SEMELE, JUPITER.

I dare not, I cannot comply.
Ah fear not; you must not deny.

Jupi. O Semele,
Why art thou thus insensible?
Were I a mortal,
Thy barbarous disdaining
Would surely end me,
And death at my complaining
In pity would befriend me.

Seme. I ever am granting,
You always complain;
I always am wanting,
Yet never obtain.

Jupi. Speak, fpeak your defire,
   I'm all over fire.
   Say what you require;
   I'll grant it——now let us retire.
Seme. Swear by the Stygian lake.
Jupi. By that tremendous flood I fwear,
   Ye Stygian waters hear,
   And thou Olympus fhake,
   In witnefs to the oath I take.
    [*Thunder heard at a diftance, and underneath.*
Seme. You'll grant what I require!
Jupi. I'll grant what you require.
Seme. Then caft off this human fhape which you wear.
   And Jove, fince you are, like Jove too appear;
   When next you defire I fhould charm ye.
    As when Juno you blefs,
    So you me muft carefs,
   And with all your omnipotence arm ye.
Jupi. Ah! take heed what you prefs,
   For beyond all redrefs,
  Should I grant what you wifh, I fhall harm ye.
Seme. I'll be pleas'd with no lefs,
   Than my wifh in excefs:
  Let the oath you have taken alarm ye:
   Hafte, hafte, and prepare,
   For I'll know what you are;
  So with all your omnipotence arm ye.

S C E N E V.

She withdraws, JUPITER *remains penfive and dejeƈted.*

JUPITER.

Ah! whither is fhe gone! unhappy fair!
Why did fhe wifh?—Why did I rafhly fwear?
   'Tis paft, 'tis paft recall,
   She muft a victim fall.

Anon, when I appear,
The mighty thunderer,
Arm'd with inevitable fire,
She needs muſt inſtantly expire.
'Tis paſt, 'tis paſt recall,
She muſt a victim fall.
My ſofteſt lightning yet I'll try,
And mildeſt melting bolt apply:
In vain—for ſhe was fram'd to prove
None but the lambent flames of love.
'Tis paſt, 'tis paſt recall,
She muſt a victim fall.

S C E N E VI.

JUNO *appears in her chariot aſcending.*

JUNO.

Above meaſure
Is the pleaſure
Which my reveage ſupplies.
Love's a bubble,
Gain'd with trouble,
And in poſſeſſing dies.
With what joy ſhall I mount to my heaven again,
At once from my rival and jealouſy freed !
The ſweets of revenge make it worth while to reign,
And heav'n will hereafter be heav'n indeed.

[*She aſcends.*

S C E N E VII.

The SCENE opening diſcovers SEMELE lying under a
canopy, leaning penſively. While a mournful ſymphony is playing, ſhe looks up and ſees JUPITER deſcend-
ing in a black cloud; the motion of the cloud is ſlow.
Flaſhes of lightning iſſue from either ſide, and thunder
is heard grumbling in the air.

2

S E M E L E.

Ah me! too late I now repent
My pride and impious vanity.
He comes! far off his lightnings fcorch me.
——I feel my life confuming:
I burn, I burn——I faint—for pity I implore——
O help, O help——I can no more.   [*Dies.*

[*As the cloud which contains* Jupiter *is arrived juft over the canopy
of* Semele, *a fudden and great flafh of lightning breaks forth,
and a clap of loud thunder is heard; when at one inftant* Semele, *with the palace and the whole prefent fcene, difappears, and*
Jupiter *reafcends fwiftly. The fcene totally changed repre-
fents a pleafant country,* mount Citheron *clofing the profpect.*

S C E N E   VIII.

Enter C A D M U S, A T H A M A S *and* I N O.

I N O.

Of my ill-boding dream
Behold the dire event.

C A D M A S,   A T H A M U S.

O terror and aftonifhment!
Ino. How was I hence remov'd,
  Or hither how return'd, I know not:
  So long a trance with-held me.
  But Hermes in a vifion told me
    (As I have now related)
    The fate of Semele;
  And added as from me he fled,
  That Jove ordain'd I Athamas fhould wed.
Cad. Be Jove in every thing obey'd [*Joins their hands.*
Atha. Unworthy of your charms, myfelf I yield;
  Be Jove's commands and yours fulfill'd.
Cad. See from above the bellying clouds defcend,
  And big with fome new wonder this way tend.

A bright cloud descends and rests on Mount Citheron, *which opening, discovers* APOLLO *seated in it as the God of prophesy.*

APOLLO.

Apollo comes to relieve your care,
And future happiness declare.
From tyrannous love all your sorrows proceed,
From tyrannous love you shall quickly be freed.
A God he shall prove
More mighty than love;
And a sovereign juice shall invent,
Which antidote pure
The sick lover shall cure,
And sighing and sorrow for ever prevent.
Then mortals be merry, and scorn the blind boy;
Your hearts from his arrows strong wine shall defend:
Each day and each night you shall revel in joy,
For when Bacchus is born, love's reign's at an end.

CHORUS.

Then mortals be merry, &c.
Dance of Satyrs.

[*Exeunt omnes.*

CONCERNING

HUMOUR IN COMEDY.

A

LETTER.

HUMOUR IN COMEDY.

A

L E T T E R.

DEAR SIR,

YOU write to me, that you have entertained yourfelf two or three days, with reading feveral comedies of feveral authors; and your obfervation is, that there is more of Humour in our Englifh writers, than in any of the other comic poets, ancient or modern You defire to know my opinion, and at the fame time my thought, of that which is generally called Humour in comedy.

I agree with you, in an impartial preference of our Englifh writers, in that particular. But if I tell you my thoughts of Humour, I muft at the fame time confefs, that what I take for true Humour, has not been fo often written even by them, as is generally believed: and fome who have valued themfelves, and have been efteemed by others, for that kind of writing, have feldom touched upon it. To make this appear to the world, would require a long and laboured difcourfe, and fuch as I am neither able nor willing to undertake. But fuch little remarks, as may be contained within the compafs of a letter, and fuch unpremeditated thoughts, as may be communicated between friend and friend, without incurring the cenfure of the world, or fetting up for a dictator, you fhall have from me, fince you have enjoined it.

To define Humour, perhaps, were as difficult as to define Wit; for like that, it is of infinite variety. To cau-

merate the several Humours of men, were a work as end-
less, as to sum up their several opinions. And in my mind
the *quot homines tot sententiæ*, might have been more properly interpreted of Humour; since there are many men,
of the same opinion in many things, who are quite different in humours. But though we cannot certainly tell
what Wit is, or what Humour is, yet we may go near to
shew something which is not Wit or Humour, and yet
often mistaken for both. And since I have mentioned,
Wit and Humour together, let me make the first distinction
between them, and observe to you that Wit is often mistaken for Humour.

I have observed, that when a few things have been wit-
tily and pleasantly spoken by any character in a comedy;
it has been very usual for those, who made their remarks
on a play while it is acting, to say, " Such a thing is very
" humourously spoken: there is a great deal of humour in
" that part." Thus the character of the person speaking,
may be, surprizingly and pleasantly, is mistaken for a character of humour; which indeed is a character of wit. But
there is a great difference between a comedy, wherein there
are many things humourously, as they call it, which is
pleasantly spoken; and one, where there are several characters of Humour, distinguished by the particular and different humours, appropriated to the several persons represented, and which naturally arise from the different
constitutions, complexions, and dispositions of men. The
saying of humourous things does not distinguish characters;
for every person in a comedy may be allowed to speak
them. From a witty man they are expected; and even a
fool may be permitted to stumble on them by chance.
Though I make a difference between Wit and Humour;
yet I do not think that humourous characters exclude wit:
no, but the manner of Wit should be adapted to the Humour. As for instance, a character of a splenetic and peevish Humour should have a satirical wit. A jolly and
sanguine Humour should have a facetious wit. The former
should speak positively; the latter, carelesly: for the former

obferves and fhews things as they are; the latter rather overlooks nature, and fpeaks things as he would have them; and his Wit and Humour have both of them a lefs alloy of judgment than the others.

As Wit, fo its oppofite, Folly, " is fometimes miftaken " for Humour."

When a poet brings a character on the ftage, commiting a thoufand abfurdities, and talking impertinencies, roaring aloud, and laughing immoderately, on every, or rather upon no occafion; is this a character of Humour?

Is any thing more common, than to have a pretended comedy, ftuffed with fuch grotefque figures, and farce fools? things, that either are not in nature, or if they are, are monfters, and births of mifchance: and confequently as fuch, fhould be ftifled, and huddled out of the way, like footerkins; that mankind may not be fhocked with an appearing poffibility of the degeneration of a god-like fpecies. For my part, I am as willing to laugh as any body, and as eafily diverted with an object truly ridiculous: but at the fame time, I can never care for feeing things that force me to entertain low thoughts of my nature. I do not know how it is with others, but I confefs freely to you, I could never look long upon a monkey, without very mortifying reflections; though I never heard any thing to the contrary, why that creature is not originally of a diftinct fpecies. As I do not think Humour exclufive of Wit, neither do I think it inconfiftent with folly; but I think the follies fhould be only fuch, as mens humours may incline them to; and not follies intirely abftracted from both humour and nature.

Sometimes, " Perfonal defects are mifreprefented for " humours."

I mean fometimes characters are barbaroufly expofed on the ftage, ridiculing natural deformities, cafual defects in the fenfes, and infirmities of age. Sure the poet muft both be very ill-natured himfelf, and think his audience fo, when he propofes by fhewing a man deformed, or deaf, or blind, to give them an agreeable entertainment; and hopes to raife their mirth, by what is truly an object of compaffion. But much need not to be faid upon this head to any body, efpecially to you, who in one of your letters to me concerning Johnfon's *Fox*, have juftly excepted againft this immoral part of ridicule in Corbaccio's character; and there I muft agree with you to blame him, whom otherwife I cannot enough admire, for his great maftery of true humour in comedy.

" External habit of body is often miftaken for Humour."

By external habit, I do not mean the ridiculous drefs or clothing of a character, though that goes a good way in fome received characters: (but undoubtedly a man's humour may incline him to drefs differently from other people :) but I mean a fingularity of manners, fpeech, and behaviour, peculiar to all, or moft of the fame country, trade, profeffion, or education: I cannot think that a Humour, which is only a habit, or difpofition contracted by ufe or cuftom; for by a difufe, or compliance with other cuftoms, it may be worn off, or diverfified.

" Affectation is generally miftaken for humour."

Thefe are indeed fo much alike, that at a diftance, they may be miftaken one for the other. For what is Humour in one, may be affectation in another; and nothing is more common, than for fome to affect particular ways of faying, and doing things, peculiar to others, whom they admire and would imitate. Humour is the life, affectation the picture. He that draws a character of Affectation fhews Humour at the fecond hand; he at beft but publifhes a tranflation, and his pictures are but copies.

But as thefe two laft diftinctions are the niceft, fo it may be moft proper to explain them, by particular inftances from fome author of reputation. Humour I take, either to be born with us, and fo of a natural growth; or elfe to be grafted into us, by fome accidental change in the conftitution, or revolution of the internal habit of body; by which it becomes, if I may fo call it, naturalized.

Humour is from nature, Habit from cuſtom ; and affectation from induſtry.

Humour, ſhews us as we are.

Habit, ſhews us, as we appear under a forcible impreſſion.

Affectation, ſhews what we would be, under a volunta-
ry diſguiſe.

Though here I would obſerve by the way, that a continued affectation may in time become a habit.

The character of Moroſe in the *Silent Woman*, I take to
be a character of humour. And I chooſe to inſtance this
character to you, from many others of the ſame author,
becauſe I know it has been condemned by many as unnatural and farce : and you have yourſelf hinted ſome diſlike
of it, for the ſame reaſon, in a letter to me, concerning
ſome of Johnſon's plays.

Let us ſuppoſe Moroſe to be a man naturally ſplenetic
and melancholy ; is there any thing more offenſive to one
of ſuch a diſpoſition, than noiſe and clamour ? Let any
man that has the ſpleen (and there are enough in England)
be judge. We ſee common examples of this humour in
little every-day. It is ten to one, but three parts in four
of the company that you dine with are diſcompoſed and
ſtartled at the cutting of a cork, or ſcratching a plate with
a knife : it is a proportion of the ſame humour that makes
ſuch or any other noiſe offenſive to the perſon that hears
it ; for there are others who will not be diſturbed at all
by it. Well ; but Moroſe, you will ſay, is ſo extravagant,
he cannot bear any diſcourſe or converſation, above a whiſ-
per. Why, it is his exceſs of this humour, that makes
him become ridiculous, and qualifies his character for comedy. If the poet had given him but a moderate proportion of that humour, it is odds but half the audience
would have ſided with the character, and have condemned
the author, for expoſing a humour which was neither remarkable nor ridiculous. Beſides, the diſtance of the ſtage
requires the figure repreſented to be ſomething larger than

the life; and fure a picture may have features larger in
proportion, and yet be very like the original. If this ex-
actnefs of quantity were to be obferved in wit, as fome
would have it in humour; what would become of thofe
characters that are defigned for men of wit? I believe if
a poet fhould fteal a dialogue of any length, from the ex-
tempore difcourfe of the two witticft men upon earth, he
would find the fceno but coldly received by the town.
But to the purpofe.

The character of Sir John Daw, in the fame play, is a
character of affectation. He every where difcovers an affectation of learning; when he is not only confcious to
himfelf, but the audience alfo plainly perceives, that he is
ignorant. Of this kind are the characters of Thrafo in
the *Eunuch* of Terence, and Pyrgopolinices in the *Miles
Gloriofus* of Plautus. They affect to be thought valiant,
when both themfelves and the audience know they are not.
Now fuch a boafting of valour in men, who are really
valiant, would undoubtedly be a Humour; for a fiery dif-
pofition might naturally throw a man into the fame extravagance, which is only affected in the characters I have
mentioned.

The character of Cob in *Every man in his Humour*, and
moft of the under characters in *Bartholomew-fair*, difcover only a fingularity of manners, appropriated in the feveral educations and profeffions of the perfons reprefented.
They are not humours, but habits contracted by cuftom.
Under this head may be ranged all country-clowns, failors,
tradefmen, jockeys, gamefters and fuch like, who make
ufe of cants, or peculiar dialects in their feveral arts and
vocations. One may almoft give a receipt for the compofition of fuch a character: for the poet has nothing to
do, but to collect a few proper phrafes and terms of art,
and to make the perfon apply them, by ridiculous metaphors in his converfation, with characters of different
natures. Some late characters of this kind have been very
fuccefsful; but in my mind they may be painted without
much art or labour; fince they require little more, than

2. good memory and fuperficial obfervation. But true Humour cannot be fhewn, without a diffection of nature, and a narrow fearch, to difcover the firft feeds, from whence it has its root and growth.

If I were to write to the world, I fhould be obliged to dwell longer upon each of thefe diftinctions and examples; for I know that they would not be plain enough to all readers. But a bare hint is fufficient to inform you of the notions which I have on this fubject: and I hope by this time you are of my opinion, that humour is neither wit, nor folly, nor perfonal defect, nor affectation, nor habit; and yet, that each, and all of thefe, have been both written and received for humour.

I fhould be unwilling to venture even on a bare defcription of humour, much more, to make a definition of it; but now my hand is in, I will tell you what ferves me inftead of either. I take it to be, " A fingular and una-
" voidable manner of doing or faying any thing, peculiar
" and natural to one man only; by which his fpeech and
" actions are diftinguifhed from thofe of other men."

Our Humour has relation to us, and to what proceeds from us, as the accidents have to a fubftance; it is a colour, tafte and fmell, diffufed through all; though our actions are never fo many, and different in form, they are all fplinters of the fame wood, and have naturally one complexion; which though it may be difguifed by art, yet cannot be wholly changed: we may paint it with other colours, but we cannot change the grain. So the natural found of an inftrument will be diftinguifhed, though the notes expreffed by it are never fo various, and the divifions never fo many. Diffimulation may, by degrees, become more eafy to our practice; but it can never abfolutely tranfubftantiate us into what we would feem: it will always be in fome proportion a violence upon nature.

A man may change his opinion, but I believe he will find it a difficulty to part with his Humour; and there is nothing more provoking, than the being made fenfible of

that difficulty. Sometimes, one shall meet with those who
perhaps, innocently enough, but at the same time im-
pertinently, will aſk the queſtion; " Why are you not merry?
" Why are you not gay, pleaſant and chearful?" Then inſtead
of anſwering, could I aſk ſuch one; " Why are you not
" handſome? Why have you not black eyes, and a better
" complexion?" Nature abhors to be forced.

The two famous philoſophers of Epheſus and Abdera,
have their different ſects at this day. Some weep, and
others laugh at one and the ſame thing.

I do not doubt but you have obſerved ſeveral men
laugh when they are angry; others who are ſilent; ſome
that are loud: yet I cannot ſuppoſe that it is the paſſion
of anger which is in itſelf different, or more or leſs in one
than the other; but that it is the Humour of the man that
is predominant, and urges him to expreſs it in that manner. Demonſtrations of pleaſure are as various; one man
has a humour of retiring from all company, when any thing
has happened to pleaſe him beyond expectation; he hugs
himſelf alone, and thinks it an addition to the pleaſure to
keep it ſecret. Another is upon thorns till he has made
proclamation of it; and muſt make other people ſenſible
of his happineſs, before he can be ſo himſelf. So it is
in grief, and other paſſions. Demonſtrations of love, and
the effects of that paſſion upon ſeveral humours, are infinitely different; but here the Ladies who abound in ſervants
are the beſt judges. Talking of the Ladies, methinks ſomething ſhould be obſerved of the humour of the fair ſex;
ſince they are ſometimes ſo kind as to furniſh out a character for comedy. But I muſt confeſs I have never made
any obſervation of what I apprehend to be true humour
in women. Perhaps paſſions are too powerful in that ſex,
to let humour have its courſe; or may be, by reaſon of
their natural coldneſs, humour cannot exert itſelf to that
extravagant degree, which it often does in the male ſex.
For if ever any thing does appear comical or ridiculous in
a woman, I think it is little more than an acquired folly,
or an affectation. We may call them the weaker ſex, but

I think the true reafon is, becaufe our follies are ftronger, and our faults are more prevailing.

One might think that the diverfity of humour, which muft be allowed to be diffufed throughout mankind, might afford endlefs matter for the fupport of comedies. But when we come clofely to confider that point, and nicely to diftinguifh the difference of humours, I believe we fhall find the contrary. For though we allow every man fomething of his own, and a peculiar humour; yet every man has it not in quantity to become remarkable by it: or, if many do become remarkable by their humours, yet all thofe humours may not be diverting. Nor is it only requifite to diftinguifh what humour will be diverting, but alfo how much of it, what part of it to fhew in light, and what to caft in fhades; how to fet it off by preparatory fcenes, and by oppofing other humours to it in the fame fcene. Through a wrong judgment, fometimes, mens humours may be oppofed when there is really no fpecific difference between them; only a greater proportion of the fame, in one than the other, occafioned by his having more phlegm, or choler, or whatever the conftitution is, from whence their humours derive their fource.

There is infinitely more to be faid on this fubject; though perhaps I have already faid too much; but I have faid it to a friend, who I am fure will not expofe it, if he does not approve of it. I believe the fubject is entirely new, and was never touched upon before; and if I would have any one to fee this private effay, it fhould be fome one, who might be provoked by my errors in it, to publifh a more judicious treatife on the fubject. Indeed I wifh it were done, that the world being a little acquainted with the fcarcity of true humour, and the difficulty of finding and fhewing it, might look a little more favourably on the labours of them who endeavour to fearch into nature for it, and lay it open to the public view.

I do not fay but that very entertaining and ufeful characters, and proper for comedy, may be drawn from affectations, and thofe other qualities which I have endea-

voured to diftinguifh from humour ; but I would not have
fuch impofed on the world for humour, nor efteemed of
equal value with it. It were, perhaps, the work of a long
life to make one comedy true in all its parts, and to give
every character in it a true and diftinct humour. Therefore, every poet muft be beholden to other helps, to make
out his number of ridiculous characters. But I think fuch
a one deferves to be broke, who makes all falfe mufters ;
who does not fhew one true humour in a comedy, but en-
tertains his audience to the end of the play with every
thing out of nature.

I will but make one obfervation to you more, and have
done ; and that is grounded upon an obfervation of your
own, and which I mentioned at the beginning of my letter,
viz. that there is more of humour in our Englifh comic
writers than in any others. I do not at all wonder at it,
for I look upon humour to be almoft of Englifh growth ;
at leaft, it does not feem to have found fuch encreafe on
any other foil. And what appears to me to be the reafon of it, is the great freedom, privilege, and liberty which
the common people of England enjoy. Any man that
has a humour, is under no reftraint, or fear of giving it
vent. They have a proverb among them, which, may be,
will fhew the bent and genius of the people, as well as a
longer difcourfe : " He that will have a May-pole, fhall
" have a May-pole." This is a maxim with them, and their
practice is agreable to it. I believe fomething confiderable
too may be afcribed to their feeding fo much on flefh, and
the groffnefs of their diet in general. But I have done,
let the phyficians agree that. Thus you have my thoughts
of Humour, to my power of expreffing them in fo little
time and compafs. You will be kind to fhew me wherein I
have erred ; and as you are very capable of giving me inftruction, fo, I think I have a very juft title to demand it
from you ; being without referve,

July 10. 1695.

Your real friend, and humble fervan',

WILL. CONGREVE.

AMENDMENTS

OF

Mr COLLIER's

FALSE and IMPERFECT CITATIONS, &c.

FROM THE

OLD BACHELOR,	LOVE for LOVE,
DOUBLE DEALER,	MOURNING BRIDE.

" Quem recitas meus eſt O Fidentine libellus,
" Sed male dum recitas incipit eſſe tuus." MART.

" Graviter, et iniquo animo, maledicta tua paterer, ſi te
" ſcirem judicio magis, quam morbo animi, petulentia iſta
" uti. Sed, quoniam in te neque modum, neque mode-
" ſtiam ullam animadverto, reſpondebo tibi : uti, ſi quam
" maledicendo voluptatem cepiſti, eam male-audiendo
" amittas." SALLUST. DECL.

AMENDMENTS

OF

Mr COLLIER's

FALSE and IMPERFECT CITATIONS, &c.

I HAVE been told by fome, that they would think me very idle, if I threw away any time in taking notice even of fo much of Mr Collier's late treatife of the immorality, &c. of the Englifh ftage, as related to myfelf, in refpect of fome plays written by me: for that his malicious and ftrained interpretations of my words were fo grofs and palpable, that any indifferent and unprejudiced reader would immediately condemn him upon his own evidence, and acquit me before I could make my defenec.

On the other hand, I have been tax'd of lazinefs, and too much fecurity, in neglecting thus long to do myfelf a neceffary right, which might be effected with fo very little pains; fince very little more is requifite in my vindication than to reprefent, truly and at length, thofe paffages, which Mr Collier has fhewn imperfectly, and, for the moft part, by halves. I would rather be thought idle than lazy; and fo the laft advice prevailed with me.

I have no intention to examine all the abfurdities and falfhoods in Mr Collier's book; to ufe the gentleman's own metaphor in his preface, " An inventory of fuch a " ware houfe would be a large work." My detection of his malice and ignorance, of his fophiftry and vaft affurance, will ly within a narrow compafs, and only bear a proportion to fo much of his book as concerns myfelf.

U 3

Leaſt of all, would I undertake to defend the corrup-
tions of the ſtage. Indeed if I were ſo inclined, Mr Collier has given me no occaſion ; for the greater part of thoſe
examples which he has produced, are only demonſtrations
of his own impurity ; they only ſavour of his utterance,
and were ſweet enough till tainted by his breath.

I will not juſtify any of my own errors ; I am ſenſible of
many ; and if Mr Collier has by any accident ſtumbled
on one or two, I will freely give them up to him, *Nullum
unquam ingenium placuit ſine venia.* But I hope I have done
nothing that can deprive me of the benefit of my clergy ;
and though Mr Collier himſelf were the ordinary, I may
hope to be acquitted.

My intention, therefore, is to do little elſe, but to re-
ſtore thoſe paſſages to their primitive ſtation, which have
ſuffered ſo much in being tranſplanted by him : I will remove them from this dunghill, and replant them in the
field of nature ; and when I have waſhed them of that
filth which they have contracted in paſſing through his very
dirty hands, let their own innocence protect them.

Mr Collier, in the high vigour of his obſcenity, firſt
commits a rape upon my words, and then arraigns them
of immodeſty ; he has barbarity enough to accuſe the very
virgins that he has deflowered, and to make ſure of their
condemnation, he has himſelf made them guilty : but he
forgets that while he publiſhes their ſhame, he divulges
his own.

His artifice, to make words guilty of profaneneſs, is of
the ſame nature ; for where the expreſſion is unblameable
in its own clear and genuine ſignification, he enters into
it himſelf like the evil ſpirit ; he poſſeſſes the innocent
phraſe, and makes it bellow forth his own blaſphemies ;
ſo * " that one would think the muſe was legion "

To reprimand him a little in his own words, if theſe
paſſages produced by Mr Collier † are obſcene and profane,
" why were they raked in and diſturbed, unleſs it were to

* Coll. p. 81. † p. 70. 71,

"conjure up vice, and revive impurities? Indeed Mr Col-
" lier has a very untoward way with him; his pen has such
" a libertine ſtroke, that it is a queſtion whether the
" practice or the reproof be the more licentious.

" He teaches thoſe vices he would correct, and writes
" more like a pimp than a p——. Since the buſineſs muſt
" be undertaken, why was not the thought blanched, the
" expreſſion made remote, and the ill features caſt into
" ſhadows?" So far from this, which is his own inſtruction in his own words, is Mr Collier's way of proceeding,
that he has blackened the thoughts with his own ſmut;
the expreſſion that was remote he has brought nearer;
and left by being brought near, its native innocence might
be more viſible, he has frequently varied it, he has new-
molded it, and ſtamped his own image on it; ſo that it at
length is become current deformity, and fit to be paid in
the devil's exchequer.

I will therefore take the liberty to exorcife this evil
ſpirit, and whip him out of my plays, where-ever I can
meet with him. Mr Collier has reſerved the ſtory which
he relates from Tertullian *; and after his viſitation of
the play-houſe, returns, having left the devil behind him.

If I do not return his civilities in calling him names, it
is becauſe I am not very well verſed in his *Nomenclatures*;
therefore for his foot-pads, which he calls us in his preface,
and for his buffoons and ſlaves in the *Saturnalia*, which he
frequently beſtows on us in the reſt of his book †, I will
only call him Mr Collier; and that I will call him as often
as I think he ſhall deſerve it.

Before I proceed, for method's ſake, I muſt premiſe ſome
few things to the reader, which if he thinks in his con-
ſcience are too much to be granted me, I deſire he would
proceed no farther in his peruſal of theſe animadverſions,
but return to Mr Collier's Short view, &c.

Firſt, I deſire that I may lay down Ariſtotle's definition
of comedy; which has been the compaſs by which all the
comic poets, ſince his time, have ſteered their courſe.

* P. 257.   † P. 81. 63. 175.

I mean them whom Mr Collier so very frequently calls
Comedians; for the distinction between *Comicus* and *Comœ-dus*, and *Tragicus* and *Tragœdus* is what he has not met
with in the long progress of his reading.

Comedy (says Aristotle) is an imitation of the worse sort
of people. Μίμησις φαυλοτέρου, *imitatio pejorum.* He does
not mean the worse sort of people in respect to their quality, but in respect to their manners. This is plain, from
his telling you immediately after, that he does not mean
Κατὰ πᾶσαν κακίαν, relating to all kinds of vice: there
are crimes too daring and too horrid for comedy. But
the vices most frequent, and which are the common practice of the looser sort of livers, are the subject matter of
comedy. He tells us further, that they must be exposed
after a ridiculous manner: for men are to be laughed out
of their vices in comedy; the business of comedy is to delight, as well as to instruct: and as vicious people are
made ashamed of their follies or faults, by seeing them exposed in a ridiculous manner, so are good people at once
both warned and diverted at their expence.

Thus much I thought necessary to premise, that by
shewing the nature and end of comedy, we may be prepared to expect characters agreeable to it.

Secondly, Since comic poets are obliged by the laws of
comedy, and to the intent that comedy may answer its true
end and purpose abovementioned, to represent vicious and
foolish characters; in consideration of this, I desire that
it may not be imputed to the persuasion or private sentiments of the author, if at any time one of these vicious
characters in any of his plays shall behave himself foolishly
or immorally in word or deed. I hope I am not yet un-
reasonable; it were very hard that a painter should be
believed to resemble all the ugly faces that he draws.

Thirdly, I must desire the impartial reader, not to con-
sider any expression or passage cited from any play, as it
appears in Mr Collier's book; nor to pass any sentence
or censure upon it, out of its proper scene, or alienated
from the character by which it is spoken; for in that

place alone, and in his mouth alone, can it have its proper and true fignification.

I cannot think it reafonable, becaufe Mr Collier is plea-fed to write one chapter of immodefty, and another of pro-fanenefs, that therefore every expreffion traduced by him under thofe heads, fhall be condemned as obfcene and pro-fane immediately, and without any further enquiry. Per-haps Mr Collier is acquainted with the *deceptio vifus*, and prefents objects to the view through a ftained glafs ; things may appear feemingly profane, when in reality they are only feen through a profane *medium*, and the true colour is diffembled by the help of a fophiftical varnifh : there-fore, I demand the privilege of the *habeas corpus* act, that the prifoners may have liberty to remove, and to appear before a juft judge in an open and an uncounterfeit light.

Fourthly, Becaufe Mr Collier, in his chapter of the pro-fanenefs of the ftage, has founded great part of his accu-fation upon the liberty which poets take of ufing fome words in their plays, which have been fometimes employ-ed by the tranflators of the holy fcriptures ; I defire that the following diftinction may be admitted, *viz.* That when words are applied to facred things, and with a pur-pofe to treat of facred things, they ought to be underftood accordingly : but when they are otherwife applied, the diverfity of the fubject gives a diverfity of fignification. And in truth, he might as well except againft the common ufe of the alphabet in poetry, becaufe the fame letters are neceffary to the fpelling of words which are mentioned in facred writ.

Though I have thought it requifite, and but reafonable to premife thefe few things, to which, as to fo many *poftu-lata*, I may, when occafion offers, refer myfelf ; yet if the reader fhould have any objection to the latitude which at firft fight they may feem to comprehend, I dare venture to affure him that it fhall be removed by the caution which I fhall ufe, and thofe limits by which I fhall reftrain myfelf, when I fhall judge it proper for me to refer to them.

It may not be impertinent in this place, to remind the reader of a very common expedient, which is made use of to recommend the instruction of our plays; which is this. After the action of the play is over, and the delight of the representation at an end; there is generally care taken, that the moral of the whole shall be summed up, and delivered to the audience, in the very last and concluding lines of the poem. The intention of this is, that the delight of the representation may not so strongly possess the minds of the audience, as to make them forget or oversee the instruction: it is the last thing said, that it may make the last impression; and it is always comprehended in a few lines, and put into rhyme, that it may be easy and engaging to the memory.

Mr Collier divides his charge against the stage into these four heads, immodesty, profaneness, abuse of the clergy, and encouragement of immorality.

I have yet written but four poor plays; and this author, out of his very particular favour to me, has found the means to accuse them every one of one or more of these four crimes. I will examine each in its turn, by his citations; and begin with the plays in the order that they were written.

In his chapter of the immodesty of the stage, he has not made any quotation from my comedies: but in general, finds fault with the lightness of some characters. He mentions slightly *, and, I think, without any accusation, Belinda, in the *Old Bachelor*, and Miss Prue in *Love for Love*. Miss Prue, he says, is represented " silly to screen her im-
" pudence, which amounts to this confession, that wo-
" men, when they have their understandings about them,
" ought to converse otherwise †." I grant it; this is in truth the moral of the character. If Mr Collier would examine still at this rate, we should agree very well. Belinda he produces as a character " under disorders of liberty ‡;" this last is what I do not understand, and therefore desire

to be excufed, if I can make no anfwer to it. I only refer thofe two characters to the judgment of any impartial reader, to determine whether they are reprefented fo as to engage any fpectator to imitate the impudence of one, or the affectation of the other; and whether they are not both ridiculed rather than recommended.

But he proceeds, " The Double-Dealer is particularly re- " markable. There are but four ladies in this play, and " three of the biggeft of them are whores *." Thefe are very big words; very much too big for the fenfe; for to fay " three of the biggeft," when there are but four in num- ber, is ftark nonfenfe; whatever the matter may be in this gentleman's book, I perceive his ftile at leaft is admirable.

Well, fuppofe he had faid——and the three biggeft, *etc.* for I am fure he cannot part with " biggeft," he has oc- cafion to ufe it fo often in the reft of his book. But mark, he gives us an inftance of his big good breeding. " A " great compliment to quality, to tell them, there is not " above a quarter of them honeft!" This computation I fuppofe he makes by the help of political arithmetic. As thus; the ftage is the image of the world; by the men and women reprefented there, are fignified all the men and wo- men in the world; fo that if four women are fhewn upon the ftage, and three of them are vicious, it is as much as to fay, that three parts in four of the whole fex are ftark naught. He who dares be fo hardy as to gain-fay this argument, let him do it; for my part, I love to meddle with my match. It was a mercy that all the four women were not naught; for that had been maintaining that there was not one woman of quality honeft. What has Virgil to an- fwer for at this rate, in his Eneis? where, for two of the fair fex that do good, *viz.* Venus and the Sybill, (for Cybelle and Andromache are but well-wifhers) he has the following catalogue, who are always engaged in mifchief, *viz.* Juno, Juturna, Dido, her fifter, her nurfe, an old witch, Alecto the fury, all the Harpies; to thefe you are

* P. 12.

reminded of Helen the firſt incendiary, Sylvia is produ‐
ced as a ſecond, next Camilla, then Amata, who deſpiſed
the decrees of the gods; nay, poor Creuſa and Lavinia are
made ſubſervient to unfortunate events. This is Boſſu's
remark [*], and he ſays that Virgil, in the characters of the
ſex, has cloſely obſerved the rule of Ariſtotle, who in his
treatiſe of poetry has ventured to affirm, that there are
more bad than good women in the world; and that they
do more harm than good.

In an epic poem ladies of quality may be uſed as Ari‐
ſtotle pleaſes; but comedy was meant to compliment, and
tickle, and flatter, and all that.

Here I take the firſt liberty to refer the reader to my
firſt propoſition. Mr Collier, [†] who talks with great inti‐
macy of ancient and modern critics, and amongſt others,
makes familiar mention of Rapin, has unluckily overſeen
a particular remark that is made by that learned critic, on
the improvement of modern comedy by Moliere, in his
raiſing his ridiculous characters. If he does not know
where to find it, I can help him to it.

*Les anciens poetes comiques n'ont que des valets pour les plai‐
ſans de leur Theatre; et les plaiſans du Theatre de Moliere, ſont,
les marquis et les gens de qualite : les autres n'ont joue dans la
comedie, que la vie bourgeoiſe et commun, et Moliere a joute tout
Paris et la Cour [‡].*

Well, this may be the French, and it may be the En‐
gliſh breeding; but Mr Collier aſſures me——" This was
" not the Roman breeding [‖]." They uſed to compliment
vice in quality; the gentle Perſius gives us an inſtance of it.

" Vos O Patricius ſanguis, quos vivere fas eſt,
" Occipite cæco, poſticæ occurrite ſannæ."   *Sat.* 1.

But Perſius was a man of quality, and perhaps might

* Traite du poem Epique. L. 4. Cap. 2.
† Vid. Col. P. 175.
‡ Rap. Reflex. ſur la poet. 26.   ‖ P. 12.

be a little familiar with his equals. As for Juvenal, he kept his diſtance, and made it as plain as the ſun.

> " Namque ibi fortunae veniam damus. Alea turpis,
> " Turpe et adulterium mediocribus ; haec eadem illi
> " Omnia cum faciant, hilares nitidique vocantur."

Satire 11.

I am finely employed, to furniſh my adverſary with two ſuch authorities againſt myſelf ; but reflecting that Mr Collier has no great eſteem for Juvenal, who he ſays, "_writes " more like a pimp than a poet *_," it is likely that he will return me his authority, to make the beſt uſe that I can of it for myſelf ; therefore I will take the liberty to ſtate a ſhort queſtion.

Juvenal, by the help of an irony, has in theſe three lines laſhed the vices of great perſons with more ſeverity than he could have done by the means of a direct and point-blank invective. Mr Collier is †, in plain terms, for having compliments paſſed on perſons of quality, and neither will allow their follies nor their vices to be expoſed. Now the queſtion that I would aſk, is only, which agrees beſt with the character of a pimp, the ſatire of Juvenal, or the complaiſance of Mr Collier ? In the concluſion of his preface he is quite of another opinion ; there " he confeſſes " he has no ceremony for debauchery, for to compliment " vice is but one remove from worſhipping the devil." Now that Mr Collier compliments vice is plain. Ergo, &c.

This is his own confeſſion, and ſo I leave him to lick himſelf with one of his own abſolutions.

When vice ſhall be allowed as an indication of quality and good-breeding, then it may alſo paſs for a piece of good-breeding to compliment vice in quality ; but till then, I humbly conceive, that to expoſe and ridicule it, will altogether do as well.

" The *Double Dealer* (he ſays), runs riot" upon ſome oc-

---

* Page 71.   † Page 12, 173, 175.

cafion or other, " and gives Lord Touchwood a mixture
" of fmut and pedantry to conclude with. *" For proof of
this, he directs the reader in his margin to the 79th page,
which is the laft of the play.   He has made no quotation,
therefore I will do it for him, and tranfcribe what Lord
Touchwood fays in that place, being the concluding lines
and moral of the whole comedy. Mellefont and Cynthia are
to be married, the villainies of Mafkwell having been detected; Lord Touchwood gives them joy, and then concludes the play as follows.

" Lord *Touch.* —Be each other's comfort;—let me join
" your hands—unwearied nights, and wifhing days, at-
" tend you both; mutual love, lafting health, and circling
" joys tread round each happy year of your long lives.

" Let fecret villainy from hence be warn'd;
" Howe'er in private, mifchiefs are conceiv'd,
" Torture and fhame attend their open birth;
" Like vipers in the womb bafe treachery lyes,
" Still gnawing that whence firft it did arife;
" No fooner born but the vile parent dies."

This, in Mr Collier's polite phrafe, " is running riot
" upon fmut and pedantry."   I hope this is fome reafon
for my having laid down my third propofition; where the
reader is defired not to rely upon Mr Collier's bare word,
but to confult the original, before he paffes his cenfure on
the Author.

Before he finifhes his chapter of immodefty, he taxes
the *Mourning Bride* with fmut and profanenefs.   If he can
prove it, I muft of neceffity give up the caufe.   If there
be immodefty in that tragedy, I muft confefs myfelf
incapable of ever writing any thing with modefty or decency.

" Had Ofmyn (fays he) parted with Almeria civilly, it
" had been much better, that rant of fmut and profane-

* Page 27.

" ness might have been spared †." What he means by civilly know I not, unless he means dully and insensibly;
neither civility nor incivility have any thing to do with
passion. Where a scene is wrought to an excess of tenderness and grief, there is no room for either rudeness or complaisance. Mr Collier is pleased to condemn the parting
of Ofmyn and Almeria, by comparing it to the meeting of
Menelaus and Helen; but I must take the liberty to tell
him, that meeting and parting are two things, and especi-
ally between two lovers. Now for the rant of smut and
profaneness;

 Ofm. " O my Almeria,
 " What do the damn'd endure but to despair,
 " But knowing Heav'n, to know it loft for ever!"

I will not here so much as refer myself to my third proposition, nor desire the reader to trouble himself so far as
to look on these lines in their proper scene and place, tho'
most of the foregoing incidents in the poem were contrived
so as to prepare the violence of this scene; and all the
foregoing part of this scene was laid as a gradation of paffion, to prepare the violence of these expressions, the last,
and most extreme of the whole, in Ofinyn's part.

For once I will let these lines remain as they are set by
Mr Collier, with his own filthy foil beneath, hemmed in
and sullied over with his own smut. And still what is
there either of profaneness or immodesty in the expression?
Is not the reflection rather moral and religious than otherwise? Does not the allusion set forth the terrors of damnation? I dare affirm that Mr Collier himself cannot so
transpose those words as to make them signify any thing
either smutty or profane; what he may be able to do with
the letters if they were disjointed, I know not; I will not
dispute his skill in anagram; and if the truth were known
I believe there lyes the-stress of the proof. Well, Mr Say-

grace, in the *D uble Dealer*, is beholden to him for his new
amufement; for the future he fhall renounce acroftics and
purfue anagrams.

As to what he fays after, that thefe verfes are a fimi-
litude drawn from the creed; I no more underftand it,
than he himfelf would believe it, though he fhould affirm
it.

In the reft of his remarks upon this fcene, his zeal
gives way to his criticifm. He had but an ill hold of pro-
fanenefs, and was reduced to catch at the poetry. The
corruption of a rotten divine is the generation of a four-
critic.

He is very merry, and as he fuppofes with me, in laughing at wafting air. Wafting, he thinks, is a fenfelefs epi-
thet for air. Truly I think fo too. I will not lofe this occafion of confenting with him, becaufe he will not afford
me any more; but where does he meet with wafting air?
Not in the *Mourning Bride*, for in that play it is printed
wafting air. So that all his aukward raillery about this
word, reflects alone upon himfelf; to fay nothing of his
honefly in making a falfe quotation, or of his becoming
affurance in charging me with his own nonfenfe.

He proceeds in his unlucky and fatirical ftrain, and
ridicules half a dozen epithets, and about as many figures,
which follow in the fame fcene, with much delicacy of
fine raillery, excellence of good manners, and elegancy of
expreffion.

Almeria, in the play, oppreffed and finking beneath
her grief, adapts her words to her pofture, and fays to
Ofmyn——

——" O let us not fupport,
" But fink each other lower yet, down, down,
" Where levell'd low, &c."

" One would think (fays Mr Collier), fhe was learning
" a fpaniel to fet."

Learning a fpaniel to fet! " Delectus verborum eft origo

" eloquentiæ," is an aphorifm of Julius Cæfar, and Mr
Collier makes it plain. This poor man does not fo much
as underftand even his own dog-language; when he fays
learning, I fuppofe he means teaching a critic to fet, a
dainty critic indeed !

A little before, Almeria is cold, faint and trembling in
her agony, and fays,

——" I chatter, fhake and faint with thrilling fears."

" By the way, (fays Mr Collier, for now he is Mr Col-
" lier emphatically) it is a mighty wonder to hear a woman
" chatter! but there is no jefting, &c."

Jefting, quotha! what, does he take the letting a pun to
be the breaking of a jeft? a whip and a bell, and away
with him to kennel again immediately.

Ay, now he's in his element, as you fhall hear.

" This litter of epithets makes the poem look like a
" bitch overftocked with puppies, and fucks the fcene al-
" moft to fkin and bone."   The comparifon is handfome,
I muft needs fay; but I defire the reader to confider that it
is Mr Collier the critic, that talks at this odd rate; not
Mr Collier the divine; I would not by any means, that he
fhould miftake the one for the other.

If it is neceffary for me to give any reafon in this place,
why I have ufed epithets and figures in this fcene, I will
do it in few words.   Firft, I defire the reader to remove
my verfes from amongft Mr Collier's interlineations of fad
drollery, and reinftate them in the fcene of the play from
whence they were torn.   If there is found paffion in thofe
parts of the fcene where thofe epithets and figures are
ufed, they will ftand in need of no vindication; for every
body knows that difcourfes of men in paffion naturally
abound in epithets and figures, in aggravations and hyper-
boles.   To this I add, that the diction of poetry confifts of
figures; by the frequent ufe of bold and daring figures, it
is diftinguifhed from profe and oratory.   Epithets are beautiful in poetry, but make profe languifhing and cold; and

the frequent use of them in profe makes it pretend too much, and approach too near to poetry *. If figures and epithets are natural to paffion and if they compofe the diction of poetry, certainly tragedy, which is of the fublime and firft-rate poetry, and which ought every where to abound in paffion, may very well be allowed to ufe epithets and figures, more efpecially in a fcene confifting entirely of paffion, and ftill more particularly in the moft violent part of that fcene. Thus much to juftify the ufe and frequency of epithets and figures in the fcene above-mentioned. Ay, but Mr Collier fays, fome of the figures there are ftiff; he fays fo, I confefs; but what then? Why, in anfwer, I fay they are not, and fo leave it to be determined by better judges.

Having fhewn that men in paffion naturally make ufe of violent figures and epithets; I will produce no lefs a man than Mr Collier himfelf for an example; if you would behold the gentleman beginning to fwell, fee him in page 80, there he puffs and blows, and deals mightily in fhort periods; at firft he is fcarce able to breathe, but at length he opens, and anon finds vent for a very odd expreffion. He is angry, with fome play or other, and fays——" Nature " made the ferment and rifing of the blood, for fuch occa- " fions." I hope he fpeaks figuratively, or elfe I am fure he fpeaks at leaft profanely; for we know who is meant by " Nature in the language of Chriftianity, and efpecially " under the notion of a maker †."

He difcovers in this expreffion, that his religion and his natural philofophy are both of a fize. He has declared the very fource of living, and the fpring of motion in the mechanical part of man, to be no more than the fountainhead of follies and paffions; and intimates very ftrongly, that Nature made it only for that purpofe.

But I think nothing that he fays fhould be confidered ferioufly; therefore I will proceed, and produce Mr Collier as he ftands advanced, both in ferment and figure.

---

* Arift. Rhet. l. 3. c. 3.　　　　† v. p. 72.

Ju p. 84. he has drawn quotations from comedies, " that
" look recking as it were from *Pandemonium*, and almoſt ſmell
" of fire and brimſtone; eruptions of hell with a witneſs! he
" almoſt wonders the ſmoak of them has not darkened the
" ſun, and turned the air to plague and poiſon. Provoca-
" tions enough to arm all nature in revenge; to exhauſt the
" judgments of Heaven," *etc.* He goes on with ſuch terrible
ſtuff for a conſiderable while together. I give this only as
a ſample of ſome of this gentleman's figures.

Methinks I hear him pronounce them every time I behold them, they are almoſt noiſy and turbulent, even in
the print. In ſhort, they are contagious; and I find he
that will ſpeak of them is in great danger to ſpeak like
them. But why does Mr Collier uſe all this vehemence
in a written argument? If he were to preach, I grant it
might be neceſſary for him to make a noiſe, that he might
be ſure to be heard : but why all this paſſion upon paper?
judgment is never outragious ;. and Chriſtianity is ever
meek and mild.

I have read it ſomewhere as the remark of St Chryſoſtom,
that the prophets of God were as much diſtinguiſhed from
the prophets of the devil by their behaviour, as by the
divine truths which they uttered. The former gave oracles
with all mildneſs and temper; the other were ever bel-
lowing with fury and madneſs; no wonder (ſays he) for
the firſt were poſſeſſed with the Holy Ghoſt; and the laſt
were poſſeſſed with the devil. So the reaſon is plain.

But I have employed too much time in digreſſing from
my purpoſe, which is chiefly to vindicate myſelf; and
only from caſual obſervation, to take notice of Mr Collier's errors, as they ſhall appear blazing up and down in
thoſe pages where I am concerned, or others into which
I may dip accidentally, in ſearching for expreſſions cited
from my own plays.

I have done with him in his chapter of immodeſty.
The reader has ſeen his charge againſt the *Mourning-Bride*,
and is a judge of the juſtneſs and ſtrength of it. I con-

fefs I have not much to fay in commendation of any thing that I have written: but if a fair-dealing man, or a candid critic had examined that tragedy, I fancy that neither the general moral contained in the two laft lines, nor the feveral particular morals interwoven with the fuccefs of every principal character, would have been overfeen by him.

The reward of matrimonial conftancy in Almeria, of the fame virtue, together with filial piety and love to his country, in Ofmin; the punifhment of tyranny in M.nuel, of ambition in Gonfalez, of violent paffions, and unlawful love in Zara: thefe it may be were parts of the poem as worthy to be obferved, as one or two erroneous expreffions; and admit they were fuch, might in fome meafure have attoned for them.

Mr Collier, in his fecond chapter, charges the ftage with profanenefs. Almoft all the quotations which he has made from my plays in this chapter are reprefented falfly, or by halves; fo that I have very little to do in their vindication, but to reprefent them as they are in the original, fairly and at length; and to fill up the blanks which this worthy honeft gentleman has left.

"In the *Old Batchelor* (fays he) Vainlove afks Bellmour, "Could you be content to go to heaven?" *

Bell. "Hum, not immediately, in my confcience not "heartily———

Here Mr Collier concludes this quotation with a dafh, as if both the fenfe and the words of the whole fentence were at an end. But the remainder of it in the play, Act 3. Scene 2. is in thefe words———"I would do a little "more good in my generation firft, in order to deferve it."

I think the meaning of the whole is very different from the meaning of the firft half of this expreffion. It is one thing for a man to fay pofitively, he will not go to heaven; and another to fay, that he does not think him-

---

* Coll. P. 64.

felf worthy, till he is better prepared. But Mr Collier
undoubtedly was in the right, to take juft as much as would
ferve his own turn. The ftile of this expreffion is light,
and fuitable to comedy, and the character of a wild debauchee of the town; but there is a moral meaning contained in it, when it is not reprefented by halves.

From Scene 3. of the 4th Act of the fame comedy,
he makes the following quotation. Fondlewife a jealous
Puritan is obliged for fome time to be abfent from his
wife:

Fond. " Have you throughly confidered how deteftable,
" how heinous, and how crying a fin the fin of adultery
" is? Have you weighed it, I fay? for it is a very weighty
" fin: and although it may lie————yet thy hufband muft
" alfo bear his part; for thy iniquity will fall upon his
" head." Here is another dafh in this quotation, I refer
the reader to the play to fee what words Mr Collier has
omitted; and from thence he may guefs at the ftrength of
his imagination.

For this quotation, the reader fees it in the fame condition that Mr Collier thinks fit to fhew it; his notes upon it are as follow.

" This fit of buffoonry and profanenefs was to fettle the
" confcience of young beginners, and to make the terrors of
" religion infignificant."

Indeed I cannot hold laughing, when I compare his
dreadful comment with fuch poor filly words as are in the
text: efpecially when I reflect how young a beginner, and
how very much a boy I was when the comedy was written; which feveral know was fome years before it was
acted. When I wrote it I had little thoughts of the ftage;
but did it to amufe myfelf in a flow recovery from a fit
of ficknefs. Afterwards through my indifcretion it was
feen; and in fome little time more it was acted: and I,
through the remainder of my indifcretion, fuffered myfelf to be drawn in, to the profecution of a difficult and
thanklefs ftudy; and to be involved in a perpetual war

with knaves and fools. Which reflection makes me return
to the subject in hand.

" Belmour desires Lætitia to give him leave to swear by
" her eyes and her lips." Well, I am very glad Mr Collier
has so much devotion for the lips and eyes of a pretty
woman, that he thinks it profanation to swear by them.
I will give him up this, if he pleases. To the next.

" He kisses the strumpet, and tells her——Eternity was
" in that moment."

To say " eternity is in that moment," is neither profane nor sacred, nor good nor bad. With reverence of my
friend the author be it spoken, I take it to be stark non-
sense; and I had not car'd if Mr Collier had discover'd it.

Something or other he saw amiss in it, and writing a
chapter of profaneness at that time, like little Bays, he
pop'd it down for his own.

Lætitia, when her intrigue was like to be discovered,
says of her lover,

" All my comfort lyes in his impudence, and, Heav'n
" be prais'd, he has a considerable portion."

This Mr Collier calls the " play-house grace." It is the
expression of a wanton and a vicious character, in the distress and confusion of her guilt. She is discovered in
her lewdness, and suffered to come no more upon the
stage.

In the end of the last act Sharper says to Vainlove :

" I have been a kind of godfather to you yonder :

" I have promised and vowed some things in your name,
    " which I think you are bound to perform."

I meant no ill by this allegory, nor do I perceive any in
it now. Mr Collier says it was meant for drollery on the
catechism ; but he has a way of discovering drollery where
it never was intended; and of intending drollery where
it can never be discovered. So much for the *Old Batchelor.*

In the *Double Dealer* (he says) " Lady Plyant cries on
" Jesu, and talks smut in the same sentence." That excla-
mation I give him up freely, I had myself long since con-

demned it, and refolved to ftrike it out in the next impref-
fion. I will not urge the folly, vicioufnefs, or affectation,
of the character to excufe it. Here I think myfelf obliged
to make my acknowledgments for a letter, which I received after the publication of this play, relating to this very
paffage. It came from an old gentlewoman, and a widow,
as fhe faid, and very well to pafs: it contained very good
advice, and required an anfwer, but the direction for the
fuperfcription was forgot. If the good gentlewoman is yet
in being, I defire her to receive my thanks for her good
counfel, and for her approbation of all the comedy, that
word alone excepted.

That Lády Plyant talks fmut in the fame fentence, lyes
yet upon Mr Collier to prove. His bare affertion, without
an inftance, is not fufficient. If he can prove that there
is downright fmut in it, why even let him take it for his
pains: I am willing to part with it.

His next objection is, that Sir Paul, who he obferves
bears the character of a fool, makes mention too often of
the word Providence; for, fays Mr Collier, " the mean-
" ing muft be (by the way, that *muft* is a little hard upon
" me) that Providence is a ridiculous fuperftition; and
" that none but blockheads pretend to religion *." What
will it avail me in this place to fignify my own meaning,
when this modeft gentleman fays, I muft mean quite contrary! I am civiler to him; I take his fenfe as he would
have it underftood; tho' his expreffion is exquifite nonfenfe; and I humbly conceive he may mean, that " a be-
" lief in Providence is a ridiculous fuperftition," when
he fays, that " Providence is a ridiculous fuperftition."

" Lady Froth is pleafed to call Jehu a hackney coach-
" man." *Ibid.*

Lady Froth's words are as follow——" Our Jehu was
" a hackney-coachman when my Lord took him." Which
is as much as to fay, that the coachman's name is Jehu:
and why might it not be Jehu as well as Jeremy, or Abra-

* P, 62.

ham, or Joseph, or any other Jewish or Christian name? Brisk desires that this may be put into a marginal note in Lady Froth's poem.

This, Mr Collier says, is meant to "burlesque the text, "and comment under one." What text, or what comment, or what other earthly thing, he can mean, I cannot possibly imagine. These remarks are very wise; therefore I shall not fool away any time about them.

Sir Paul tells his wife, "he finds passion coming upon "him by inspiration *."

The poor man is troubled with the *flatus*, his spleen is puff'd up with wind; and he is likely to grow very angry and peevish on the sudden; and desires the privilege to scold and give it vent. The word *inspiration*, when it has *divine* prefixed to it, bears a particular and known signification; but otherwise, to *inspire* is no more than to *breathe into*; and a man without profaneness may truly say, that a trumpet, a fife, or a flute, deliver a musical sound, by the help of inspiration. I refer the reader to my fourth proposition in this case. For a dispute about this word, would be very like the controversy in Ben Johnson's *Bartholomew Fair*, between the Rabbi and the Puppet; it is profane, and it is not profane, is all the argument the thing will admit of on either side.

"The *Double Dealer* is not yet exhausted." *Ibid.*
That is, Mr Collier is not yet exhausted; for to give double interpretations to single expressions, with a design only to lay hold of the worst, is double-dealing in a great degree.

"Cynthia the top lady grows thoughtful" Cynthia, it seems, is the top lady now; not long since, the other three were the three biggest †. Perhaps the gentleman speaks as to personal proportion, Cynthia is the tallest, and the other three are the fattest of the four.

Well, "Cynthia is thoughtful, and upon the question "relates her contemplation."

* P. 64.   † P. 12.

"*Cyn.* I am thinking, that tho' marriage makes man
" and wife one flesh, it leaves them two fools."

Here he has filched out a little word so slily, it is hardly
to be missed; and yet without it, the words bear a very
different signification. The sentence in the play is printed
thus: " Tho' marriage makes man and wife one flesh, it leaves
" them (still) two fools." Which by means of that little
word *still*, signifies no more, than that if two people were
fools before or when they were married, they would continue in all probability to be fools still, and after they were
married. Ben Johnson is much bolder in the first scene of
his *Bartholmew Fair.* There he makes Littlewit say to his
wife———" Man and wife make one fool;" and yet I do
not think he designed even that for a jest either upon Ge-
nesis ii. or St Matthew xix. I have said nothing compa-
rable to that, and yet Mr Collier in his penetration has
thought fit to accuse me of nothing less.

Thus I have summed up his evidence against the *Double
Dealer.* I have not thought it worth while to cross-exa-
mine his witnesses very much, because they are generally
silly enough to detect themselves.

In *Love for Love*, Scandal tells Mrs Foresight, he will
" die a martyr rather than disclaim his passion *." The word
martyr is here used metaphorically to imply perseverance.
Martyr is a Greek word, and signifies, in plain English,
no more than a witness. A holy martyr, or a martyr
for religion, is one thing; a wicked martyr, or martyr for
the devil, is another : a man may be a martyr, that is,
witness to folly, to error, or impiety. Mr Collier is a
martyr to scandal and falsehood quite through his book.
" This expression, (he says) is dignifying adultery with the
" style of martyrdom;" as if any word could dignify vice.
These are very trifling cavils, and I think all of this kind
may reasonably be referred to my fourth proposition,

* P. 74.

" Jeremy, who was bred at the univerſity, calls the na-
" tural inclinations to eating and drinking, whoreſon
" appetites *."

Jeremy bred at the univerſity! who told him ſo? What
Jeremy does he mean, Jeremy Collier, or Jeremy Fetch?
The laſt does not any where pretend to have been bred
there. And if the other would but keep his own counſel,
and not print M. A. on the title page of his book, he
would be no more ſuſpected of ſuch an education than his
name-ſake. Jeremy, in the play, banters the coxcomb
Tattle, and tells him he has been at Cambridge : whereupon Tattle replies————

" It is well enough for a ſervant to be bred at an uni-
" verſity."

Which is ſaid to expoſe the impudence of illiterate fops,
who ſpeak with contempt of learning and univerſities.
For the word " whoreſon," I had it from Shakeſpeare and
Johnſon, who have it very often in their low comedies;
and ſometimes their characters of ſome rank uſe it. I have
put it into the mouth of a footman. It is not worth ſpeak-
ing of. But Mr Collier makes a terrible thing of it, and
compares it to the " language of the Manicheans who made
" the creation to be the work of the devil." After which
he civilly ſolves all by ſaying, " the poet was Jeremy's
" tutor, and ſo the myſtery is at an end." This, by a pe-
riphraſis, is calling me Manichean : well, let him call
me what he pleaſes, he cannot call me Jeremy Collier.

His next quotation is of one line taken out of the middle
of eight more in a ſpeech of Sir Sampſon in the ſecond act
of this comedy : he repreſents it as an aphoriſm by itſelf,
and without any regard to what either precedes or follows
it. I deſire to be excuſed from tranſcribing the whole
ſcene or ſpeech. I refer to my third propoſition, and deſire the reader to view it in its place. Mr Collier's citation is————" Nature has been provident only to bears
" and ſpiders." I beg the reader to peruſe that ſcene,

* Ibid.

and then to look into the 139th Pſalm, becauſe Mr Collier ſays it is paraphraſed by me in this place. I wonder how ſuch remote wickedneſs can enter into a man's head. I dare affirm the ſcene has no more reſemblance of the Pſalm, than Mr Collier has of the character of a Chriſtian prieſt, which he gives us in page 127, 128, of his own book. Towards the end of the third act, Scandal has occaſion to flatter old Foreſight. He talks to him, and humours him in the cant of his own character, recites quotations in favour of aſtrology, and tells him the wiſeſt men have been beholden to that ſcience *———

"Solomon (ſays he) was wiſe, but how? By his judge-" ment in aſtrology." So ſays Pineda in his third book and eighth chapter. But the quotation of the authority is omitted by Mr Collier, either becauſe he would repreſent it as my own obſervation to ridicule the wiſdom of Solomon, or elſe becauſe he was indeed ignorant that it belonged to any body elſe.

The words which gave me the hint are, as above cited. *Pin. de rebus Salom.*

———" Illum judiciariam aſtrologiam calluiſſe circa "naturalia, circa inclinationes hominum, etc."

Does Mr Collier believe in prognoſtications from judicial aſtrology? does he think that Solomon had his wiſdom only from thence? If he does not, why will he not permit the ſuperſtitions growing from that ſcience to be expoſed? Why will he not underſtand that the expoſing them, in this place and manner, does not ridicule the wiſdom of Solomon, but the folly of Foreſight?

Scandal, he ſays, continues his banter, and ſays, " The " wiſe men of the Eaſt owed their inſtruction to a ſtar, " which is rightly obſerved by Gregory the great, in fa-" vour of aſtrology "

Scandal, indeed, banters Foreſight, but he does not banter the audience, in mentioning Gregory the Great: take his own words.

* P. 75.

Y 2

" Deus accommodare ad eorum fcientiam docuit, ut qui
" in ftellarum obfervatione verfabantur ex ftellis.
" Chriftum difcerent."

The reft of the banter is what Scandal relates from Al-
bertus Magnus, who makes it the moft " valuable fcience,
" becaufe it teaches us to confider the caufation of caufes
" in the caufes of things."

I am but a bare tranflator in this place: for example.
 —— " Nos habemus unam fcientiam mathematicam,
" quæ docet nos in rerum caufis caufationem caufa-
" rum confiderare *."

Is not all this ftuff, and fit to be expofed? yet thefe, and
fome other like fayings, have I fometimes met with as au-
thorities in vindication of judicial aftrology.

In page 76. Mr Collier is very angry that Sir Sampfon
has not another name; becaufe Sampfon is a name in the
Old Teftament.

He fays, it is burlefquing the Sacred Hiftory, for Sir
Sampfon to boaft of his ftrength; becaufe Sampfon in the
Old Teftament is faid to be very ftrong. The reft that he
quarrels at is a metaphorical expreffion or two, of lefs con-
fideration if poffible than any of his former cavils.

I refer the reader to the fcene, which is the laft in the
play: and for an anfwer to what has before been faid on
the word *martyr*. When I read in this page thefe words
of Mr Collier—— " to draw towards an end of this play,"
I thought he had no more to fay to it; but his method
is fo admirable, that he never knows where to begin, nor
when to make an end. Five or fix pages farther I find
another of his remarks.

In *Love for Love*, Valentine fays, " I am truth †."

If the reader pleafes to confult the fourth act of that
comedy, he will there find a fcene, wherein Valentine
counterfeits madnefs.

One reafon of his counterfeiting in that manner, is,

* Albert. Mag. Tom. 5. P. 659.   † Coll. P. 83.

that it conduces fomewhat to the defign and end of the play. Another reafon is, that it makes a variation of the character; and has the fame effect in the dialogue of the play, as if a new character were introduced. A third ufe of this pretended madnefs is, that it gives liberty to fatire, and authorifes a bluntnefs, which would otherwife have been a breach in the manners of the character. Madmen have generally fome one expreffion which they ufe more frequently than any other. Valentine, to prepare his fa-tire, fixes on one which may give us to underftand, that he will fpeak nothing but truth; and fo before and after moft of his obfervations fays——" I am truth." For example; Forefight afks him,

——" What will be done at court?

Val. " Scandal will tell you——I am truth, I never " come there."

I had at firft made him fay, " I am Tom-tell-troth;" but the found and meannefs of the expreffion difpleafed me : and I altered it for one fhorter, that might fignify the fame thing. What a charitable and Chriftian-like conftruction my dear friend Mr Collier has given to this expreffion, is fit only to be feen in his own book; and thither I refer the reader : I will only repeat his remark as it perfonally aims at me——" Now a poet, that had not been fmitten " with the pleafure of blafphemy, would not have furnifhed " frenzy with infpiration, etc." Now I fay, a prieft, who was not himfelf furnifhed with frenzy inftead of infpira-tion, would never have miftaken one for the other.

In his next chapter he charges the ftage with the abufe of the clergy He quotes me fo little in this chapter, and has fo little reafon even for that little, that it is hardly worth examining.

The *Old Batchelor* has a throw (as he calls it) at the diffenting minifters *.

Now his throw, in his own words, amounts to no more than that a pimp provides the habit of a diffenting mini-

* P. 101.

ster, as the safest disguise to conceal a whoremaster; which is rather a compliment than an affront to the habit.

" Barnaby calls another of that character Mr Prig." Calls him Mr Prig? Why, what if his name were Mr Prig? Or what if he were not? This is furiously simple! " Fondle- " wife, to hook in the Church of England into the abuse, " tacks a chaplain to the end of the description."

How this pretty little reasoner has (as he calls it) hooked-in the Church of England! Cannot a man be a chaplain unless he is of the Church of England?

Father Dominic the second, he is for bringing in Heaven and the Church by hook or crook into his quarrel. If a Mufti had been tacked to the description, he would have been equally offended; for Mufti, in the language of the theatre, he says, signifies Bishop[*].

Maskwell in the *Double-Dealer*, has a plot, and is for engaging Saygrace in it[†], He is for "instructing the Levite," and says, " without one of them have a finger in it; no " plot, public or private, can expect to prosper."

Perhaps there is a mistake; many damnable plots have miscarried, wherein priests have been concerned.

After this, he has transcribed a broken piece of a dialogue between Maskwell and Saygrace, which I leave to shift for itself; having nothing in it worth an accusation, or needing a defence.

Mr Collier is very florid in this chapter; but it is very hard to know what he would be at; he seems to be apprehensive of being brought upon the stage, and in some places endeavours to prove, that as he is a priest, he should be exempted from the correction of the Drama[‡].

In other places he does not seem to be averse to treading the stage; but he would do it in buskins; he would be " all gold, purple, scarlet, and embroidery; and as rich as " nature, art, and rhetoric, can make him[§]."

[*] p. 103. [†] p. 102. [‡] p. 124. 127.
[§] p. 118.

We will first enquire whether he may be brought on the stage or not; and then shew both how he would, and how he should, be represented; granting the representation of his character to be lawful.

Here he lays down something with the appearing face of an argument, under three heads, to shew that the clergy have a " right to regard and fair usage *." I am sure I will never dispute that with him in the general terms. But I suppose he is particular here; and means that they have a right to be exempted from the theatre. Whether they have or not I will not pretend to determine; this I know, that the custom of the theatre in all ages and countries is against this opinion; which in this chapter is sufficiently proved by the examples which himself has produced.

If Mr Collier is in earnest of that opinion, he has behaved himself either very treacherously or very weakly, in offering to assert it by a false and sophistical argument. His proof begins.

1. Because of their relation to the Deity.

" Now (says he) the credit of the service always rises in " proportion to the quality and greatness of the master." Upon this position he builds all the argument under this first head. The position is sophistical, and his inferences consequently false. The trick lyes here. It being granted him that the credit of the Service rises in proportion, *etc.* he slily infers, that the credit of the Servant also rises in proportion to the credit of the service; which is false: for every body knows that an ill servant both discredits his service, and is discredited by it. And by how much the more honourable the service is in which he is employed, so much the more is he accounted an ill man who behaves himself unworthily in that service.

If an offending servant is punished by the law, the honour of the service is not by that means violated; so far from that, that it is rather vindicated: neither on the stage is the divine service ridiculed, only the ridiculous servant is exposed.

* p. 127.

2. Becaufe of the importance of their office. And,

3. They have prefcription for their privilege, their function has been in poffeffion of efteem in all ages and countries.

Thefe two are but branches of the firft head; for " their " relation to the Deity implies the importance of their " office:" and befpeaks that privilege and efteem which ever ought to be paid to their holy function.

But here again Mr Collier confounds the function with the perfon, the fervice with the fervant : he is father Dominic ftill.

I would afk Mr Collier, whether a man, after he has received holy orders, is become incapable of either playing the knave, or the fool?

If he is not incapable, it is poffible that fome time or other his capacity may exert itfelf to action.

If he is found to play the knave, he is fubject to the penalties of the law, equally with the lay-man; if he play the fool, he is equally, with a lay-fool, the fubject of laughter and contempt.

By this behaviour the *man* becomes alienated from the *prieft* ; as fuch actions are in their own nature feparate and very far removed from his function; and when fuch a one is brought on the ftage, the folly is expofed, not the function; the *man* is ridiculed, and not the *prieft*.

Such a character neither does nor can afperfe the facred order of priefthood, neither does it at all reflect upon the perfons of the pious and good clergy : for as Ben. Johnfon obferves on the fame occafion from St Hierome, " Ubi " generalis eft de vitiis difputatio, ibi nullius effe perfonae " injuriam:" where the bufinefs is to expofe and reprehend folly and vice in general, no particular perfon ought to take offence. And fuch bufinefs is properly the bufinefs of comedy.

That this may not look like a fophiftical diftinction in me, to fay that the *man* does, by his behaviour, as it were, alienate himfelf from the *prieft*, and become liable to an ill character, apart from his office; I desire it may be observed that the church itself makes the same distinction.

It was foreseen by the reverend bishops and clergy of this realm, in their convocations for establishing the thirty-nine articles of our religion in the year 1562, and 1604, that evil men (unperceived to be such) might creep into the ministry of the church. That afterwards they might become openly profligate, and notoriously scandalous in their lives and conversation; even to that degree, that some scrupulous Christians, and of a very tender conscience, might probably take such offence at the unworthiness of their minister, as dangerously to avoid his administration of the holy word and sacraments; to refrain from public worship, and to lose the real benefit of the communion, through a misconceived opinion of the invalidity of it when administered by unclean and wicked hands.

They might (and not without some reasonable grounds) doubt, whether the same man, who was personally impious, could be spiritually sacred; whether he, who by his example would seduce them to the devil, could by his precepts be conducing to their salvation. This, I say, they might doubt; and not without some reasonable grounds; and not without the opinions of two of the fathers, viz. St Cyprian and St Origen, to authorize their distrust.

But to remove this doubt, and to invalidate the authorities of those fathers, the six-and-twentieth article of religion was thus established by the convocations above-mentioned.

A R T I C L E XXVI.

" Although in the visible church the evil be ever mingled
" with the good, and sometime the evil have chief autho-
" rity in the ministration of the word and sacraments:
" yet for as much as they do not the same in their own
" name, but in Christ's, and do minister by his commission
" and authority, we may use their ministry both in hear-
" ing the word of God, and in receiving the sacraments.
" Neither is the effect of Christ's ordinance taken away

" by their wickednefs, nor the grace of God's gifts dimi-
" nifhed from fuch, as by faith, and rightly do receive
" the facraments miniftered unto them, which are effec-
" tual, becaufe of Chrift's inftitution and promife, altho'
" they be miniftred by evil men.

" Neverthelefs it appertaineth to the difcipline of the
" church, that enquiry be made of evil minifters : and
" that they be accufed by thofe that have knowledge of
" their offences ; and, finally being found guilty, by juft
" judgment be depofed."

Here is a moft manifeft diftinction made between the
man and the prieft ; between the regard to his perfon,
and the refpect to his function.

I will fhew anon, that Mr Collier himfelf has made this
very diftinction, when he is pleafed to approve of the characters of Joida and Mathan in the Athaliah of Racine.

If any man has in any play expofed a prieft, as a prieft,
and with an intimation, that as fuch, his character is ridiculous, I will agree heartily to condemn both the play
and the author. I am confident no man can defend fuch
an impiety : and whoever is guilty of it, my advice to him
is, that he acknowledge his error, that he repent of it and
fin no more.

I confefs I do not remember any fuch character. Mr
Collier, who is more converfant with bad plays than any
man that I know, perhaps may.

Mr Collier in this chapter produces many inftances of
the characters of priefts in the poems of heathen writers ;
he is extremely delighted with the diftinctions of their habits, with the fhow and fplendour in which they appeared.
The crown and gilt fceptre of Chryfeis, with the valuable ranfom which he had in his power, are objects that
gratify his vain imagination extremely. He is indeed
fo rapt with his fplendid ideas of Chryfeis, Laocoon, and
Chloreus, that to ufe his own phrafe, he *runs riot* upon
their defcription from page 112 to 118. He feems to have
quite laid afide the thoughts of the " twelve poor men

" who over-bore all the oppofition of power and learning,"
in page 81.

He now talks of nothing but great families, great places,
wealthy and honourable marriages, fine clothes, and in
fhort, of all the pomps and vanities of this wicked world.
To give him his due, as in fome places of his book he
criticizes more like a pedant than a fcholar, argues more
like a fophifter than a right reafoner, and rallies more like
a waterman than a gentleman; fo in this place he talks
more like a herald-painter than a prieft, and infifts more
upon pedigrees and coats of arms, than on moral virtues,
or a generous education.

He tells us the Jewifh and Egyptian priefts, the Perfian
Magi, and Druids of Gaul, were all at the " upper-end
" of the government," p. 131. What then? What is that
to us, any more than if they were ufed to fit at the upper-
end of the table? No doubt this gentleman's affection for
fuch a feat. furnifhed him with this florid and metaphorical expreffion.

In p. 132. he fays, " the priefthood was for fome time
" confined to the Patrician order." Very well: we know
the reafon of that; but, with fubmiffion, that is not the
fame thing as if the Patrician order had been confined to
the priefthood. However, this gentleman's meaning is
plain: certainly if he were Pope, he would renounce the
title of " fervus fervorum Dei."

He quotes Tully for his approbation of the fame perfon's
being fet at the head both of religion and government *.
What does he mean by this? What occafion is there of
this quotation in our country? Is not our king both at
the head of our religion and government? When Mr Collier allows him one, perhaps he will not deny him the
other.

But to come to his meaning (if he has any) through all
this vain ftuff. I take it, he would give us to underftand,
that in all ages the function of a prieft was held to be a

* Page 133.

very honourable function. Did Mr Collier ever meet with
any body fool enough to engage him to affert that?

He tells us the men of the firft quality, nay, kings and
emperors, have been employed in the facred miniftry : and
I can tell him that kings and emperors have been in all
ages expofed on the ftage; their ambition, tyrannies and
cruelties. All the follies and vices which were confe-
quences of their arbitrary power and ungoverned appetites,
have been laid open to the people's view. They have been
punifhed, depofed, and put to death on the ftage; yet
never any king complained of the theatre, or the poets.
On the contrary, all great princes have cherifhed and fup-
ported them fo long as they themfelves were great; till
they have diminifhed in their own characters, and turned
to bigotry and enthufiafm; and of this a living inftance
might be given.

Yet, 1ft, Kings have a relation to the Deity.

They are his deputies and vicegerents on earth.

2dly, They are poffeffed of a very important office.
And,

3d'y, Their function has been in poffeffion of efteem in
all ages and countries.

That men of quality have always been, and are now
employed in the facred miniftry, is evidently true; and
I could heartily wifh that more were ftill employed in it :
fo fhould the moft honourable office be executed by the
moft honourable hands. So fhould we behold men of
birth, title and heraldry, defpifing tinfel fhew, pageantry,
and all Mr Collier's beloved bells, bawbles, and trinkets ;
and preferring decency, humility, charity, and other Chriftian virtues to fhining ornaments ; or even the " upper-
" end of the government." How ill fuch temporal pride
agrees with the perfon and character of a truly pious and
exemplary divine, I will not pretend to determine. I will
only tranfcribe the words of a learned and honoured mini-

ſter of the church, to this purpoſe; and that is the reverend Mr Hales of Eaton *.

" For we have believed him that hath told us, That in
" Jeſus Chriſt there is neither high nor low; and that in
" giving honour, every man ſhould be ready to prefer an-
" other before himſelf; which ſayings cut off all claim
" moſt certainly to ſuperiority, by title of Chriſtianity, ex-
" cept men can think that thoſe things were ſpoken only
" to poor and private men. Nature and religion agree in
" this, that neither of them hath a hand in this heraldry
" of *ſecundum ſub et ſupra;* all this comes from compoſition
" and agreement of men among themſelves. Wherefore
" this abuſe of Chriſtianity, to make it lacquey to ambition,
" is a vice for which I have no extraordinary name of ig-
" nominy, and an ordinary I will not give it, left you
" ſhould take ſo tranſcendent a vice to be but trivial."

Here is not one ſyllable of " heraldry regulated by"
garter, " and blazoned by" ſtones †. I would deſire the
reader, immediately after this paragraph from Mr Hales, to
conſult Mr Collier in p. 136, and to obſerve how he ſtickles
for place, and thruſts himſelf before the gentleman.

" The addition of clerk is at leaſt equal to that of gentle-
" man." How ſnappiſh and ſhort his clerkſhip is in his
periods! mark him, " were it otherwiſe, the profeſſion
" would in many caſes be a kind of puniſhment." Good
Heaven! to profeſs the ſervice of God would be a puniſhment, if the title of clerk were not at leaſt equal to that
of gentleman. Well,—" The heraldry is every jot as ſafe
" in the church as it was in the ſtate. When the laity are
" taken leave of, not gentleman but clerk is uſually writ-
" ten." And, a little after, " The firſt addition is not
" loſt but covered." Good reader, return to Mr Hales,
that you may be reminded of the true reſpect and veneration that is due to his memory; and to the reſt of the
meek, the modeſt, and the humble miniſters of the church:

* Vid. his Tract concerning Schiſm. p. 224, 225.
† Coll. p. 135.

for while Mr Collier is before you, you will be very apt to forget it.

I know many reverend clergymen now living, whofe names I cannot hear without awe and reverence : and why is that ? Not from their heraldry, but their humility, their humanity, their exceeding learning, which is yet exceeded by their modefty; their exemplary behaviour in their whole lives and converfations ; their charitable cenfures of youthful errors and negligence, their fatherly and tender admonitions, accompanied with all fweetnefs of behaviour ; and full of mild, yet forcible perfuafion.

He were next to a Manichean that would not hold fuch mens perfons in a degree of veneration, next to their profeffion. But a Mr Prig, a Mr Smirk, and, I am afraid, a Mr Collier, are names implying characters worthy of averfion and contempt.

Now let us take a view of Mr Collier as he appears upon him as one who has eloped from his pulpit and ftrayed within the inclofures of the theatre ; and I do not fee why the players fhould not lay hold of him, and pound him till he has given them abfolution. Why does he abandon his gown and caffoc to come capering and frifking, in his lay-doublet and drawers, behind the fcenes ? Is he mafter of the revels ? Is the ftage under his difcipline ? " And is " he fit to correct the theatre who is not fit to come into " it *?" He is not fit to come into it. Firft, becaufe his office requires him to another place. And, fecondly, becaufe he makes naughty of innocent plays, and writes baudy and blafphemous comments on the poets works.

Well, he has at length difcovered a play which is " an " exception to what he has obferved, in France," (Coll. 124.) The play is the *Athalia* of Racine. In this play are the characters of two priefts, Joida and Mathan ; of both which Mr Collier is pleafed to admit. By enquiring into his reafons for licenfing this play, we fhall fee in what man-

* v. Coll. p. 139.

ner he will allow a prieſt to be repreſented on the ſtage; and from thence we may gueſs how he himſelf would be contented to appear there alſo.

" Joida," ſays he, " the high-prieſt, has a large part, but " the poet does him juſtice in his ſtation; he makes him " honeſt and brave, and gives him a ſhining character " throughout." That is well. " Mathan is another prieſt " in the ſame tragedy, he turns renegado, and revolts from " God to Baal." That is not altogether ſo well. But has not the poet done him juſtice too, in giving him the character that belonged to him? Whether he has or not, Mr Collier thinks he has made him ample reparation and more than amends, as you ſhall ſee. He goes on. " He is a very " ill man; but"——ay, now for the *but*.—He has turned renegado, has revolted to God from Baal, is poſitively a very ill-man. But, what? O, but " he makes a conſiderable " appearance." There, now it is out, and all is well. If he has but " a gilt crown and ſcepter, ſcarlet and embroidery in " abundance," let him rebel or revolt, he makes a good figure, and it becomes him very well. Your ſervant, Mr Racine, it was well for you that Baal gave good benefices, and his prieſts could afford to make a conſiderable appearance, or Mathan's revolt had not been ſo well taken at your hands. But hold, Mr Collier goes on.

I am afraid the reputation enlarges, and the compliment riſes. For the ſake of connection let us repeat.——

——" But makes a conſiderable appearance." And,—

Ay, now, what can follow this And, in the name of climax?

You ſhall ſee.——" And is one of the top of Athalia's " faction."

Nay, then there is no more to be ſaid. If he had fine cloaths, and was ſet at the top, or rather at the upper end of a faction too, he had his heart's content: a reaſonable Mathan would have been ſatisfied with any one of thoſe bleſſings. Though 1 would not anſwer for Mr Collier's continence, at this time eſpecially; he is ſo tranſported with Mr Racine's bounty to Mathan, that he excuses him frankly for shewing him a renegado.

He goes on.————" As for the blemishes of his life, " they stick all upon his own honour, and reach no farther " than his person."

I think I have now kept the promise that I made not long since, to shew that Mr Collier himself, when he is in the humour, will allow of the distinction betwixt the man and the priest, the person and the function.

But to shew that I can be as cross as he; now when he would admit of this distinction, I should rather say when he alledges, it shall not by any means be granted him. Here is a renegade priest, that revolts from the true God to Baal; and this man is only branded with a blemish on his person. What, is it no affront to his function then? I take it to be no excuse for him that he should afterwards become a priest of Baal. Sure Mr Collier does not mean to make use of Mr Dryden's key, as he calls it, and say, that " priests of all religions," &c. Well, it is only a blemish upon his person; or, if Mr Collier pleases, because he delights in phrases of heraldry, it is only a blot in his escutcheon. Let Mr Collier answer for this, to those who have authority to examine him further. He is in every line growing more and more gracious to Mr Racine. And now he is come to the very top or upper-end of his civility; and says with a bon grace and belle air, that
————" in fine, the play is a very religious poem "

Indeed! why then " in fine," we are tacked about; then, a play, " in fine," may be a religious poem, it seems: why then Sir Martin with his, " in fine," here has quite unraveled his own plot. Ay, ay, the play is a very religious poem; if faction and fine cloaths will not make a religious poem, it must be made of strange stuff indeed.
————" It is upon the matter all sermon and anthem"————

O Lord! nay, now I protest, Mr Collier, this must not be; nay, now you are so infinitely obliging! fye, this is

too much on the other side : you quite forget the fathers indeed, Sir, and the bishop of Arras.

——"And if it were not designed for the theatre"——
Out with it, man.——"I have nothing to object."

Why, that is well, now he has come to himself. On
my word, I was half afraid he would have played the
Mathan, and have revolted to the theatre. The mischief
is, this naughty theatre will be interloping; when sermon
and anthem become the stage as ill as faction and fine
cloaths do the pulpit : but men sometimes travel into foreign countries for variety.

I cannot forbear enquiring into one example more,
which this gentleman offers in the very next page.

"In the history of Sir John Oldcastle, Sir John, parson of
   "Wrotham, swears, games, wenches, pads, tilts and
   "drinks ; this is extremely bad."

Extremely bad ? Can any thing be worse ? and yet, says
he, "Shakespear's Sir John has some advantage in his
"character." Now who can forbear enquiring what advantage a character can possibly have consistent with such
abominable vices ? First, "He appears loyal and stout;
"he brings in Sir John Acton, and other rebels, prisoners."
So ! as it is in the *Spanish Friar*, a manifest member of the
church militant ! that he was stout, was plain before, from
his padding and tilting. But this will not do; the advantage does not yet appear. No ! why then,

——"He is rewarded by the King, and the judge uses him
   "civilly and with respect."

This advantage appears still but coldly. Kings reward
spies and executioners, and necessary instruments of policy
and punishment. And judges are generally men of years,
temper and wisdom, and use all gentlemen with civility.
Ay, say you so ? why then——"in short"——ay, now
for the Iliads in a nut-shell. Here is the *but* coming again,
I had a glimpse of him just now, *ex gr.* "In short, he is
"represented lewd, but not little."

There is an advantage for you now ; "in short, lewd,
"but not little."

Concife and pretty! the gentleman had beft take it for a motto, and have it annexed to his coat-armour, when he can get " his heraldry regulated by garter, and blazon- " ed by ftones."

Well, I confefs I have been in an error; I thought a man never appeared fo very little, as when he appeared ex-tremely lewd. If I have undervalued lewdnefs, I afk ,Mr Collier's pardon.

" And the difgrace falls rather on the perfons than the " office."

Here again, you fee he will allow this diftinction to all his favourites. Here is the perfon and the function fepa-rated again; the prieft and the man: in fhort, he anfwers himfelf fo often, that I will difpute this point no more with him.

But you may fee what this poor gentleman, in the wretched pride of his little heart, thinks a fufficient alloy to make current a moft diffolute or impious character. Though you expofe a prieft revolted from God to Baal, yet, if you let him make a confiderable figure, and place him at the head of a faction, all is well enough; and the poem may be a " religious poem," &c. Shew another in comedy, let him fwear, game, wench, pad, tilt and drink, but withal let him keep good company; let a judge, or fome great man treat him with refpect, that he may not appear little, though he appear lewd, and you give " fome " advantage to his character;" at leaft you will fhew that he " underftands his poft, and converfes with the freedom " of a gentleman *."

In page 112, our author has obferved " how the hea- " then poets behaved themfelves in the argument. Priefts " feldom appear in their plays; and when they come, it " is bufinefs of credit that brings them. They are treated " like perfons of condition; they act up to their relation, " neither fneak, nor prevaricate, nor do any thing unbe- " coming their office."

Indeed when men neither fneak nor prevaricate, nor do any thing unbecoming their office in the world, they ought

* Ibid.

not to be reprefented otherwife on the ftage : nay, they ought not to be expofed at all in comedy; for the characters expofed there, fhould be of thofe only who mif-behave themfelves.

Let us fuppofe that the character of this author were to be fhewn upon the ftage; he who fhould reprefent him behaving himfelf as he ought, would be to blame, and that for thefe reafons.

Firft, To reprefent him behaving himfelf as he ought, would be to reprefent him in the difcharge of fome part of his holy office, which is fit by no means to be fhewn on the ftage; efpecially in comedy, where men's vices and follies are expofed; that would be to bring Mr Collier's function, not his perfon, on the ftage, which is not to be permitted.

Secondly, He that fhould reprefent Mr Collier behaving himfelf as he ought, would very much mifreprefent Mr Collier, in refpect to the manner of his character.

Let us take a flight fketch of him as he prefents himfelf to us in his book. Let Mr Collier be reprefented as he is, not as he ought to be; that by feeing what he is, Mr Collier may be afhamed of what he is, and endeavour at what he ought to be.

And that the inftruction of the reprefentation may not be loft, let us borrow that diftinction which feveres the prieft from the man; if Mathan, and fir John of Wrotham have done with it, they may lend it to us; it is for the ufe of an humble fervant of theirs, and whenever the hu-mour takes them to revolt, pad, tilt, wench, drink, and foforth, let them give us a quarter of an hour's notice, and they fhall have it again.

Well, our author being thus divided, we will defire the better part of him to take his place in the pit, and let the other appear to him like his evil genius on the ftage.

Suppofe the gentleman in the fcene to appear very in-tent upon the very obfcene comedies of Ariftophanes; Quære, * Whether the perfon in the pit, beholding how

_____
* Coll. p. 40, 44.

very ill this becomes him, will not think that he might
with much more decency, betake himself to his feptua-
gint?

Mr Collier on the ftage fhall anathematife the poets,
and tell them in plain terms, they fhall be excommuni-
cated, and that " they are not fit to come into the
" Church *." Quære, Whether Mr Collier in the pit, will
not think it had been more becoming his character, to have
invited and exhorted them to it?

Mr Collier on the ftage fhall behave himfelf with all the
arrogance, and little pride of a fpruce pedant, that the
gentleman in the pit may be induced to practife the meek-
nefs and humility of a Chriftian divine †. The former
fhall pervert and mifconftrue every thing that is faid to
him, that the latter may learn to ufe juftice, candour, and
fincerity, in his interpretations ‡.

The player Collier fhall call the gentlemen that he converfes with, foot-pads, buffoons, flaves, &c. that the fpectator Collier may remember they are Chriftians, and fhould
be catechifed by other names §.

Mr Collier, on the ftage, fhall rake baudry and obfcenity out of modeft and innocent expreffions; and having
extorted it, he fhall fcourge it, not out of chaftifement but
wantonnefs; he fhall forget, " that fometimes to report a
" fault is to repeat it **." The fpectator in the pit fhall
plainly perceive, that he loves to look on naked obfcenity;
and that he only flogs it, as a finful pedagogue fometimes
lafhes a pretty boy, that looks lovely in his eyes, for reafons beft known to himfelf ††.

" Caftigo te non quod odio habeam fed quod amem."

Mr Collier, on the ftage, fhall ridicule, rail at, and condemn all plays whatfoever; he fhall tire himfelf, and his
audience, with his inveteracy and exclamations againft
them. Which done, he fhall all on a fudden, and, that

* Coll. 139. † Page 136. ‡ V. moft part of Mr Collier's
quotations. § V. Pref. 81, 63, 175. ** page. 77.
†† Coll ch. 1, 2.

there may be something surprising, and " præter expecta-
" tum" in his character, from a perfecutor, become a pro-
moter of the drama; he shall be as furious a critic as he is
a bigot ; and give the best rules and instructions of which
he is capable for the composure of comedy. He shall talk
in all the pedantical cant of fable, intrigue, discovery, of
unities of time, place, and action *. But lest this behaviour in Mr Collier's character should appear inconfistent,
and a violation of the precept of Horace,

——" Servetur ad imum,
" Qualis ab incepto procefferit; et fibi conftet."

His vanity shall bear proportion with his diffimulation;
his ignorance shall be as great as his malice ; and he shall
not be able to deviate from his inveterate zeal against plays;
for he shall not appear to understand one syllable of the
rules of writing, but shall mislead poetry as much by his
instructions, as he has perverted it by his interpretations ;
he shall favour his adversaries without obliging them ; the
zeal of his character shall be preserved even in his own de-
spite ; and his devotion, in this particular, shall be the
child of his ignorance ; for he can make but
——" Lame mischief though he mean it well † "
And if plays are pernicious, Mr Collier shall only be wicked in his withes, he shall be acquitted in his performances; his instigations to poetry shall prove checks upon
it. He shall appear mounted upon a false Pegafus, like a
Lancashire witch upon an imaginary horse, the phantom
shall be unbridled, and a broomstick made visible ‡.
At this cataftrophe, Mr Collier, in the pit, shall exclaim,
like Flecknoe, and with very little variation;.

" O why didft thou on learning fix a brand,
" And rail at arts thou didft not understand?"

Now, lest the poet who shall undertake this character,

* V. from p. 206, to 228, and forwards.   † P. 204.   ‡ P. 230.

should be gravelled in the imitation of the style of this ela-
borate writer, let him take these few instances of his allu-
sive and highly metaphorical expressions, for patterns; *viz.*
" running riot upon smut; a poem with a litter of epi-
" thets, like a bitch overstocked with puppies; sucking
" the sense to skin and bone; a fancy slip-stocking high;
" the upper end of a government; a whole kennel of beaux
" after a woman," &c. For his elegancy, these are origi-
nals; " learning a spaniel to set : this belike is the mean-
" ing : three of the biggest of four : big alliances : men of
" the biggest consideration for sense, &c. to marry up a top-
" lady:" cum multis aliis *.

  It is a strange thing that a man should write such stuff
as this, who is capable of making the following observa-
tion.

  " Offensive language, like offensive smells, does but make
" a man's senses a burden, and affords him nothing but
" loathing and aversion †."

  " For these reasons it is a maxim in good-breeding ne-
" ver to shock the senses or imagination ‡."

  Indeed there are few things which distinguish the manner of a man's breeding and conversation, more visibly
than the metaphors which he uses in writing, I mean, in
writing from himself, and in his own name and character.
A metaphor is a similitude in a word, a short comparison ;
and is used as a similitude, to illustrate and explain the
meaning. The variety of ideas in the mind furnish
it with variety of matter for similitudes; and those ideas
are only so many impressions made on the memory, by
the force and frequency of external objects.

  Pitiful and mean comparisons proceed from pitiful and
mean ideas; and such ideas have their beginning from a
familiarity with such objects. From this author's poor
and filthy metaphors and similitudes, we may learn the
filthiness of his imagination ; and from the uncleanness of
that, we may make a reasonable guess at his rate of edu-

---

* See p. 12, 27, 34, 92, 131, 132, 225, 233, &c. † Coll. 205. ‡ Ibid.

cation, and thofe objects with which he has been moft converfant and familiar.

To conclude with him in this chapter, I will only fay
that no man living has a greater refpect for a good clergyman, nor more contempt for an ill one, than myfelf; the
former I have often been proud to fhew, the latter never
fell in my way till now. I never yet introduced the character of a clergyman in any of my plays, excepting that
little apparition of Saygrace, in the *Double Dealer*; and I
am very indifferent whether ever the gown appear upon
the ftage or not; if it does, I think it fhould not be worn
by the character of a good man; for fuch a one ought
not to be made the companion of foolifh characters. If
ever it is fhewn there, it ought to be hung loofely on the
fhoulders of fuch a one as I have lately inftanced; but to
no other end, than to demonftrate that even the facred
habit is abufed by fome; that by their characters and
manners the audience may obferve what manner of men
they are. And no queftion but if our author in the pit,
did behold his counterpart on the ftage, thus egregioufly
to play the fool in his pontificalibus, " the rebuke would
" ftrike ftronger upon his fenfe," and prove more effectual
to his reformation *.

I come now to his chapter of the immorality of the
ftage.

His objections here are rather objections againft comedy
in general, than againft mine, or any body's comedies in
particular. He fays the fparks that " marry up the top
" ladies †," and are rewarded with wives and fortunes in
the laft acts, are generally debauched characters. In anfwer to this, I refer to my firft and fecond propofition. He
is a little particular in his remarks upon Valentine, in *Love
for Love*. He fays,

" This fpark, the poet would pafs for a perfon of virtue;
" but he fpeaks too late ‡."

I know who, and what he is, that always fpeaks too

---

* Coll. III.   † P. 152,   ‡ Ibid.

foon. Why is he to be paffed for a perfon of virtue? or
where is it faid that his character makes extraordinary pretenfions to it? Valentine is in debt, and in love; he has
honefty enough to clofe with a hard bargain, rather than
not pay his debts, in the firft act; and he has generofity
and fincerity enough, in the laft act, to facrifice every
thing to his love; and when he is in danger of lofing his
miftrefs, thinks every thing elfe of little worth. This, I
hope, may be allowed a reafon for the lady to fay " he has
" virtues:" they are fuch in refpect to her; and her once
faying fo, in the laft act, is all the notice that is taken of
his virtue quite through the play.

Mr Collier fays he is prodigal. He was prodigal, and is
fhewn in the firft act under hard circumftances, which are
the effects of his prodigality. That he is unnatural and
undutiful, I do not underftand: he has indeed a very unnatural father; and if he does not very paffively fubmit
to his tyranny and barbarous ufage, I conceive there is a
moral to be applied from thence to fuch fathers. That he
is profane and obfcene, is a falfe accufation, and without
any evidence. In fhort, the character is a mixed character;
his faults are fewer than his good qualities; and as the
world goes, he may pafs well enough for the beft character
in a comedy: where even the beft muft be fhewn to have
faults, that the beft fpectators may be warned not to think
too well of themfelves.

He quotes the *Old Batchelor* twice in this chapter *. His
firft quotation is made with his ufual affurance and fair-
dealing.

" If any one would underftand what the curfe of all ten-
" der-hearted women is, Bellmour will inform him. What
" is it then? It is the pox."

Here he makes a flourifh upon ill-nature's being recommended as a guard of virtue and of health, &c.

The whole matter of fact is no more than this:

Lucy to Bellmour, Act V. Scene ii.

* Page 171, 172.

" If you do deceive me, the curſe of all kind tender-
" hearted women light upon you.

" *Bell*. That is as much as to ſay, the pox take me."

It is his interpretation; and it is agreeable to his character. He is a debauchee, and he thinks there is but one
way for a woman to be kind and tender-hearted; and I
think his threatening them with ſuch a curſe as the conſe-
quence of ſo much eaſineſs, does not ſeem to recommend
the vice at all, but rather to forbid it : his very lewdneſs,
in this place, is made moral and inſtructive.

I am very glad our author is in ſuch circumſtances, in
this chapter, that he can bear the ſight of that helliſh mono-
ſyllable, pox; and prevail with himſelf to write it at its
full length. Non ita pridem. In page 82 he loves his love
with a p—— but no naming : that is not like a cavalier.
What ermine was ever an inſtance of ſuperfine nicety com-
parable to Mr Collier? I will not ſay, what cat? though
if I ſhould, I can quote a Spaniſh proverb to juſtify the
comparison.

" El gato ſcaldado tiene miedo de agua fria.

He makes one quotation more *, to what purpoſe indeed
I know not; but I will repeat it, in juſtice to him, becauſe
it is the laſt that he has made, and the firſt fair one.
Old Bachelor, Act IV. Belinda to Sharp.

" —Where did you get this excellent talent of railing ?

" *Sharp*. ——Madam, the talent was born with me.—I
" confeſs I have taken care to improve it, to qualify me
" for the ſociety of ladies."

Theſe are the words juſt as the gentleman quotes them,
but why, or wherefore, he is not pleaſed to diſcover; for
he ſays not one ſyllable for nor againſt them; I ſuppoſe
he thinks the proof plain, and the evidence firm without a
corroborator.

I hope the reader will not forget, that theſe inſtances
are produced, to prove that I have encouraged immorality
in my plays. I thought the expreſſion above-mentioned,

* P. 172

had been a gentle reproof to the ladies that are addicted
to railing; and since Mr Collier has not said that it must
mean the contrary, I do not see why it may not be under-
stood so still.

I have now gone through with all Mr Collier's quotations; I have been as short as I could possibly in their vindication; I have avoided all recriminations, and have not
so much as made one citation from any of my plays
in favour of them; whatever they contain of morality or
invective against folly and vice, is no more than what
ought to be in them; therefore I do not urge it as a merit.

My business was not to paint, but to wash; not to shew
beauties, but to wipe off stains.

Mr Collier has indeed given me an opportunity of re-
forming many errors, by obliging me to a review of my
own plays.

" Dum relego scripsisse pudet, quia plurima cerno
" Me quoque qui feci, judice, digna lini."

But I must affirm, that they are only errors occasioned
by inadvertency or inexperience, and that I am conscious
of nothing that can make me liable to his censure, or rather slander. I am as ready to own the advantages I have
received from his book, as to demonstrate the wrongs; if
I resent the latter, it is because they were intended me;
and if I do not thank him for the other, it is because
they were not: he would have poisoned me, but he
overdosed it, and the excess of his malice has been my security.

To give him his due, he seems every where to write
more from prejudice than opinion; he rails when he
should reason, and for gentle reproofs uses scurrilous reproaches. He looks upon his adversaries to be his enemies; and to justify his opinion in that particular, before
he has done with them, he makes them so. If there is
any spirit in his argument, it evaporates and flies off unseen, through the heat of his passion. His passion does
not only make him appear in many places to be in the

wrong, but it also makes him appear to be conscious of it. That which shews the face of wit in his writing, has indeed no more than the face; for the head is wanting. Wit is at the best but the sign to good understanding; it is hung out to recommend the entertainment which may be found within: and it is very well when the invitation can be made good. As the outward form of godliness is hypocrify, which very often conceals irreligion, and immorality; so is wit also very often an hypocrify, a superficies glazed upon false judgment, a good face set on a bad understanding.

It is a mask which Mr Collier sometimes wears, but it does not fit the mould of his face; he presumes too much on the security of his disguise, and very often ventures till he is discovered: he does not know himself in his foreign dress, and from thence concludes that no body else can. His anceftor of honoured memory, recorded in Æsop, miscarried through the same self-sufficiency. Mr Collier, when he clothed himself in the lion's skin, should have thought of an expedient of concealing his ears: but, it may be, he is proud of them, and thinks it proper to shew that he has them both, and at their full length.

He has put himself to some pain to shew his reading; and his reading is such, that it puts us to pain to behold it. He discovers an ill taste in books, and a worse digestion. He has swallowed so much of the scum of others, that the overflowing of his own gall was superfluous to make it rise upon his stomach. But he ought in good manners to have stept aside, and not to have been thus nauseous and offensive to the noses of the whole country. But as his reading would not stay with him, so his writing ran away with him.

Ben Johnson, in his Discoveries, says, " There be some " men are born only to suck the poison of books *." *Habent venenum pro victu imo pro deliciis.* " And such are they that " only relish the obscene and foul things in poets; which

---

* Johnf. Difc. p. 702.

" makes the profeffion taxed: but by whom? Men that watch
" for it," &c. Something farther in the fame Difcoveries,
he is fpeaking again very much to our purpofe; for it is in
juftification of prefenting vicious and foolifh characters on
the ftage in comedy. It feems fome people were angry at
it then; let us compare his picture of them, with the characters of thofe who quarrel at it now *. " It fufficeth,"
fays he, " I know what kind of perfons I difpleafe, men
" bred in the declining and decay of virtue, betrothed to
" their own vices; that have abandoned or proftituted
" their good names; hungry and ambitious of infamy, in-
" vefted in all deformity, enthralled to ignorance and ma-
" lice, of a hidden and concealed malignity, and that hold
" a concommitancy with all evil."

It is ftrange that Mr Collier fhould overfee thefe two
paffages, when he was fimpling in the fame field where
they both grow. This is pretty plain; becaufe in the
51ft page of his book he prefents you with a quotation
from the fame Difcoveries, as one entire paragraph, though
feverally collected from the 706 and 717th pages of the
original; fo that he has read both before, and beyond
thefe paffages. But a man that looks in a glafs often,
walks away, and forgets his refemblance.

Mr Collier's vanity, in pretending to criticifm, has extremely betrayed his ignorance in the art of poetry; this
is manifeft to all that underftand it. And methinks his
affectation of feeming to have read every thing, fometimes
betrays him to confeffions that are not much to his advantage. I wonder he is not afhamed to own, that he is fo
well acquainted with the ἐκκλησιαζύσαι of Ariftophanes.
The dialogues of Aretine, or Aloifa, are not more obfcene
than that piece. The author there, as Mr Bayes fays,
" does egad name the thing directly," and that in above a
hundred places. But perhaps Mr Collier meant to veil
that play under a *mifnommer* (to ufe his own phrafe †);
and when he called it *concianotores*, thought we could not
difcover, that in fpite of his artifice, or his ignorance, he

---

* Johnf. Difc. p. 114.   † Coll. p. 44.

muft mean no other than the lewd concionatrices, or parliament women of Ariftophanes. He has indeed raked together a ftrange number of authors names: but as Gide-
on's army of two-and-thirty thoufand was ordered to be
reduced to three hundred; fo his rabble of citations, without any lofs to him, might be reduced to a much lefs number; but his bufinefs is not difcipline, but tumult. He
appears like Captain Tom at the head of a people that are
fhuffled together, neither the world, nor they, nor he, can
tell why: but fince they are met, plunder is the word, and
the playhoufe is firft to be demolifhed.

He has outdone Bays in his grand dance; nay, the heathen philofophers, in their notions of the grand chaos, never imagined a greater confufion. All religions, all countries, all ages are jumbled together, to explode what all
religions, all countries, and all ages have allowed. He is
not contented with his batalia, compounded of Bramins,
Brachmans, Mufties, councils, fathers, the Bifhop of Arras, &c. But the philofophers, nay, the very poets themfelves are preffed into the fervice.

Cicero endeavoured with all his might to get himfelf a
name in poetry; and Ariftotle preferred tragedy even to
philofophy. But Mr Collier has converted them both; in
fhort, between him and the Bifhop of Arras, they have
been feduced and inveigled over to the other fide..

He pretends to triumph in the heart of Parnaffus, and
has fown diffention in the bofoms of fome of the chief
proprietors. Ovid and the Plain-Dealer are revolted, and
take arms againft their brethren, while Mr Collier fings,
with Lucan and Hudibras of—civil fury, &c.

——" Populumque potentem,
" In fua victrici converfum vifcera dextra :
" Cognatafque acies——
" Bays againft Bays—et pila minantia pilis."

I wifh his feeds of fedition were fcattered elfewhere;
for here I think they will hardly thrive. What effect his
doctrine in private families will have, I know not, when
the fuperiority comes to be difputed between the country

gentlemen and their chaplains; or rather, as Mr Collier has established it, between the chaplains and their country gentlemen.

I am not the only one who look on this pamphlet of his to be a gun levell'd at the whole laity, while the shot only glances on the theatre : what he means by the attack, or what may be its consequences, I know not, and I suppose he cares not. "Bellum inchoant inertes, fortes finiunt." But there are those who will not be displeased at an occasion of making recriminations. With respect to his parts, it is no wise thing to give any body an example of searching into books for negligent and foolish expressions. Divines have sometimes forgot themselves in controversial writings; disputes begun, or pretended to have been begun on points of faith, have ended in scurrilous and personal reflections; and from tracts of divinity have degenerated into pasquils and lampoons. That Mr Collier has laid the foundation of such a controversy, I think is apparent; but I hope his credit is not sufficient to engage any body to go on with the building.

He has assaulted the town in the seat of their principal and most reasonable pleasure. Down with the theatre right or wrong. "Delendo est Carthago," let the consequence be what it will. That was a very rash maxim; and if Cato had lived to have seen its effects, he would have repented it. To prosecute an ally (and that desires no more than to continue in our alliance) as an enemy, is a weak and barbarous piece of policy.

Persecution makes men persevere in the right ; and persecution may make them persist in the wrong. Men may, by ill usage, be irritated sometimes to assert and maintain even their very errors. Perhaps there is a vicious pride in triumphing in the worst of the argument, which is very prevailing with the vanity of mankind. I cannot help thinking that our author is not without his share of this vanity. I think truly he had a fair appear-

* P. 139.

ance of right on his fide in the title page of his book; but with reafon I think I may alfo affirm, that by this mifma-pagement he has very much weakened his title. He that goes to law for more than his right, makes his pretenfions, even to that which is his right, fufpected; as a true ftory lofes its credit, when related from the mouth of a known liar.

Mr Collier's many falfe citations make his truth fuf-pected; and his mifapplication of his true citations very much arraigns both his judgment and fincerity. His au-thorities from the fathers (with all due refpect to them) are certainly no more to the purpofe, than if he had cited the two Attic laws againft the licentioufnefs of the old co-medy; in truth not fo much : for the invectives of the fathers were levelled at the cruelty of the gladiators, and the obfcenity of the pantomimes. If fome of them have eonfounded the drama with fuch fpectacles, it was an over-fight of zeal very allowable in thofe days; and in the in-fancy of Chriftianity, when the religion of the heathens was intermingled with their poetry and theatrical reprefen-tations; therefore Chriftians, then, might very well be forbidden to frequent even the beft of them. As for our theatres, St Auftin and Lactantius knew no more of them, than they did of the Antipodes; and they might with as much difficulty have been perfuaded, that the former would in after-times be tolerated in a Chriftian ftate, as that the latter would be received for a manifeft and com-mon truth, and made intelligible to the capacity of every child [*].

To what end has he made fuch a bugbear of the theatre? Why would he poffefs the minds of weak and melancholic people with fuch frightful ideas of a poor play? unlefs to four the humours of the people of moft leifure, that they might be more apt to mif-employ their vacant hours It may be there is not any where a people, who fhould

---

[*] Vid. St Auft. de Civ. Dei. L. 16. C. 9. et Lact. de falf. fap. 23.

lefs be debarred of innocent diverfions, than the people of England.   I will not argue this point; but I will ftrength-en my obfervation with one parallel to it from Polybius. That excellent author, who always moralizes in his hiftory, and inftructs as faithfully as he relates; in his fourth book, attributes the ruin of Cynethia by the Ætolians, in plain terms, to their degeneracy from their Arcadian anceftors, in their neglect of theatrical and mufical per-formances.   The Cynethians, fays my author, had their fituation the fartheft north in all Arcadia; they were fubjected to an inclement and uncertain air, and for the moft part cold and melancholic; and, for this reafon, they of all people fhould laft have parted with the innocent and wholefome remedies, which the diverfions of mufic admi-niftred to that fournefs of temper, and fullennefs of difpo-fition, which of neceffity they muft partake from the dif-pofition and influence of their climate; " For they no " fooner fell to neglect thefe wholefome inftitutions, than " they fell into diffentions and civil difcords, and grew at " length into fuch depravity of manners, that their crimes " in number and meafure furpaffed all nations of the " Greeks befide [*]."

He gives us to underftand, that their chorufes on the theatres, their frequent affemblies of young people, men and women, mingling in mufical performances, were not inftituted by their anceftors out of wantonnefs and luxury, but out of wifdom; from a deliberated and effectual po-licy, and for the reafons above noted.   Much more might be cited from Polybius, who has made a very confiderable digreffion on this occafion.

The application of what I have borrowed is very plain. Is there in the world a climate more uncertain than our own? and which is a natural confequence, is there any where a people more unfteady, more apt to difcontent, more faturnine, dark and melancholic, than ourfelves? Are we not of all people the moft unfit to be alone, and

---

[*] Vid. Tranfl. by Sir H. Sheer, Vol. 2. P. 49.

most unsafe to be trusted with ourselves? Are there not more self-murderers, and melancholic lunatics in England, heard of in one year, than in a great part of Europe besides? From whence are all our sects, schisms, and innumerable subdivisions in religion? whence our plots, conspiracies, and seditions? who are the authors and contrivers of these things? Not they who frequent the theatres and consorts of music. No: if they had, it may be Mr Collier's invective had not been levelled that way; his "gunpowder-treason plot upon music and plays (for he says " music is as dangerous as gunpowder *") had broke out in another place, and all his false-witnesses been summoned elsewhere.

* P. 279.

T H E   E N D.